PRAISE FOR KENNY KLEIN'S
THROUGH THE FAERIE GLASS

"Think you know Faeries? This well-researched, compelling book will have you looking twice at shadows and tying bits of red thread around your bedposts for protection."

—Jennifer McMahon, author of *Promise Not to Tell*

"Kenny Klein's writing has always inspired, stimulated, and informed. I'm very excited about his latest effort, a book about scary Faeries. He writes as well as he sings—which is to say, superbly!"

—Ariel Monserrat, editor and publisher *of Green Egg Magazine*

"This book is a perfect next step for Harry Potter readers who are now teenagers and young adults. The green-eyed beauty staring out of the shadows on the cover will let them know that. The book will also be an invaluable resource for writers of those epic adventure tales that are ultimately headed to the big screen, laden with special effects."

—Anna Jedrziewski, www.SpiritConnectionNewYork.org

FAIRY TALE
Rituals

ABOUT THE AUTHOR

Kenny Klein is a musician, performer, and lecturer who has been active in the Pagan community and on the Renaissance festival and folk-music circuits for over twenty years. He is also the author of the books *Through The Faerie Glass: A Look at the Realm of Unseen and Enchanted Beings* and *The Flowering Rod: Men and Their Role in Paganism*. He lives in New Orleans.

Kenny has recorded numerous CDs of music and performs year-round. Please visit him online at www.kennyklein.net.

FAIRY TALE
Rituals

Engage the Dark, Eerie & Erotic
Power of Familiar Stories

KENNY KLEIN

Llewellyn Publications
Woodbury, Minnesota

First Edition
First Printing, 2011

Cover art © Esao Andrews
Cover design by Lisa Novak
Llewellyn is a registered trademark of Llewellyn Worldwide Ltd.

Library of Congress Cataloging-in-Publication Data
Klein, Kenny, 1955–
  Fairy tale rituals : engage the dark, eerie & erotic power of familiar
stories / Kenny Klein. — 1st ed.
      p. cm.
  Includes bibliographical references and index.
  ISBN 978-0-7387-2305-1
  1. Fairy tales—History and criticism. 2. Fairy tales—Psychological aspects.
  3. Psychoanalysis and fairy tales. 4. Ritual. 5. Magic. I. Title.
  GR550.K64 2011
  398.2—dc22
                              2010045134

Llewellyn Worldwide Ltd. does not participate in, endorse, or have any authority or responsibility concerning private business transactions between our authors and the public.

All mail addressed to the author is forwarded, but the publisher cannot, unless specifically instructed by the author, give out an address or phone number.

Any Internet references contained in this work are current at publication time, but the publisher cannot guarantee that a specific location will continue to be maintained. Please refer to the publisher's website for links to authors' websites and other sources.

Cover model used for illustrative purposes only and may not endorse or represent the book's subject matter.

Llewellyn Publications
A Division of Llewellyn Worldwide Ltd.
2143 Wooddale Drive
Woodbury, MN 55125-2989
www.llewellyn.com

Printed in the United States of America

CONTENTS

"[Little Red Riding Hood] was my first love. I felt that if I could have married Little Red Riding Hood, I should have known perfect bliss."
—Charles Dickens, "A Christmas Tree" (1850)

"I used to be Snow White, but I drifted."
—Mae West, *I'm No Angel* (1933)

FAERIES AND FAIRY TALES

Hungry and cold, lost in a deep forest, a brother and sister hear the voice of a bird. They understand the creature's song, which tells them that just ahead is the answer to their prayers: they will find a house made of food. But the prophetic bird warns them they must be careful, for eating that food could cost them their lives!

A girl stands by the side of the road. She is impossibly beautiful, with skin like snowy cream and hair that falls in raven-black ringlets. She seems to be lost, alone, frightened. A carriage drives by. On the door is the royal crest. She peers into the coach, and meets the eye of a king. He signals the driver to stop, and takes the girl inside. His wife looks away, an impassive expression on her face, her deepest feelings hurt by this strange girl's very presence.

A teenage girl wanders playfully through her father's castle. She knows this place intimately, for she has lived here all her life. She has stepped upon every stair, opened every ornate doorway, sat upon each window bench looking out upon the fields of her father's kingdom. But oddly, today, on the birthday that will mark her as a woman, she finds a door where she has never seen one before. Her face flushed with curiosity and excitement, she opens it, peering into a tiny room. An old woman sits there, working away at something the girl has never beheld: a wooden wheel that spins flax into linen thread. The girl draws closer, thrilled and flushed with wonder, and reaches out her finger to touch the strange whirring wheel . . .

A man has made a promise to his youngest daughter, a promise to bring her a rose. But it is winter, and snow lies on the roads and pathways. He despairs that he will never find a rose for his lovely, pious girl, who asks for so little. Yet as the man walks from town along the road home, he sees a garden behind a wall—blooming, verdant, full of life in this deathly cold. And in the center of the garden, a red rose blooms. He walks slowly into the gated garden, picking his way carefully through flowers and ripe fruits. Now he is at the center. The man looks about, once, twice, and sees no one. He gently, carefully picks the rose. Suddenly a gruff voice roars: "That rose is mine!"

Do you recognize these stories? Are they familiar? The tales of your childhood? Stories you cherished as a youth? Perhaps you still refer to them. Do you call someone a "sleeping beauty"? Do you wait for your "prince to come" or have to "kiss a lot of frogs"? You recall the magic of these stories, the way they made you feel as you listened—intent, tensed, waiting for the girl to escape, for the boy to triumph, for the sister to push the wicked sorceress into the oven to save her brother from being cooked and eaten.

These tales shaped us, molded us, helped make us who we were to become. They taught us to analyze; they taught us morality and virtue. They gave us a sense of self.

But most of us have never heard these tales the way they were first collected, from peasants, milkmaids, and spinning midwives. As children, we were not told these tales by old women who cooked porridge in a cauldron over a hearth fire, reciting as they stirred. Or by a German hausfrau churning butter as she told stories she'd grown up with. No, we watched them on television, or saw them as we sat in movie theaters, thrilling over celluloid renditions that were the creations of Disney and other cinematic icons. We watched them again and again. The characters in them became our friends and acted as playmates in our fantasies and our dreams. We came to know the tales so well that we can recite them by heart to this day.

Or at least we think we can.

These tales are old. Much older than Wilhelm and Jacob Grimm, the brothers who spent their lives collecting and cataloging hundreds of these strange narratives. Much older than the Victorian and Edwardian illustrators who dressed their characters in royal garb and peasant clothes. They come from the dimmest recesses of time. They come from the storytelling of Black Forest wives and French peasants, who lived through decades of war and starvation. They hearken back to a dim past—before the pleasantries of the Victorian era, before the troubadours of the Renaissance, before the winding bardic tales of the Middle Ages. They are as ancient as Rome, as Greece, as Persia, and as the Celts who wandered across Europe in search of game and adventure. Within the pretty tales of Snow White and Sleeping Beauty are the seeds of stories in ancient tongues, languages no longer spoken or even known of, sounds so alien to our ears that to hear them would make us shrug and declare them utter nonsense.

Passed from mother to daughter, father to son, told to children around the fires of ancient hovels, in yurts on the tumbled plains, or at the hearth of rustic Slavic farmhouses, the tales have been cherished from time beyond memory. They have changed with the tools, fashions, and tastes of each generation of storyteller, losing and gaining elements as people's religious and moral beliefs ebbed and flowed.

Perhaps they seem like innocent, harmless tales? They are, after all, the memories of our earliest years, the common thread that all children shared. What little girl did not dream of marrying her prince? What boy did not wish for the chance to save a helpless maiden from her wicked stepmother?

But these tales are creepier, darker, filled with more mystery than the versions you may know. At their core these tales contain deep magic, the kernel of the most ancient myths and beliefs. Through them we glimpse Faeries and immortal beings—Nixies, Kobolds, and Nymphs—changelings who were transformed into our childhood playmates. When we scratch the surface of these tiny heroes' and heroines' tales, we find a bedrock of myth, magical ritual, Goddesses and Gods, enchanted beings, and ancient lore.

Scattered lore related to fairy tales may be found across the British Isles, the French countryside, the Alps, the Urals, across the Baltic coasts and the Russian wilderness. Stories of enchanted horse Faeries, mysterious changelings, wayside urchins, Pookahs, Pixies, sea demons, Lorelie, Naiads, Dryads, and dwarfs. Beings that inhabit a land whose laws and realities are far different from the ones we take for granted. Where a taste of food or a cup of wine might trap you forever. Where a girl can disappear into the branches of a pear tree. Where the picking of a flower can mean your life, or the life of your daughter.

The tales we know today have come to us over centuries, navigating rivers of language, belief, and culture. They have lived on while the myths, sagas, and legends that spawned them have fallen away. Some deep magic in these tales preserves them, makes them seem both harmless enough and important enough to pass down over countless generations.

And here we are, frozen at a moment in time, a link in the long, flowing chain of these stories' histories. From here we can study the distant road these tales have traveled, and seek to reconnect with the magic of them. The Nymph who is Snow White, the deep bond between Rose-Red and her bear consort, the prophetic trance of Sleeping Beauty, the changeling bargain of Beauty: all of these lay buried beneath the prettiness and sanitizing with which the Grimms and Disney and countless others have burdened these tales.

We are armed with the knowledge that the Faeries and enchanted beings in these narratives are subtle, seductive, sexual, sublime, stubborn, erotic, enticing, emotionally distant, dark, drear, and deadly.

We can handle the sinister truth behind these lovely characters. We can shed light on the deep forest where the wolf hides. We can caress the Nymphs there, knowing they may wish to grab us and pull us to a watery death. We can speak to the birds, though they may lie. We are not tempted by the food there—that bunch of grapes, that house made of candy—as we know that very feast may trap us for a hundred years. Those are simply the chances we take as seekers of the enticing, enchanted places.

We can use these dark mysteries as a basis for shaping our own lives through ritual, that magical dream shaper that is as old as humankind, that lurks in the shadows behind Christianity, Judaism, and all other "civilized" faiths. After all, wasn't it the worship of Gods, Goddesses, Nymphs, Pookahs, the dark fay, and creatures hidden or half-seen that first caused humankind to create its rituals?

Above all, let us see that what our parents told us—that these were figments of our imagination, invisible playmates, fantasies—is simply not true. Let us see for ourselves that they are real and can run with us again into the enchanted forest, in search of treasure, love, and adventure!

USING THIS BOOK

You might be someone who has always loved fairy tales. These tales were crucial in shaping you as a child, and the characters haunted you as you grew. They took hold, and became a part of your very psyche. Perhaps you still call upon them as game characters, for inspiration in your dress and your style, or as denizens of stories and songs that you create?

Maybe you were inspired by their magic to seek out magic in your own life. You may be drawn to spells and rituals. In later years, perhaps you sought out religions or systems like Paganism, Ceremonial Magic, or Qabalah.

Whether you are an experienced ritual magician, or whether you are someone who has never done anything like a ritual and just enjoys fairy tales, you may find something of interest in this book.

Each tale here is related in two ways: first we look at the tale itself, with an eye toward the mythic roots and the magical elements of the story. Each of the Grimms' tales has evolved from older sources that come to us from Greek, Roman, Germanic, and Celtic roots, and we'll take a look at these ancient threads of the tales we know; we'll also examine the ways the characters have changed and transformed over the centuries that the story has been told. So, if you are a person who simply loves the romance and magic of these tales, each discussion will help you come to a better understanding of what the tale is and how you can read more deeply into it.

Next we will borrow from such magical traditions as Wicca, Ceremonial Magic, and Qabalah; we will consider a ritual or a spell based on the characters or events of the tale, which you may use to create change in your life. The characters of these tales, you see, are so much a part of our psyche, and have been with us in our deepest mind for so long, that we can easily access our childhood self, which is the part of us that simply feels and that allows magic to happen. So if you have never done a ritual or a spell before, and want to give it a try, the workings here are thoroughly explained step by step, and you can attempt to follow them and unleash the part of you that believes in these ancient tales to help transform your reality. And if you are an experienced ritual magician, these spells may be used as they are, or as a basis to create new and more elaborate workings—tapping into these fairy tale archetypes that live in our innermost selves.

Let's look at the notion of magic, and explore why and how it works.

MAGIC AND RITUAL

The characters in fairy tales are an indelible part of our psyche. We grew up with them; in fact, we cannot remember a time when we did not know them. Who did not thrill at the danger when Red Riding Hood opened the door, not knowing, as we knew, that a wolf lay in Grandma's bed? Who did not feel that lump in the pit of their stomach when Snow White took the apple from the disguised peddler, who we knew so well was really her own jealous stepmother? Who did not hope beyond hope that Beauty would see through the veil of the physical, and realize that the hideous Beast before her was her own true love?

We have lived with these creatures of folklore for so long that their names call to mind instant images of their stories, and of the ways they formed our own personalities as we spent our childhoods in their company. We learned to navigate the difficult world of reality by considering the exploits of these fantasy heroines and heroes. When danger threatened us, we learned from Gretel to use our brains, or from Cinderella to be patient, and things would work as they were supposed to.

As archetypes we may call on these fairy tale denizens to aid us. By doing so, we access the childish portion of our mind that first came to know these characters. That childish mind is more open and accepting than the adult mind: it has not become as disillusioned with the world as our adult minds might have. Using these iconic figures to open the childish mind, ritual and magic will work more easily, and achieve results faster.

But wait: there's more to these fairy tale icons than just archetype. They are a shadow of Faerie creatures and mythic figures, sanitized and handed down to us as Snow White, the Dwarfs, Rose-Red, and the Beast. As a distant memory of actual Faerie beings, these characters are real, and inhabit this world as we do. Those who believe in the truth of Faeries—not cutesy Tinker Bell Faeries, but true enchanted creatures of the lands beyond our sight—may call upon these creatures for aid and magic in the form of the fairy tale denizens we will consider. While we may call upon Snow White, we will see that it is just one name for a Nymph, a Faerie creature of the ancient world who may aid us to take on sexual confidence and sensual bearing. And when we call upon the bear in "Snow-White and Rose-Red," we are conjuring up an Underworld creature that has aided shamans for thousands of years.

So we will evoke these ancient Faerie creatures, in their guise as the heroines and heroes of the Grimms' tales, for aid in achieving our real-world goals. We will do this in the form of spells and rituals.

Rituals, or structured ceremonies, have been performed by people throughout the world since the dawn of humankind. Most rituals carry spiritual or religious significance, and are performed as ceremonies to Goddesses, Gods, spirits, and natural forces. Most of us grew up with rituals such as Mass, Shabbos, or other religious services of some kind. In most belief systems, ritual is done in essentially the same way each time (which is what makes it a ritual rather than a service or a ceremony). The Catholic Mass, for instance, is done the same way every time, throughout the world. One reason this works is that when you do a special set of actions the same way each time, the actions begin to "wake" the subconscious mind, enabling you to enter a trance state. Using fairy tale denizens also opens the "child mind," which will allow the same thing to happen—the child mind is less judgmental and analytical than the adult mind, and tends to just "let things happen." These elements combined—doing ritual in the same format each time, entering a child-like state (no matter how old you are), and enticing your mind into a trance state—will allow you to create a magical environment where inner change can occur, and where enchanted beings may enter your world and bond with you.

The rituals we will perform here are based on Ceremonial Magic and Wiccan ritual. Ceremonial Magic is an old magical system that is at the root of Catholicism, Qabalah, and the practices of the ceremonial Masons; Wicca is European Paganism, the worship of ancient European Goddesses and Gods. You do not need to believe in either discipline for the ritual to work. They are simply a blueprint for the ritual's structure.

You will spend some time preparing yourself to do each ritual, by thinking carefully about the desired outcome. If you want a ritual to bring you a long-term result—such as a lifelong lover, lasting confidence, an enduring relationship with Nature, or a deep understanding of some aspect of your life—then be prepared to put some time into preparing for the ritual. It's just not logical to expect to find a lover who will commit to you for decades simply by performing a twenty-minute ritual: you may find you will need to perform the same ritual again and again over time, every full moon for six months for example, to feel that the magic is truly affecting your life. That is the nature of ritual; it is meant to be done over and over, the same each time, and each time you perform the ritual you will gain a deeper understanding or feel a deeper magic.

We live in a "fast food" culture, where people expect immediate results, but magic does not work like that. For instance, preparation for some workings here may include long-term activities like keeping a journal or a dream diary, or waiting until the moon is in the correct phase. Prolonged preparation like this may be necessary for a spell to work. The more energy you put into your desires, the more the magic will aid you. Be patient and focused, and you will get results.

GETTING STARTED WITH RITUALS: WHERE, HOW, AND WHEN?

If you are new to doing rituals and spells, you'll end up with quite a few questions. Here are some basics:

Rituals are very effective when done outdoors, but indoor rituals are good, too—as long as you have a quiet, private place where you will not be disturbed or distracted. The rituals in this book are usually recommended for the day or evening of a full or new moon. You will be instructed on how to set up your altar; an altar can be a table, a tree stump, a large rock, or a cloth laid on the ground or the floor. There will be certain tools needed: a wand, a knife (called an *athame* in magic), and a chalice or cup; almost all of these tools can be found in your house or in Nature (a wand should simply be a stick about the length of your inner arm from your elbow to the tip of your middle finger).

Some of the rituals in this book are written for one person, but two or three people, or a group, can perform them simply by taking turns speaking the lines and performing the actions. Some rituals are written for a group, but can be adapted to one person. Rituals may be performed skyclad (nude) if you are comfortable that way, robed, or dressed in loose clothes (like a flowing skirt or cloth pants such as those worn in martial arts). Street clothes are least preferable, because your dress, like your mindset, should be different from what you present to the mundane world each day. Skyclad is good because you are presenting yourself to the enchanted ones in your most natural state. Loose clothing allows you to move freely, and is different from most people's everyday wear. The only steadfast rule here is not to perform ritual dressed the way you would on a typical day.

It is important to say here that while ritualized magic will work for the inexperienced magician, practice makes your skills and senses more powerful. Doing ritual regularly (for instance, every full moon or every new moon) will make you a skilled magician able to effect concrete changes in your life.

After performing any ritual, it's important to eat something. This will help you ground the magical energy; if you don't ground, you may go about the next few days feeling dizzy or having trouble focusing. A good magician grounds the energy and "keeps silence," meaning you do not talk about the spell to anyone who was not in the ritual.

If you are doing ritual with others, sharing a nice meal afterward is not only grounding, but will bond the group. Laugh, feast, and make merry after any ritual. If you are alone, simply meditate on the magic you have done as you eat, and then feel yourself grounded and satisfied.

Ritual, like anything worth doing, takes practice and dedication. Do not expect amazing results after a first try. Learn as you go, think about rituals before performing them, and take care to take each step with thought and exactitude. It will not be long before you feel the magic in yourself and begin to develop psychic skills you never imagined you had.

There are many great books on the practice of ritual, and I recommend perusing a few. Here are a few I like, though this should not be seen as the ultimate list. There are many books on ritual and magic, and each has its own merits. To get you started, I suggest:

Eight Sabbats for Witches, by Janet and Stewart Farrar

Transcendental Magic: Its Doctrine and Ritual, by Eliphas Levi

Ceremonial Magic: A Guide to the Mechanisms of Ritual, by Israel Regardie

The Tree of Life: An Illustrated Study in Magic, by Israel Regardie

The Training and Work of an Initiate, by Dion Fortune

Many other books on the subject are out there that may resonate with you. Read as much as you can, and seek out responsible teachers of magic and ritual.

LET'S BEGIN . . .

Now it's time to take a look at fairy tales, enchanted beings, and ritual magic. Be warned: these are not the Grimms' tales the way your mother told them! These tales are eerie, dark, sexual, and perverse.

I know, perfect, huh?

GRIMMS' TALES

When we talk about fairy tales, we always seem to use the word *Grimms.* Who were the Grimms, and why are many of our childhood stories associated with them?

Two hundred years ago, two brothers named Wilhelm and Jacob Grimm set out on what would become a lifelong quest: to collect the tales and folklore of the German Black Forest. Jacob (January 4, 1785–September 20, 1863) and Wilhelm (February 24, 1786–December 16, 1859) had both studied law in school, and might have become a couple of lawyers that no one in our time would even remember. But that was not to be: while at university, the brothers were inspired by a professor to take a look at the old tales and legends of the Black Forest, a wild and untamed part of Germany.

Wilhelm and Jacob and their four sisters lived in privilege near Frankfurt, until their father died while the brothers were in their preteen years. When their grandfather died a little while later, their mother moved her brood into more modest urban living quarters, where she struggled to survive. In spite of their circumstances, Jacob and Wilhelm attended university in the city of Kassel. There they were inspired by a Professor von Savigny to take an interest in all things ancient, especially early languages and old folk stories. The professor helped both brothers become scholars in ancient languages. In fact, Jacob created a protocol meant to identify specific pronunciation shifts that occurred when the ancient Indo-European tongues evolved into Germanic languages. His protocol is still used today, and is still called Grimm's Law. And the brothers worked together on a definitive German dictionary, which was published in 1854.

But the work that was their lifelong passion began in their early years, in 1807. The brothers were taught by their professor to be fascinated with folklore and folktales. They began to get to know local storytellers in their own area of Germany and to write down the tales they told. It wasn't all hard work: "Little Red Cap" (Little Red Riding Hood) was told to Wilhelm by Henriette Dorothea Wild, the girl he would eventually marry.

In 1812 the brothers published their first collection of these narratives, *Kinder- und Hausmärchen* (Children's and Household Tales). From 1816 to 1818 they published a group of five hundred and eighty-five German tales as *Deutsche Sagen* (German Legends). The brothers continued compiling and editing collections of folklore until their deaths, ranging into French and Italian tales as well as the German tales they had grown up on.

The Grimms were very different from other folklore collectors of the era. For example, Francis James Child (1825–96) and Cecil Sharp (1859–1924), both English folklorists, observed a sort of golden rule that one printed songs and tales just as they were collected. But the Grimms were well known for editing tales, giving them new characters (such as changing *fee*, meaning "Faerie," to *enchantress* or *sorceress* in several stories). They often turned malicious mothers into step-mothers, or created other justifications for characters who did wicked deeds. In several cases, they mixed collected tales from oral sources (stories told to them) with similar tales from printed sources, like those of Charles Perrault (1628–1703), a French author who a century earlier had committed many French fairy tales to print. In short, they often made folklore soup.

Even though the Grimms' tales have come to be immensely popular (often because of later adaptations, like Disney films), the versions many of us know today are often not what the tale was like when it was told in the Black Forest. In our discussions of these tales, we'll look back at a time before the Grimms—at versions that come to us from Germany, Italy, France, and England—but we will use the Grimms' version as a final model (so it is well worth looking at the tales as the Grimms published them; they are easy to find on the Internet or in print form).

Note that the Grimms referred to these tales as sagas, folk tales, or just as stories. The misleading term *fairy tale* was applied to them much later, when publishers began using them in books intended for very young children. Another phrase that came into use for these types of folk stories is *Mother Goose stories*. Mother Goose was originally a term simply used for an older country woman, who could often be seen herding her domestic geese. Under these terms, publishers made a sort of folklore mishmash out of the Grimms' tales and other stories. The terms tend to trivialize these narratives, giving them an air of being nonsense meant simply to entertain children. The truth is, these stories were told to adults and children alike, and were known by their audiences to contain very potent magic and ancient lore.

Now let's take a look at the most popular tales gathered by the Grimms, and peer into the eerie, dark, erotic roots of those tales.

Chapter 1

SNOW WHITE: THE NYMPH; A RITUAL FOR SEXUAL ATTRACTION

"Snow White" is the well-known story of a girl whose mother, a queen, becomes filled with jealousy as her daughter blossoms into a beauty; the queen orders the girl killed, but the girl is spared by a hunter and finds refuge with seven dwarfs. Her mother pursues her and tries three times to murder her, but the dwarfs save her twice. In her mother's third attempt, the girl appears to have died, but she is saved by a visiting prince. In our ritual, we will call upon Snow White's gift of attractiveness and allure, and harness these qualities for ourselves. All story quotes are from the Grimms' 1812 printing of Children's and Household Tales.

Once upon a time in midwinter, when the snowflakes were falling like feathers from heaven, a beautiful queen sat sewing at her window, which had a frame of black ebony wood. As she sewed, she looked up at the snow and pricked her finger with her needle. Three drops of blood fell into the snow. The red on the white looked so beautiful, that she thought, 'If only I had a child as white as snow, as red as blood, and as black as this frame.' Soon afterward she had a little daughter that was as white as snow, as red as blood, and as black as ebony wood, and therefore they called her Little Snow-White."

So begins the Grimms' telling of the story we have come to call "Snow White."

On the surface, "Snow White" is the story of a poor girl caught in the crosshairs. Seemingly through no fault of her own, she has incurred the wrath of her jealous stepmother, who vows to kill the girl. She is spared by a hunter in defiance of his queen's orders, and she takes refuge with seven dwarfs who live in a cottage in the forest. She is discovered by her stepmother through a magic scrying mirror, and poisoned. She seems dead but is rescued and brought back to life by a handsome prince.

At least that is the story we grew up with in books and in the Disney movie. We will see that Disney has made the story very safe and pretty. There are many versions of the story, quite a few much older than the Grimms' version, and not all are quite as sweet.

In the Grimms' version, a woman wishes for a child (we see that in the quote above), and soon has a little girl. In this version the mother dies giving birth to the girl, and her father the king marries again a year later. Of this new wife the tale says: "She was a beautiful woman, but proud and haughty, and she could not bear that anyone else could surpass her in beauty. She had a wonderful looking-glass, and when she stood in front of it and looked at herself in it, she said, 'Looking-glass, looking-glass, on the wall, who in this land is the fairest of all.'"

Of course we know the response given by the mirror.

But when Snow White reaches the age of seven, the mirror gives a different response, telling the queen that Snow White is more beautiful than she: "Then the queen was shocked, and turned yellow and green with envy. From that hour, whenever she looked at Snow-White, her heart heaved in her breast, she hated the girl so much."

The queen asks a hunter to take the girl into the forest and kill her, but the hunter finds he cannot because Snow White is so beautiful (giving us the message that ugly girls are fully expendable). He rationalizes that the wild beasts will kill the girl, and he kills a bear and takes its lungs and liver to the queen. (In some versions it is a heart, in others a toe.)

Snow White wanders through the forest, where the beasts do not hurt her, until she finds a small cottage. It is very neat and laid out with seven place settings, seven chairs, seven beds (of which the Grimms give us the odd description "Against the wall stood seven little beds side by side, and covered with snow-white counterpanes"). Snow White eats a little food from each plate, and falls asleep in one of the beds after saying a prayer.

The dwarfs arrive home and find that someone has been eating their food, sitting in their chairs, and curling up in their beds. When they find Snow White in one bed, the dwarfs, like the hunter, are struck by her astounding beauty: "Oh, heavens, oh, heavens, cried they, what a lovely child. And they were so glad that they did not wake her up, but let her sleep on in the bed. And the seventh dwarf slept with his companions, one hour with each, and so passed the night."

In the morning the dwarfs make their pact with Snow White. "The dwarfs said, 'If you will take care of our house, cook, make the beds, wash, sew, and knit, and if you will keep everything neat and clean, you can stay with us and you shall want for nothing.' 'Yes,' said Snow-White, 'with all my heart.'" This is very like a marriage vow, and Snow White assumes the role of wife to all seven dwarfs. The Faerie creatures leave the house to her care each day as they mine in the earth.

Now the queen consults her mirror and discovers that Snow White is alive. She disguises herself as a peddler, and sells Snow White a set of corset stays. In lacing the girl, she suffocates her, and leaves her for dead. When the dwarfs return, they undress Snow White, reviving her.

A second time the mirror tells the queen that Snow White has survived, and now the disguised queen sells Snow White a comb dipped in poison. As soon as Snow White places the comb in her hair, she falls over, seemingly dead. Again she is rescued by the dwarfs, and again the queen discovers this in her mirror.

The third and final time the queen dresses as a farmer's wife, and this time gives Snow White an apple poisoned on one side. The queen bites the healthy side, but Snow White is left eating the poison: the girl takes a nibble and keels over. When the dwarfs return, they cannot revive her.

Unable to live without seeing her astounding beauty, they place her in a glass coffin and set her on display. The dwarfs take turns watching the casket at all times, and birds also watch over the dead girl.

A king's son is passing through the forest, and plans on spending the night at the dwarfs' home. He sees the glass coffin and decides he must have it. The dwarfs say they will not sell it, but when the prince asks for it as a gift, strangely, they give it to him.

The prince's men take up the coffin to carry it away, and they trip and fall with it. The fall dislodges the apple from Snow White's throat, and she wakes. The prince explains the situation to her, and she agrees to marry him.

Her mother comes to the wedding, where iron shoes heated in a fire are put on her feet, and she is made to dance until she dies.

It's likely that from hearing the tale in childhood or seeing movie and television versions, you recall the tale differently from the version here. For instance, you might remember the prince kissing

Snow White to wake her, or everyone living happily ever after. As you can see, the story is a little different from the way most people remember it: The prince does not kiss Snow White awake (more on that later). And the queenly mother is killed in horrible ways. Oh, and Snow White comes out of her coma, turns her back on her seven dwarfly husbands, and marries a total stranger.

WHO IS SNOW WHITE?

Snow White is a bit of an enigma. She is something totally different to each character in the story. In the Grimms' version, we are told that her stepmother wished for her to be exactly as she herself was, but later that she became insanely jealous of Snow White's beauty. (We all grew up with the Grimms' version, which calls her a stepmother, but the Grimms replaced the mother of older versions with a stepmother to make this situation a little less creepy.) So, to her mother Snow White was a source of frustration, jealousy, and loathing. To the hunter, to whom the mother issued orders to kill Snow White, she was a ravishing beauty. ("And as she was so beautiful the huntsman had pity on her and said, 'Run away, then, you poor child.'") To the dwarfs, with whom she comes to live, she is a wife. And to the prince who finds her asleep and rescues her, she is a lover. How can one girl, who several versions of the story tell us is seven years old ("But Snow-White was growing up, and grew more and more beautiful, and when she was seven years old she was as beautiful as the day, and more beautiful than the queen herself") be these very different things?

The answer lies in an older version of the story. In this tale, a king and queen are riding their carriage through their realm while snow is falling and ravens fly overhead (a very common setting in central Europe). The king wishes for a daughter as white as the snow and as black as the ravens. There beside the road such a girl suddenly appears, and the king takes her into his carriage and declares that she will be his daughter.

Let us imagine the scene for a moment: The king and queen ride through a gloomy European mist, watching ravens overhead. The king verbalizes his thoughts: "Look at those ravens, my queen. And at the shining white of the snow around us. If only we had a child as white as the snow, and as black as those ravens . . . " The queen says nothing, nodding at the king's idle wish. But suddenly, the king gasps, pointing out the window of the carriage. There, by the side of the road, stands a girl. She is young, perhaps seven years old. She wears an old frock coat of pink cream color, with a fox fur collar and a muff of black fur. Her skin is as pale as cream, and her cheeks red like the bloom of an apple. Her pallor is so pale, you might not see her against the snow that falls around her but for her hair and eyes. Her hair is black as the raven's wing, cut in delicate bangs that frame her pale face, and falling in loose curls around her shoulders. And as the king nears, he sees her eyes, also black as midnight.

The king's heart sings out, that is the child I have wished for! He bangs his walking stick on the carriage roof, signaling the coachman to stop. He opens the coach door, beckoning to the child. "Come in from the cold and wet, my darling. I am your king. Come into my carriage." The girl steps daintily aboard the coach. The queen looks away, out the window, onto the scene of dismal snow and deathly bare trees.

We have a very different kind of story now, where the girl appears out of nowhere, seemingly by chance, and assumes her place in the royal family. While the version we know well seems not to mention a father, here the father seems to have created the adventure that is about to take place. In this version there is no mention of either the king ascertaining that the child actually has parents, or any question of the queen's opinion of the situation. Well, after all, he's the king. He can do as he likes.

The appearance of Snow White on the side of the road in answer to the king's wish fits the behavior of an enchanted creature called an urchin. Urchins often appear as wayward children, timing their appearance to just the right moment to be taken up by human families. Another name for this is a changeling, a Faerie who assumes a human life. Keep that in mind; we'll talk more about it in a moment.

In the Grimms' version, we see the birth of Snow White. Her mother conceives after a little sewing accident, where she pricks herself with a needle (representing sex and loss of virginity), and three drops of her blood fall on the white snow. She wishes for a child as white as the snow, as red as blood, and as black as her ebony frame. This wish is powerful magic. She has given three drops of her blood in exchange for her wish, and we can see that a Faerie, a changeling, might answer that wish and take on the life of a human child with pale skin, red cheeks, and black hair and eyes. Stories of beautiful changeling children are quite common throughout Europe, and a wish accompanied by blood would certainly bring such a Faerie child into one's life—with a deadly outcome of jealousy, rage, poison, and death. Such is the hold Faeries have over us.

Another odd aspect of the story is that, although Snow White is quite young, she is seen as a romantic interest by many characters in the story. The hunter sees her as so beautiful he is willing to defy a queen's direct order so he may spare her. Huntsmen, no matter how smitten they are by the beauty of a young woman, seldom defy a queen's orders. And the dwarfs take her to their beds. Her mother, as I've said, sees Snow White as a sexual competitor, and becomes so jealous of her daughter that she is willing to kill her. (In the older version, the queen/mother is justified in being jealous, as the girl has replaced her in her husband's affection. That mother seemed to have little choice in accepting the urchin girl from the roadside as a daughter.)

Take a look at yet another older story, which seems to be a version of Snow White told from a very different perspective, and with a very different outcome. This version of our tale of sweet little Snow White was collected in Switzerland:[1]

> On one of the high plains between Brugg and Waldshut, near the Black Forest, seven dwarfs lived together in a small house. Late one evening an attractive young peasant girl, who was lost and hungry, approached them and requested shelter for the night. The dwarfs had only seven beds, and they fell to arguing with one another, for each one wanted to give up his bed for the girl. Finally the oldest one took the girl into his bed.
>
> Before they could fall asleep, a peasant woman appeared before their house, knocked on the door, and asked to be let inside. The girl got up immediately and told the woman that the dwarfs had only seven beds, and that there was no room there for anyone else. With this the woman became very angry and accused the girl of being a slut, thinking that she was cohabiting with all seven men. Threatening to make a quick end to such evil business, she went away in a rage.
>
> That same night she returned with two men, whom she had brought up from the bank of the Rhine. They immediately broke into the house and killed the seven dwarfs. They buried the bodies outside in the garden and burned the house to the ground. No one knows what became of the girl.

Here it is a peasant woman, not a queen, who falls into a deadly rage inspired by our sweet heroine. What has little Schneewittchen got going on that makes her the object of so much lust and envy?

---

1. Ashliman, trans., "Death of the Seven Dwarfs. A Legend from Switzerland." Translated by D. L. Ashliman. ©2009 by D. L. Ashliman. Used here with permission. Please see the bibliography for more complete information on this source.

SEX AND THE SINGLE NYMPH

The answer is simple, and lies in the mystery of Snow White's birth or conjuring from deep Faerie magic: our little Snow White is a Nymph, a Nature deity, spoken of often in Greek and other European myth! Found on the road, or conjured up during a magical wish for which her mother's virginity and three drops of her blood have been offered, the young beauty who appears exactly as described in the wish is a changeling, a Faerie who chooses to live a human life. Often a changeling exchanges her life for that of a human child, sending the human into the Faerie world in her place, but in some legends the Faerie will simply appear on the roadside. In these tales, where the Faerie is an urchin, she can often transform into a hedgehog.

Snow White fits every circumstance of a Nymph. She is unthinkably beautiful and looks exactly the way each character wishes her to look: the mother or father describe a girl as white as snow, as red as blood, and as black as wood or three ravens (there's that number three in the wish again), and the girl looks just that way. We can only imagine that Snow White must have very pale skin (white as snow), very dark hair (black as wood or as the ravens), and striking red cheeks (the color of blood). As the daughter of a king or queen, she would be very noble, royal in her bearing, and proper in her conduct.

But wait. A huntsman's idea of beauty would be quite different from the aesthetic of a king or queen: in rural nineteenth-century Germany or Switzerland, a beauty of the common people might have been on the plump side (a sign of health and fertility), with a complexion revealing hours working in the sun (not creamy skin and blushing cheeks), and, as a German icon of beauty, certainly a shining blond. Yet the hunter finds seven-year-old, pale, brunette Snow White so beautiful that he simply disobeys the queen he serves (herself a ravishing beauty if we believe the Grimms' story). Is it possible he saw Snow White in the same way as the mother and father saw her? We are even told that "the wild beasts ran past her, but did her no harm." Snow White apparently had enough magic to subdue bears and wolves.

And what about the dwarfs? We are told by the Grimms that when they first meet her, they cry out: "'Oh, heavens, oh, heavens,' cried they, 'what a lovely child.'" So lovely that they invite her to live with them, doing the chores of a wife. The Grimms tell us that the dwarfs make alternate sleeping arrangements for the lovely child, though we know from the Swiss story that, in at least some versions, the dwarfs treat Snow White as an actual wife, with the eldest dwarf exchanging her sexual favors for her room and board. If you know anything at all about Nymphs, you know this arrangement would be no problem at all for this type of Faerie. In the Germanic myth of Freya, for instance, that Nymph-like Goddess laid with four dwarfs—Dvalinn, Alfrik, Berling, and Grer—one per night, to earn her gold and amber necklace Brísingamen. Perhaps there is a touch of Freya passed down to us in the character of Schneewittchen.

Even in death, the dwarfs are in awe of Snow White's beauty. "Then they were going to bury her, but she still looked as if she were living, and still had her pretty red cheeks. They said, we could not bury her in the dark ground, and they had a transparent coffin of glass made . . . And now Snow-White lay a long, long time in the coffin, and she did not change, but looked as if she were asleep, for she was as white as snow, as red as blood, and her hair was as black as ebony." The animals of the forest were stunned by this beautiful dead Nymph: "Birds came too, and wept for Snow-White, first an owl, then a raven, and last a dove." Ravens usually eat dead people.

Now the prince comes along, sees this sleeping Nymph, and asks the dwarfs for Snow White in her coffin as a gift. "He saw the coffin on the mountain, and the beautiful Snow-White within it, and read what was written upon it in golden letters. Then he said to the dwarfs, 'Let me have the coffin, I will give you whatever you want for it.' But the dwarfs answered, 'We will not part with it for all the gold in the world.' Then he said, 'Let me have it as a gift, for I cannot live without seeing Snow-White. I will honor and prize her as my dearest possession.'"

Is it me, or are these people a little creepy?

Well, no, not if you realize that Faerie beauty is irresistible. The Nymph enchants all of those around her with her ethereal visage; the dwarfs, the prince, even the animals of the forest fall in love with the Nymph. And Mom, with her insecurities at getting a bit older, is inspired by the Nymph to act out her own rage and turmoil.

Nymphs are Faeries who come to us from Greek lore, and are spoken of in the lore of nearly all European cultures. Sexual, beautiful, seductive, and sensuous, they can also be aloof, chaste, and even virginal when they want to be. In Greek myth, Artemis was surrounded by an entourage of Nymphs who had the appearance of nine-year-old girls, and who in some cases were chaste. Three of Artemis's retinue had been mortal girls turned into Nymphs after they died defending their virtue. But in most myths, Nymphs are wanton and celebrate their sexuality, engaging in sexual unions with male and female humans, Gods (such as Bacchus/Dionysus), and animals. Many Nymphs are tied to one of the elements, living in water, sky, or trees. Among these are Naiads (river Nymphs), Dryads (tree Nymphs), and Lorelei (stream Nymphs, specifically German Nymphs of the Rhine River). Each is gorgeous and seductive.

The term *Nymph* may come from a Greek work meaning a rose that is blooming, likening the color of the rose to the blush of a maiden's cheek (Snow White's cheeks and lips are as red as blood), and the bloom of the rose to the shape of a woman's vaginal lips. Innocence and sexual allure rolled into one divinely beautiful creature.

Snow White is a Nymph in every respect. She has certain virtuous qualities. Her goodness is partly reflected in her name: snow falls from the sky and therefore connects us to Heaven. Like her namesake element, we see Snow White as clean, chaste, and innocent. This is seen in the old saying "pure as the driven snow." There is another aspect as well, as Maria Tatar points out: "Snow suggests cold and remoteness, along with the notion of the lifeless and inert . . . and Snow White in the coffin does indeed become not only pure and innocent but also passive, comatose, and ethereally beautiful."[2] While seemingly dead, she is chaste, aloof, unattainable. All see her Divine beauty, but none may have her (until her one worthy suitor, the prince, shows up).

Snow White is very much the virtuous daughter, fitting all of her parents' expectations (either being born just as her mother wished, or appearing to her royal father in fulfillment of his desires). She is later the perfect wife, caring for the dwarfs by cooking, cleaning their home, and satisfying them in all ways. But she is also sexual, sensual, wanton, and seductive. While the urchin story of the father finding her by the wayside is in fulfillment of the king's wish, Snow White usurps the queen's role, placing herself exactly where the adult man will see her and desire her. She is his perfect vision of beauty, which the human queen can never hope to be. She goes willingly into the king's carriage with no objection, an act that might be seen as naïve but also as wanton. In our culture, it is in fact common for women to feign innocence or naïveté when acting seductively. And young women often know that while adult men might feel protective and fatherly, they also feel lustful and desirous of a young, vulnerable female.

Next comes the huntsman. Snow White, the Nymph, seduces him with beauty and tears. She begs for her life, as anyone would. But her begging may be read as more than simply fear and pleading: "She began to weep, and said, 'Ah dear huntsman, leave me my life. I will run away into the wild forest, and never come home again.'" Imagine insanely beautiful Snow White gently, innocently taking this very strong, masculine hunter's hand, looking up at him with her dark eyes, and saying these words in her soft, girlish voice, merely a

---

2. Tatar, "Introduction. Snow White" in the Grimms' *Children's Stories and Household Tales*, 240.

whimper, slowly moving her torso from side to side in fear and excitement. Her soft white hand grips the rough fabric of his sleeve, and on her pale face a single tear falls. She places his calloused hand over her own heart, tearful eyes saying, "This fragile life is yours now to destroy or redeem. Will you destroy me, or will you allow me to flee?"

I think you get the picture. (I may have mentioned that these people are a little creepy.)

JOLLY DWARFS AND JEALOUS MOMS

Let's move on to the dwarfs. Before the dwarfs are even present, the Nymph begins her selection process. She lies in each dwarf's bed, sensing him, feeling one is not right, then another, and finally settling on the bed of the most perfect companion. Indeed, when they return, each finds that this tender, trembling beauty has lain under his blanket: the bed of each still warm with her fragile impression, each pillow touched by the scent of her sweet perspiration and of the blossoming forest flowers she has walked through.

Then one of those grizzled earth dwellers cries out, as he sees her lithe, pale form stretched sleeping across his own bed, the cream-colored skin of her bare thigh protruding from the tousled hem of her grass-stained dress. The Grimms tell us that one dwarf shared his brothers' beds that night, but the Swiss story is quite different. By virtue of his seniority, the eldest dwarf in that story was allowed to do what each creature there was dying to do, to claim this nubile prize and possess her all the long, dark night by candlelight in the wild, deep, thorn-tangled forest.

But the Grimms' Snow White is not a story of a Nymph's sexual relationship with these muscular, swarthy creatures of Earth; it is a story of a human woman fighting a Nymph for the attention of her man. So the mother acts, trying three times to kill the Nymph and forever draw her lover's advances back to herself. For as long as Snow

White lived in the world, she would be the image in her husband's mind each time he lay down beside the human woman: that is the nature of Faerie obsession.

The human woman hatched a plan. She dressed as a peddler and went "over the seven mountains to the home of the seven dwarfs." (Seven, like three, is a magical number used in spells.) She told Snow White she had "stay laces" for sale. Stays would have been used on a corset, so when the human queen offers to lace the Nymph, she is tightly binding the Nymph's breasts. Breasts are, of course, an outward sign of the Nymph's maturity and sexuality, a clear indication of a woman's attractiveness and her ability to engage in sex and its outcome, birthing and nursing a child. When the queen binds Snow White's chest, she is binding or destroying this outward sign of the Nymph's beauty, not only cutting off her breath but also giving her a childish, sexually immature physique. Snow White falls to the ground, seemingly dead. But when the dwarfs return home, they rip the laces from her. To do this they must undress her. When she comes alive, partially disrobed, the dwarfs certainly cannot help but notice her breasts. The dwarfs help the Nymph reassert her sexual allure. Her Faerie lust and beauty is in antithesis to the queen's spell: Snow White is unbound, her ripe sexuality reasserted. The spell is broken.

The scrying mirror, itself the essence of Faerie magic (magic tied to the Underworld or to Faerie, an often dark magic that gives these creatures power over us), alerts the queen-mother to Snow White's survival. Now the queen appears again, with a poisoned comb.

Hair is another feature of feminine beauty and desirability. Women work tirelessly to make their hair attractive, and many women feel that hair is a feature over which they have great control, perhaps unlike their figure or facial features. Since the dawn of time, seductive hairstyles have been worn to attract a lover. In many cultures, women are required to cover their hair, because it is well known how tempting it looks to men. (In Orthodox Judaism, married women shave their head and wear a wig, so as to no longer be sexually attractive to men other than their husband; in Islam, women cover their heads to avoid appearing attractive to men.) From Lady Godiva's tresses to Twiggy's pixie cut, Farrah Fawcett's wings, Betty Page's bangs, Marilyn's styled blond halo, or Jennifer Aniston's feathery shag, every generation's Aphrodite has worn her hair as a signature symbol of her sexuality. And the Nymph Snow White, with her incredible coloring, must have had a beautiful mane that flowed like dark water over rosy red cheeks and framed ruby lips. (We'll speak about this more when we get to "Rapunzel").

So the queen goes to work, attempting to destroy her daughter's hold on dwarfs and men by placing a poisoned comb into the beautiful hair, turning that lush fountain into a poisoned well. The poison is loosed, and Snow White falls dead. But the dwarfs, her lovers, thwart the queen by removing the comb, restoring Snow White to life, and allowing her unbound locks to excite the earthy creatures and keep them aroused.

At the very core of a woman's attractiveness, and of a Nymph's exquisite beauty, is the promise that her lover may possess her, which means entering her in a sexual embrace. While the Swiss story spells this out without much room for confusion, the Grimms' version has the queen enter Snow White in the orifice of her mouth. Of course oral gratification is the first urge we humans feel from birth, and we spend our lives satisfying our mouths with food, talk, tastes, lipstick, and, of course, our sexual desires. So finally, on the third try (three being the magical number of fulfillment), the queen must penetrate Snow White, taking the place of her lover, substituting poison for her lover's gift.

It does not take a biblical genius to see that the apple the queen offers is a symbol of Snow White's sexual wantonness, the fruit of the garden that gave Eve the revelation that she was a sexual being, that her body was nude and desirable, that Adam was not just her brother and companion but the object of her lust. And, like Eve, Snow White's apple would bring the consequences of sexual awareness: pain, heartbreak, and eventually death, in two senses: orgasm is a state of death, a glimpse into the journey to the other side. The French call orgasm "the little death," and the Catholic Church sees it as a mortal, or deadly, sin for a woman to be wantonly aroused; and the apple itself brings Snow White's demise, or so the dwarfs think.

Snow White and the mother-queen act out the biblical scene of temptation and sin here—mother taking the role of serpent, the Nymph taking Eve's part. Like Eve, sensuous Snow White is tempted by the apple, and desires it. Like the serpent of Eden, the crafty queen tricks Snow White by tasting it herself (showing that sex with an adult man will not injure the adult queen as it will the Nymph), and Snow White is lulled into biting the fruit. She falls, seemingly dead: an analogy to Eve's fall from grace, or a spiritual death; in either case, we know or come to learn that the Nymph is not dead, but sexualized.

While the dwarfs have been able to undress her and to caress her hair to find the cause of the last two "deaths," they are not Adam: they cannot fully enter the Nymph's orifices to find the cause of this disease. Snow White becomes aloof, unattainable, a monument to her desirability and beauty that none can possess.

None, that is, but her true lover. After her body has lain for some time on display, a human prince comes. He may play the part of Adam and may take the object from Snow White and replace it with his own sexual presence, the thing that will bring the Nymph back to life because she will be allowed to live fully—to be a sexual creature, granting her lover his unbridled desire.

There is another aspect to the stepmother's destructive actions: she is attempting to undo Snow White's magic. The three conditions of the compact made by her mother at her birth were that Snow White would be white as snow, red as blood, and black as ebony.

The stepmother attempts to eradicate each. The stay laces bind the Nymph's snow-white skin; the comb poisons her ebony black hair; and the poisoned apple is red as blood. The stepmother nearly succeeds, but for the efforts of the human prince.

The prince orders the stepmother to be killed horribly: " . . . iron slippers had already been put upon the fire, and they were brought in with tongs, and set before her. Then she was forced to put on the red-hot shoes, and dance until she dropped down dead." She is punished quite severely for seeing her daughter as a sexual competitor rather than nurturing the girl's sexuality and sensuality, as a true mother should. While many girls go through a stage during which they become intensely attached to their fathers,[3] a nurturing mother turns a blind eye to this and helps the growing girl redirect her desire toward potential lovers outside the family circle. In time, a nurturing mother encourages her daughter to seek out love and romance, and ultimately to bond with a lover and create a family. Our queen, faced with a Nymph daughter, could not do this, and fell to obsession and finally death for her shortcomings.

Despite her mother's efforts to subdue her daughter's sexuality and femininity, Snow White's sexual nature leads her to maturity, and after a "dormant" period of being adored from afar (in sleep), Snow White may take a lifelong lover, the prince.

Notice that in the Grimms' version it is not a romantic kiss that wakes Snow White, but the prince's servants' very human bumbling: "And now the king's son had [the coffin] carried away by his servants on their shoulders. And it happened that they stumbled over a tree-stump, and with the shock the poisonous piece of apple which Snow-White had bitten off came out of her throat. And before long she opened her eyes, lifted up the lid of the coffin, sat up, and was once more alive. 'Oh, heavens, where am I,' she cried." Snow White, through her sleepy visit to the Underworld and her transformation through

---

3. See, for example, Sigmund Freud's *Three Essays on the Theory of Sexuality.*

death, is now able to leave her Nymph life behind, and live a human life with the prince, complete with human mistakes and bumbling. She awakens into her human life with this dramatic bumble.

In the Grimms' version, as with many stories, the Nymph's life with the prince is never described. The prince simply tells Snow White, "I love you more than everything in the world, come with me to my father's palace, you shall be my wife." Notice that the prince falls in love with Snow White without conversation or any meeting of the minds; it is Snow White's beauty alone that seals the deal, and that is the way with Faerie beauty. Their looks, sexuality, and charisma seduce us, even when they are inert.

SLEEP, TRANCE, AND INITIATION

The element of sleep in the story of Snow White is interesting. We see it in several of the Grimms' tales, especially "Sleeping Beauty." But the sleep element also appears in "Beauty and the Beast," where the Beast falls asleep as if dead under a cabbage while awaiting Beauty's return to his castle. We also see it in "Snow White and Rose-Red," in which the bear sleeps with the two young girls each night.

Sleep is a time that binds us to dreams, and to death. Just like Snow White, we appear inert or deathly when we sleep, and worried parents often check on sleeping infants to be sure they are breathing. We sleep at night, which is the domain of the Goddess, the subconscious, and is ruled by the moon. Night is seen as the death of day and of the sun. Sleep is our nightly visit to the Underworld, the land of both death and youth. It is a place ruled over by such Underworld Goddesses as Hel, Hecate, and Persephone. Persephone is herself a Nymph whom Hades, the Death World God, fell in love with when he glimpsed her naked beauty while she bathed. (Water is another symbol of dreams and the unconscious.)

Shakespeare likens sleep and death in what is perhaps his most famous soliloquy, when Hamlet postulates:

To die, to sleep;
To sleep: perchance to dream: ay, there's the rub;
For in that sleep of death what dreams may come
When we have shuffled off this mortal coil,
Must give us pause . . . (*Hamlet*, III.i, 65–69)

As Hamlet observes, while we appear to be dead in sleep, our minds are quite active, connecting us to the Underworld through dreams.

Dreams have been seen throughout time as messages from the Gods, prophetic visions, omens from dead intercessors, or glimpses of past lives. In all cases, they connect us to the Gods, to the Underworld, and to death. In many religious ceremonies, a seeker will willingly enter a deep dream state in order to receive information from Gods or spirits (the most widely known of these religious practices might be Siberian Shamanism, though we see it in almost all world religions, including Judaism and Christianity). In death we are able to see through the veil between our world and the Underworld, and glimpse things our human perspective will not allow.

Many rituals are meant to bring on prophetic dreaming. In Keats' long poem "The Eve of Saint Agnes," we are shown a medieval ritual that will do just that. According to the folklore, on Saint Agnes Eve (January 20) if a young woman were to go to bed without any supper, undress herself so that she was completely naked, and lie on her bed with her hands under the pillow and looking up to the heavens, and not to look behind her, then her future husband will appear in her dream, kiss her, and feast with her.

In Greek, British, Celtic, and Norse myth, dreams are ruled over by Underworld Gods and Goddesses. The Greeks credit the God Morpheus, who is able to take the form of any human and appear in that person's dreams. He is the son of the sleep God Hypnos and the night Goddess Nyx, and he sleeps in a cave upon an ebony bed, surrounded by poppies. In British myth, Queen Mab rules dreams, and especially nightmares. Shakespeare paints an image of Mab in *Romeo and* Juliet as a lovable, diminutive Faerie, riding across the night in her tiny chariot and visiting people's dreams:

> O, then, I see Queen Mab hath been with you.
> She is the fairies' midwife, and she comes
> In shape no bigger than an agate-stone
> On the fore-finger of an alderman, . . .
> And in this state she gallops night by night
> Through lovers' brains, and then they dream of love;
> (*Romeo and Juliet*, I.iiii, 53–85)

But older mythology paints Mab quite differently, as the Queen of Night who commands ravens and wolves, creatures of death and darkness. She rides a white mare wildly through the British forest, gathering souls of the hunted and harvested. The term we use today for bad dreams comes from her legend: those who, in sleep, become aware of her passage and have hideous visions are said to be "riding the night mare."

What each of these mythic accounts of sleep and dreaming have in common is the notion that dreams tie us to death and to Otherworldly visions. While asleep we are helpless, controlled by Goddesses and Gods who have our destinies in their hands, and who may play with our souls as they like while we are in their dark realms. From the teachings of Shamanism, Qabalah, and other religions, we learn that these experiences change us and allow us to grow, mature, and come to understand ourselves. We see our destinies through dreams and understand our own yearnings and desires. These death-like experiences are rituals of initiation.

In many religious traditions, a student must face a deathlike experience and feel the energies of the Underworld to be considered an initiate. In Wicca and other Pagan religions, the initiatory rite is finely crafted, representing a visit to the Underworld. In many traditions of Shamanism, the seeker must enter a trance state and commune with creatures from the realms of death. Even the Christian tradition of baptism carries with it the threat of drowning, overcome by the ecstatic spirit of Jehovah. At the end of the initiatory ritual, through the deathlike experience, the seeker is reborn, or transformed.

For Snow White, the nap she takes after tasting the apple is a return to the Underworld from which she first came. We know Snow White is a Faerie creature, who appeared in fulfillment of a magical wish; in some versions of the story, the wish is bound with three drops of blood. That she appeared fairly immediately (especially to the king in his carriage) means this Nymph was watching, waiting for an opportunity to take human form in our world. To completely transform into a human life, Snow White must face death at the hands of her mother (who may not be evil incarnate, but may be a stern initiating priestess . . . on the other hand, she may just be really nasty), and through death, be transformed into sexual and emotional maturity.

The tale of Snow White's sleep is very reminiscent of another, mythic tale: the Welsh tale of the horse Faerie Rhiannon.

The story of Rhiannon, as told in the *Mabinogion*, begins with Pwyll (pronounced "push"; yes, Welsh is an odd language), a human who has been to the Underworld. He is told that if he stands upon a certain Faerie mound, he will either "receive blows or see a wonder."[4] Pwyll takes his men up to the crest of the mound and sees a beautiful woman on a horse ride by on the road below. He sends one of his men to greet her, but no matter how fast the man spurs his horse he cannot catch up with the strange rider, even though the woman seems to be riding at a leisurely pace. Pwyll makes his own attempt to overtake her, with the same results. Finally, Pwyll calls out to the woman, who stops and tells him, "If you had called to me before, it would have been better for your horse."

---

4. Megli, "An Introduction to the Four Branches."

The woman is Rhiannon, and she tells Pwyll she has come to our world to find him. They fall in love and are married quickly. Rhiannon is soon pregnant.

When Rhiannon bears a son, she is set to nurse, guarded by several women. But the women fall asleep, and in the dead of night the child disappears. The women, afraid of being killed for sleeping on guard duty, smear dog's blood on their mistress, and claim Rhiannon ate her own child.

As punishment, Rhiannon must wear a saddle and bridle, and carry people on her back to Pwyll's castle, telling them of her crime. In short, she must act as a horse.

In time, the child is brought back to our world when a local knight battles an Otherworldly being over a colt that being was attempting to steal. In the bargain, a little blond boy was left on the knight's floor. The knight and his wife come to realize that this was Pwyll's changeling son, and return the child to their king, ending Rhiannon's service as a horse.

Let's compare this story to the events of Snow White.

Snow White and Rhiannon both appear in response to a ritualized magical wish. In Rhiannon's case, Pwyll and his men enter a Faerie space, and perform the ritual that would allow them to "see a wonder." In the case of Snow White, a magical wish is made, either bound with three drops of blood or sworn upon three flying ravens. In each case, a beautiful, mysterious Underworld creature appears, almost instantly in the case of Rhiannon and of the king in his carriage, ready to assume a place in the wishing person's human life and in our human world.

Both figures undergo an experience that involves closeness to death: for Rhiannon, her son disappears, and she finds herself smeared with blood and accused of eating the tyke; for Snow White, she is taken into the forest and nearly killed, the life of a wild animal substituted for her life.

For both, in order to restore the balance of their lives as humans, an initiatory journey back to their own world must be made. For Rhiannon, a horse Faerie, that journey is made by assuming the form (or at least the function) of a horse in our world. She connects to her true Faerie nature, riding humans on her back, living in both worlds at once. This allows her to change the course of events in her world, and bring back her son.

For Snow White, she must go through a deathlike initiatory experience of visiting her Underworld origins before she can accept mature love. In her state of sleep/death, she journeys back to Faerie, where she confronts her Faerie nature and is allowed a choice of remaining Nymph-like—being adored for her beauty but unattainable (asleep/dead)—or returning to our world and living a fully human life. If she chooses the second, she may accept the love of a human with all of his faults (we see the prince has faults by the fact that he does not realize Snow White is still alive, and by the fact that his servants are clumsy).

Snow White chooses a human life, and through the imperfections of her prince's men, comes back to life in our world. Through her initiatory deathlike experience, brought about by her mother, she is able to accept human love: not adoration for her Faerie beauty alone, but a mundane life as a wife.

One last note about the story, and this is something we'll see in several of the Grimms' tales and comment on again: in this story, the father is a nonentity. He appears briefly in the "king in his carriage" version, and in the better-known Grimms' version he only appears long enough to marry a new wife. He is not present at all to aid Snow White when her stepmother goes berserk. This is because the tale is centered around the struggle between the two females: death versus life, the Underworld against our world, night against day, dark versus light. Dad is a fleeting sexual object who disappears into the background as the two girls duke it out, because that's all he is required to do. How sad for him.

THE SNOW WHITE RITUAL

Snow White is an icon of beauty and attraction, loved by all who encounter her (well, almost all). Whether you visualize her as the Disney maiden, or allow yourself to see her as described in the Grimms' tale and other older sources, the image conjured up by the Nymph is one of allure, charm, and smoldering sensuality. We will use the icon of Snow White in a ritual that will help the magician assume these characteristics: in essence, the magician will feel alluring, attractive, stunning, and desirable—either in general or to a particular person. It can work for anyone, female or male, and it will work whether or not the magician believes herself or himself to be attractive naturally.

Everyone has attractive qualities, and no one on earth is 100 percent desirable to everyone. Speaking from my own experience, I often find the standard of American beauty fairly plain and many times quite unattractive, and I am often attracted passionately to women whom many American men would consider funny-looking, nerdy, or plain. That's how my brain is wired. The trick to being desirable is confidence, accepting one's flaws, knowing one's desirable traits, and knowing what to do with them! Self-confidence is the biggest aphrodisiac there is, and when any person has confidence, he or she will convey this in terms of sexual appeal.

Snow White is stunningly beautiful, to be sure. But what is unique about the Nymph is that she can be anyone's ideal of beauty, from a king to a huntsman, from a dwarf to a mirror. It is obvious to anyone with common sense that these disparate characters could not possibly have shared the same aesthetic. It was Snow White's charm, bearing, and utter self-confidence, even in the face of death (with the huntsman), that led each character to find such beauty in her.

This ritual will bring that sort of charm, charisma, and confidence to the magician, and aid in finding a perfect lover or cementing an existing relationship.

Never never never (was *never* written enough times?) cast a spell upon someone who is unaware or unwilling to have magic worked on them! It is very bad for them, and it is very bad for you. I know this from bitter experience, so take my word on it. If someone asks you for a healing spell, or for aid in finding a job, by all means do magic for them. But in looking for the right lover, it is never wise to name a particular person. The Gods know much better than you do how your future looks, and if you leave the identity of your one true love in their hands, things will go much more smoothly. It's fine to say, "I'd like a lover who has the qualities of so-and-so, their looks, their sense of humor," but asking specifically for a relationship with so-and-so is never good. And, yes, I know you believe so-and-so is your one true destined love now and forever, but I warn you it may not work out that way . It's a much better idea to leave yourself open to see if so-and-so will answer the call, or if there is someone else lurking in the magical shadows. You will thank me for this advice.

PREPARING FOR THE RITUAL

If you want a lover who will be with you for the long haul, be ready to put some time and energy into finding that person. It is unrealistic to think that a one-hour ritual will yield a person willing to commit decades to your exclusive company. You should think about committing months or even a year to doing magic that will bring that one special person into your life.

That said, there is some homework involved in preparing for this ritual.

Keep a journal of what you feel makes you attractive to someone and write in it a little each day. List traits and physical features: "I feel that my sense of humor makes me attractive." "I have beautiful eyes."

No one will read this but you and the Gods, so be brutally honest. If you are a woman who feels she has lovely breasts, or a man who feels he has a nice butt, say so. Or perhaps you're someone who feels your strength or intellect is attractive. But also be honest about your intelligence, honesty, truthfulness, and also your odd quirks and neuroses. Remember that what one person finds annoying another will find alluring. Perhaps you've had potential lovers turn off to you because you were too smart or too nerdy? Another lover will adore you for these traits.

If you are just doing magic to be incredibly attractive, with no intention of falling into a lifelong affair just now, that's fine, too. You should still list the things that are attractive about you, and the types of people you would like to see attracted to you. This may keep the "wrong" type away—always a good precaution (see chapter 7, on Red Riding Hood).

If you are looking for love, then also include in your daily list some trait or feature you are looking for in a mate. Again, include appearance, character, beliefs; the more you list, the stronger your projection will be when performing magic. Use photographs cut from magazines and media, such as photos printed from the Internet (only to display an ideal, not to win the love of that wolf guy from *Twilight*). Use stories of successful relationships as a standard: it's certainly a lovely idea to hold "The Gift of the Magi" or *The Taming of the Shrew* as examples of romantic scenarios you'd like to live out in a relationship. (Use Anaïs Nin's *Diaries* or Pauline Réage's *Story of O* at your own discretion.) List things you'd like to do with your future lover: walks, hockey games, passionate baths, target practice.

When you've put quite some time into your journaling (perhaps a month or two, from new moon to new moon), it is time to prepare for the ritual itself.

During the ritual you will need to be in a quiet, private place. Your room, the forest, the beach are all good places if you feel you will not be disturbed. The ritual is best done skyclad (nude) or in a sheer robe, but if you are uncomfortable this way, a closed front robe or loose-fitting clothes (like a loose dress or martial-arts pants) will also work. Remember that this spell is meant to help you feel attractive, confident, and sensual, so your own nudity should be proudly embraced, no matter what you have felt in the past about your looks and physique. This is a spell about embracing your beauty or handsomeness, and that starts right here.

You will need an altar, which could be any table. I like a round altar, as I feel it corresponds to the Wheel of the Year, the cycle of life, and the ritual format of a circle, but many Ceremonial Magicians use a square or rectangular altar, which works just as well. In lieu of a table, I find a tree trunk or a large, low boulder works well. The large industrial cable spools make great round altars. You may certainly use a cloth laid on the ground or the floor, a snack tray, or a wooden breakfast barstool. The intent of the ritual is more important than the money you spend on accoutrements.

You will need these tools:

- Two white seven-day candles
- Rose oil
- An apple
- A knife to cut the apple (your ritual athame, or any kitchen knife)
- Floral incense (rose would be very good)
- A wooden wand (do not use copper, metal, or crystal; the wand for this ritual should be a simple branch of wood)
- A chalice of red wine (or grape juice)
- Four small locks of your hair (if doing the ritual with two or more, each participant should have locks of hair on the altar, and each person's hair should be given at each direction)

- A compass to determine east, south, west, and north, if you do not already know. (Watching the sun rise or set would also be a good way of determining the directions.)

This ritual should be done at the new moon, the time when the moon is dark or is just a slim crescent. This is a time when the moon will begin to grow to full, and so the effects of the spell will grow with the waxing moon. You will also be doing a small follow-up ritual on the full moon.

Since you are calling upon Snow White, a Nymph, to give you sexual confidence and attractiveness, and to bring love, passion, and romance into your life, you will be calling upon the mythic record of Nymphs. In Greece, young women made gifts to Nymphs of locks of their hair, and the Nymphs who attended Bacchus or Dionysus were given wine (grape juice may substitute if you do not drink alcohol). So you will be giving the Nymphs these gifts in our ritual: the ritual calls for you to place these gifts on the ground; if you are indoors, simply place them in a dish or tray, and at the end of the ritual, bring the gifts and your chalice outdoors and offer them there.

You should know the name of each Nymph you are calling, and how to pronounce each name correctly: Nephelae are sky or cloud Nymphs, pronounced NEF-*el*-A; Sirens are Nymphs of the sea and rivers, but here they represent south (fire and passion) because they are passionate and sexual; Naiads (NI-*ads*) are Nymphs of oceans and other bodies of water; Dryads (DRI-*ads*) are tree Nymphs. The mistletoe Dryad was chosen because of that plant's association with love, kissing, and passion. While the custom is observed here in the Americas only on Yule or Christmas, in eastern Europe meeting under mistletoe at any time of the year elicits a kiss.

The ritual is written for a single person, but you may easily do the ritual with two, three, or more, and each action and line may be done and spoken in turn by each participant. Sharing the energy of the circle can make the magic more powerful, but do not perform the ritual with anyone with whom you cannot be honest and completely yourself.

Set the altar with the incense in the east, the wand in the south, the chalice in the west, and the apple in the north. Place the seven-day candles at the center.

Take a small drop of the oil and dab it on your forehead, saying:

"I cleanse myself with oil. Purify my mind, that I may let go of past shyness and discomfort, and embrace the me that is to be." (If you are doing the ritual in a group, each magician should repeat this as they anoint.)

Dab a drop on your throat and say, "Let my words be magic, and may the Gods hear my will."

Dab a drop over your heart, and say: "May my heart guide me, and may love find me."

Dab a drop on your loins, saying: "May passion have me, and may I have passion!"

Place a drop on each of your feet, saying: "May my footsteps guide me to adoration and fulfillment!"

Move to the east of the altar, and light the incense. Pick up your wand, and begin to move three times around the circle, clockwise (called deosil in magic), saying:

(First time) "Cast the circle three times round, once for seed beneath the ground."

(Second time): "A second time the circle tread, for sun and rain-cloud overhead."

(Third time): "Cast the circle, go times three, with wooden wand grown from the tree."

Now return to the east, and replace the wand on the altar. Pick up a lock of your hair, and present it to the east by holding it to the sky in that direction. (If more than one person is doing the ritual, pick up a group of locks.) Place the lock of hair on the ground in the east, saying:

"Daughter of clouds, Nephelae,
Accept my gift to you this day
Turn my mind to passion fair
that love and romance may appear."

Bow with your arms in a cross on your chest, and recover (stand back up straight).

Move to the south, offering a lock of hair. Place the hair on the ground in the south, saying:

"Sirens, Nymphs of passion's flame
Accept my gift to you this day
May your song enchant my heart
That my love and passion start."

Bow with your arms in a cross on your chest, and recover.

Move to the west, offering up the lock of hair, and place it on the ground, saying:

"Gentle Naiads, Nymphs at play
Accept my gift to you this day
Fill my heart with merry laughter
For love's embrace is what I'm after!"

Bow with your arms in a cross on your chest, and recover.

Move to the north, offering the lock of hair and placing it on the earth, saying:

"Dryad of the mistletoe
Accept the gift I here do show
Bless me with a thousand kisses
Touches, fondles, and passionate wishes!"

Now return to the east and say, "The directions are called, and So Mote It Be!"

Turn to the center of the circle, and light one of the seven-day candles, saying: "Snow White, Nymph girl, icon of love, beauty, sensuality, and passion, I call upon you. I ask your aid in making myself like you: confident, joyous, sexual, and proud. Be with me, Snow White, Nymph creature, as I walk this world in enchantment and beauty. So Mote It Be!"

Next, take the apple from its place on the altar. Use the knife to cut the apple in half from side to side (*not* from stem to calyx; the calyx is found at the apple's bottom). If you do this cut correctly, there should be a star on each half of the apple.

Take the bottom half of the apple (the half with the calyx) and hold it to your chest, saying:

"This half of the apple is poison! It is my old life, filled with doubt and insecurity. Thinking I am not pretty (handsome) enough! Thinking I am not smart enough! Not funny enough! Believing that others will not find me beautiful, pleasing, charming, sexual, or desirable! Hiding when I wish to be seen. Staying quiet when I wish to be heard. Cloaking my sensuality when I want to be desired!

"I take the poison out of myself, as you, Snow White, spit out the poison of the apple. I wake from my long sleep and enter the world reborn. I am confident and sure. I will show the world my beauty (ruggedness), my strength, my charm, and my most lovely (most handsome) attributes. I throw this apple away, and with it I wake from my sleep!"

If outdoors, throw the apple as far as you can, as long as it is into some wild place. If indoors, drop it into your bowl or tray. You will throw it into a natural place later.

Next, pick up the top of the apple, containing the stem.

"Here is the start of my new life. Here I see myself in the mirror of truth: the truth of my beauty (good looks), the truth of my sensuality, the truth of my sexuality! I will show those who would adore me the charms of my flesh, the greatness of my intellect, the fury

of my wit, and the wholeness of who I am. I will not hide myself.
When those I am attracted to pass by, I will show myself to them,
unafraid of rejection. What care I if they do not want me? There are
others who will see me for the prize that I am! I am Nymph, I sing
the song of love and lust! I sing the song of life! Those who have a
soul will hear my song, and adore me."

Bite a piece of this apple (if doing the ritual with others, each of
you should take a bite of the apple) and say, "So Mote It Be!"

As you take a bite (or bites) of the apple, carefully take the seeds
out. Use your knife if you need to. Place them on the altar.

"Snow White, these seeds are the start of my new life, walking
with you, Nymph girl, in sensual passion and delicious beauty! Let
us plant these seeds and begin the growth of a new joy!"

Carefully gather the seeds into a bag, or onto a small plate or bowl.
Later you will plant them in a natural place: your yard or garden, a
friend's yard, an open field, or a public park or forest. Whether they
grow or not is not as important as the effort you put into planting
them.

Now take the chalice of wine or juice, and hold it up toward the
east.

"Nymph girl, Snow White, let us drink together to seal this bond.
I offer you fruit of the vines that grow in the vineyard and the deep
forest where you dwelt in safety."

If outdoors, pour a small amount of the liquid onto the ground;
if indoors, pour it into the bowl containing the apple seeds. Then
drink of the wine yourself; if others are in the circle, share the drink.
When the chalice is emptied, say, "Blessed Be!"

Next, look through the journal you have kept to prepare for this
ritual and reflect on how you will act differently from this moment,
and what sort of person or people you want to bring into your life.
You may also speak to Snow White and to the elements as you read
over your journal.

This meditation should last as long as is comfortable. Then place the journal under or near the altar, face the center of the circle, and say, "Snow White, Nymph of the deep forest, you who are sensual and beautiful, I thank you for joining me (us) in this rite. Walk with me (us) now as I bring into my life the lessons you have taught me. Blessed Be!"

Turn to the east, and say, "Daughter of clouds, Nephelae, I thank you for joining me in this rite. As you return to the enchanted lands, I bid you hail and farewell." Bow in respect, with your arms crossed upon your chest, and then recover.

Turn now to the south, and say, "Daughter of passion, Siren, I thank you for joining me in this rite. As you return to the enchanted lands, I bid you hail and farewell." Bow in respect, with your arms crossed upon your chest, and then recover.

Turn to the west, and say, "Gentle Naiads, Nymphs at play, I thank you for joining me in this rite. As you return to the enchanted lands, I bid you hail and farewell." Bow in respect, with your arms crossed upon your chest, and then recover.

Move to the north, and say, "Dryad of the mistletoe, I thank you for joining me in this rite. As you return to the enchanted lands, I bid you hail and farewell." Bow in respect, with your arms crossed upon your chest, and then recover.

Now take the knife you used to cut the apple, and walk widder-shins (counterclockwise) around the circle while saying, "May this circle be returned unto the earth until I have need to call upon its powers again."

You are now finished. If you are with another person or several other people, all of you should hug and feast together. If you are alone, then you should relax, eat something, and feel the "zing" of magical energy in the area or the room.

RITUAL FOLLOW-UP

At full moon, put your journal in a place where it will not be disturbed, and burn the second white candle placed on the altar in the Snow White ritual beside it. Let the candle burn out, then resume writing and collaging in your journal as desired. Anytime you've performed the Snow White ritual again at a new moon, you should follow up this way on the full moon. Do this ritual several times over several months, for up to a year.

The ritual we just did is structured after a Wiccan ritual and is the basic structure for most of the rituals we will do in this book. Read it over, and familiarize yourself with some of the terms (*altar, wand, elements*). You'll see them again. Remember that the more you do rituals, the better you will get at doing them. You'll also begin to see patterns of how ritual is structured, how it flows, and how you feel while doing it. These will all help you become a good magician.

Chapter 2

SNOW-WHITE AND ROSE-RED: CONNECTING WITH YOUR TOTEM ANIMAL

Two sisters live with their mother deep in the forest. One girl is passionate and athletic, preferring summer and the outdoors; the other is quiet and gentle, preferring winter and the hearth side. One wintry night a bear comes to their door, and begins a nightly ritual of sleeping with the girls. When summer comes, the girls find a dwarf who seems to hate them even though they help the creature at every turn. In the end, the dwarf leads the two girls to a treasure. Our ritual will examine the girls' relationship with the bear as a model for a magical technique of using a totem animal to explore the world of dreams and the subconscious. Story quotes are from the Margaret Hunt translation of the 1812 printing of the Grimms' Children's and Household Tales.

There was once a poor widow who lived in a lonely cottage. In front of the cottage was a garden wherein stood two rose trees, one of which bore white and the other red roses. She had two children who were like the two rose trees, and one was called Snow-White, and the other Rose-Red."

So begins story of "Snow-White and Rose-Red," two sisters living in a cottage deep in the woods with their widowed mother. The story will go on to involve a bear, a dwarf, lambs, doves, and talking birds, all leading up to a treasure and, in some versions, a marriage to a convenient pair of princes.

The Snow-White in this story is not the same character as Snow White the Nymph. In fact, their original German names are somewhat different. The Snow White of Disney fame is *Schneewittchen* in German. The word *Weiss* (white) has been altered to make her name mean "Little Snow White." Snow-White in this story is *Schneeweißchen*, literally meaning "white as snow."

Many of the Grimms' tales play upon a struggle between a mother and her daughter, or a father and his son. Others feature orphaned children as their main characters. "Snow-White and Rose-Red" is one of the few Grimms' stories to feature a happy, loving family. It is also one of the few Grimms' tales that gives us a description of the domestic, day-to-day life of its characters. The mother is a widow; more often in Grimms, we have a father who is a widower and who has remarried. The sisters are devoted to their mother and love each other deeply, another very different situation than those we see in most Grimms' tales (think of Cinderella and her stepsisters). While they live modestly, they appear to be educated: in one passage, we learn that "Snow-White sat at home with her mother, and helped her with her housework, or read to her when there was nothing to do." In another passage of the story, we are told that "they sat round the hearth, and the mother took her spectacles and read aloud out of a large book, and the two girls listened as they sat and spun." They are very happy with their lives in the forest, and happy with each other. Unlike most Grimms' characters, they seem to want for nothing.

When siblings appear in fairy tales, they are often two halves of a whole or two aspects of a single person. Indeed, Snow-White and Rose-Red have very different personalities and complement each other perfectly. Snow-White is a bit of an agoraphobic; she prefers to stay in the cottage helping her mother with the work of the home. Like her namesake element, Snow-White is pale. We also learn that "Snow-White was more quiet and gentle than Rose-Red," as snow dampens sound and creates a still quiet when it blankets the earth. White is the color of purity and chastity, and indeed our little Schneeweißchen is gentle, pure, and virtuous. Her identity is bound up in caring for her home and her family, and we see throughout the story that she is invested in helping others.

Rose-Red, *Rosenrot* in German, is a very different girl: "Rose-Red liked better to run about in the meadows and fields seeking flowers and catching butterflies." Red is the color of passion and sensuality. In magical systems, red often represents noon and adolescence, a time of intense energy and lustful urges. Rose-Red is a wild child, roaming the forests and seeking sensations and experiences among the animals who dwell there. She comes to know the forest creatures and fears nothing.

The association of Snow-White with snow and winter, and Rose-Red with summer and passion, is made clear in this passage: "Snow-White and Rose-Red kept their mother's little cottage so neat that it was a pleasure to look inside it. In the summer Rose-Red took care of the house, and every morning laid a wreath of flowers by her mother's bed before she awoke, in which was a rose from each tree. In the winter Snow-White lit the fire and hung the kettle on the hob." Notice that Rose-Red is active in household chores in summer, a time of heat and passion, while Snow-White cares for the hearth in winter's snowy cold. The two are complementary, and represent the conflicting feelings that inhabit all young women: the lusty feelings of a growing young woman (Rose-Red) and the strong societal pressure to still her passions and be the good girl who sits quietly by her parents' side and who takes care of the home and family (Snow-White). Here the contrasting urges work together: Snow-White cannot leave her comfort zone of home and hearth without passionate Rose-Red to encourage her.

With Rose-Red by her side, Snow-White ventures out into the world, where the animals of the forest come to know the girls and befriend them: "They often ran about the forest alone and gathered red berries, and no beasts did them any harm, but came close to them trustfully. The little hare would eat a cabbage leaf out of their hands, the roe grazed by their side, the stag leapt merrily by them, and the birds sat still upon the boughs, and sang whatever they knew."

This is an interesting passage: notice that the berries are red again, showing their passion for the forest and its creatures. The cabbage leaf and the hare can both represent sexuality and fertility. The cabbage is a head, like lettuce, whose folds and creases can represent the lips of a woman's vagina (as does the rose, after whom the girls were named).

The hare has long been associated with sexuality and fertility, and represents the return of growth and sex in the spring (which is why the Pagan hare of spring continues to be associated with Christian Easter). The stag is also sexual and complements the Hare Goddess, representing the antlered male fertility God. We also see two halves of the year represented here: the hare is associated with spring and the growth of new greenery after the winter snows melt; the stag is autumn and the hunt, when summer's passionate growth falls prey to the scythe and the bow or gun. We see a full year represented in all four characters: Snow-White (winter); the hare (spring); Rose-Red (summer); and the stag (autumn). Indeed, we are being clued in on some level that the story represents a cycle of one year, from the winter hibernation of the bear, through the growth cycle of the year, to the autumn finding of a treasure (gold, the color of autumn leaves, and the treasure or prosperity of the hunt and the harvest).

Most importantly for our chapter here, the birds sing to the girls, who understand their song. In Faerie lore it is often birds who foretell the future and pass information. We remember this in the phrase *a little birdie told me.*

Now the story develops. One winter's night (Snow-White's domain) there is a knock on the door. It is Rose-Red, the adventurous girl, who answers it. The visitor is a bear, who enters the house. While the girls are alarmed at first, the bear can speak to them, and assures them that he will not harm them.

Immediately a sexual tension appears to grow between the bear and the girls: "They tugged his hair with their hands, put their feet upon his back, and rolled him about, or they took a hazel-switch and beat him, and when he growled they laughed. But the bear took it all in good part; only when they were too rough he called out, 'Leave me alive, children, Snow-White, Rose-Red, will you beat your wooer dead.'" The girls become very rough and physical with the bear, hitting and taunting him in much the same way many young teens will punch each other, pull each other's hair, or tease each other as they start to develop feeling of attraction and lust for the opposite sex. In fact, in the last line of the passage, the bear states that the bond between himself and the girls is romantic and sexual, when he calls himself their "wooer" (other translations treat this as "lover").

The bear returns nightly, and though the Grimms take great pains not to state it, there is the implication that the girls sleep each night with the bear: we see this same treatment in the way the Grimms carefully explain that the seven dwarfs made a bed for Snow White to sleep alone, while older versions describe her sleeping with the dwarfs. That the girls sleep with the bear, literally, is implied in Snow-White's relationship with the creature: bears hibernate, and

Snow-White represents winter, sleep, and quiet. The bear has come to lay with Snow-White through the winter, in his dormant state.

The sisters spend the winter sleeping and making rough horse-play with the bear. When summer comes, Rose-Red's time, the bear must return to the forest. While Snow-White may consummate her love for the creature during its hibernation, Rose-Red must explore her relationship with the bear in lustful summer, in the wild of the forest.

This is where the girls meet their enemy, the dwarf.

While Little Snow White meets seven dwarfs who seem benign and fatherly (except for the implied sex part), older versions of the story paint the dwarfs as cannibals and thieves. In another Grimms' tale, "The Robber Bridegroom," we see a Little Snow White–like figure in the Miller's Daughter. She goes into the deep woods like Little Snow White to find a house filled with men (like the dwarfs), one of whom agrees to marry her. But she learns that the men are cannibals, and plan to devour her. The folk ballad "Reynardine" tells a similar story, of a cannibalistic fox-man. In each story, the house in the forest full of dwarfs or trolls is dangerous, and the denizens of the house mean harm to the story's heroine. This is the case here. The dwarf in this story is mean, and intends the two girls no good.

Dwarfs are also hoarders of treasure. They often mine deep into the earth to find precious metals to shape (such as the Norse *Dvergar*, who created Odin's spear, Gungnir; and *Reginn*, a blacksmithing dwarf—and of course Tolkien places his dwarfs in the mines of Moria deep beneath the earth). But they will also steal treasure: the dwarfs of "Little Snow White" may be said to have stolen the treasure of Snow White herself.

Which brings us back to the dwarf in this tale. Indeed, we learn that the dwarf the two girls encounter has stolen a treasure. Several inhabitants of the forest try to capture or kill the thieving dwarf, but to no avail. Each time the forest tries to swallow him up for his misdeeds, the girls rescue him. But he is ungrateful, and curses them each time.

Finally, the bear must rescue the girls from the dwarf and kill him to retrieve his treasure.

The Grimms seem to have completely changed the storyline here from the tale they originally collected, adding the element of the bear becoming a prince and the girls marrying the bear prince and his very convenient brother. In older versions, the bear is just a bear (all right, just a talking bear who makes love to humans), and when the dwarf is killed, it is the girls who take the treasure home to live in wealth, acquiring land and education with their find.

Now as romantic as the Grimms' meddling may be, for our purposes the bear needs to be a bear, and the girls need to keep the treasure. As we will see, the story as a magical entity, and as a pathway to bonding with a totem animal, makes far more sense in the original version!

DANCES WITH BEARS

While the sisters have friendships with many animals, there are two special bonds: the birds sing to them in the forest and they can understand the song ("... and the birds sat still upon the boughs, and sang whatever they knew"), and of course the bear, who is their companion, lover, and protector.

Birds have always been animals of prophecy, especially birds with black feathers, such as ravens, crows, and blackbirds. In countless myths and songs, these fliers foresee the future and share their visions with humans trained to understand them. It is believed of these birds that they fly to the Underworld and back, and are able to see beyond the veil between our world and the supernatural world. This is especially true of ravens and crows, who feast upon the remains of the dead, and, it is believed, carry the souls of the dead to the Underworld. For this reason, ravens are often depicted with

Underworld Goddesses and Gods, such as Mab, the Morrigan, and Odin.

Bears are burrowers. They burrow into caves or holes in the earth, and hibernate throughout the long winter. In the last chapter we talked about sleep as a deathlike state, connecting us with the Underworld and the Faerie world. Dreams are our connection to those lands, giving us a glimpse into other realities. The bear as a burrowing hibernator is connected to these surreal realms, and may bring prophecy and information back to our world from these places in the forms of dreams and visions.

Throughout mythology there are stories of bears and other burrowing creatures giving omens of the future. In Siberia, the Mansi and Khanty people prepare a huge bear feast before the traditional hunting season, hoping the bear spirit will bring a vision of the best places to hunt; American Indian and Inuit people see the Big Dipper constellation as the Great Bear. This is seen in British myth as well: King Arthur's name, in an older form of Welsh, means "Bear-Man," and the same constellation is called Arthur's Chariot. Bears are observed in these cultures to foretell planting and hunting cycles, lead nomadic peoples to temporary camps, and to lead shamans and healers to plants that will cure diseases.

Here in the United States we look to a burrowing animal to foretell the future every year. Rather than the bear or the hedgehog (the prophetic burrowing animal of Ireland), we call upon the groundhog each year on February second. This little hibernating burrower is believed to predict the timing of the coming of spring—something of great importance to farmers across America who need to know when to begin planting.

Knowing the nature of birds and bears as we now do, let us look at the story of Snow-White and Rose-Red from a different, more ancient point of view.

The sisters are girls of the forest: one sister bold and physical, following her adolescent lust and passion, and acutely aware of her body and its desires; the other sister spiritual and deeply aware of her inner, psychic self, tied to the Underworld by her hibernation and her association with winter and trance. In autumn, the time of equinox when the power of the two girls is equal or neutral, the sisters wander the forest where they hear the speech of birds. With her knowledge of the Underworld, Snow-White is able to understand the birds' speech. The birds foretell that a stranger, a creature of great strength and prophecy, will come into their lives. When a knock comes on the door, passionate Rose-Red opens the gate between the worlds, and allows the bear in. But it is Snow-White who curls up beside the bear, becoming his lover and companion: her trance-like winter sleep will allow her to follow the hibernating bear into the dream world, the Underworld, where she will gather the knowledge she needs to seek a great treasure. Because of Rose-Red's influence, the girls tease their lover, and punch, hit, and taunt him as any lustful teen might.

Snow-White sleeps beside her lover through the long winter, and in spring, bear and girl awaken and move from the Underworld (the winter cottage) to the physical world (the forest). Snow-White has been given visions of a great treasure. The bear tells the sisters to beware of a dwarf. This dwarf, he tells them, is the key to the treasure they seek.

FISH, DWARFS, BEARDS, AND TREASURES

Like bears, dwarfs are burrowers, mining the earth for treasures. Like the bear, the dwarf has the ability to visit the Underworld in dreams, and has likely found the bear's treasure through his own shamanic wanderings. The forest tries to punish or kill the dwarf for his trespass; first, a tree tries to trap the dwarf while he is chopping wood, but the goodhearted sisters rescue him. It is Snow-White, the winter dreamer and virtuous daughter, who cuts the dwarf's beard to save him.

The dwarf's beard is probably a source of his strength. We see this often in myth, most notably in the biblical story of Samson. We also see it in the Greek Medusa, a gorgon whose hair is in the form of poisonous snakes; if this maiden looks into your eyes, you will turn to stone.

The dwarf is quite ungrateful to the sisters, probably because in rescuing him they have diminished his strength by trimming his beard. He storms away, calling the girls perverse names (believing their true virtuous nature). This lack of gratitude is a clue to the listener revealing the dwarf's cloaked evil, a standard device in fairy tales. It often happens in "Snow-White"–type tales, where the girl who has followed her suitor into the forest is given hints that her suitor is actually a cannibal or ogre. For instance, in "Little Red Riding Hood," the girl notices grandma's big ears, big eyes, etc., but does not flee. In the ballad "Reynardine," the fox-man tells the girl he is "searching for concealment / from the judge's men," yet she follows him to his castle anyway, where she will be seduced and devoured.

Like the characters of these other tales and myths, the sisters are clued in to the dwarf's evil nature, but they continue to rescue him with no apparent thought of harm. In one sense, as a tale, this builds tension for the listener; as in "Red Riding Hood," we know the heroine is in big trouble, but, as in versions of "Little Red Hat," we watch helplessly as she continues to climb into bed with the wolf rather than run away. This is a device used in countless horror movies, in which the audience sees the killer approach but the intended victim does not. But as a magical tale, we understand that the nature of the sisters, virtuous and helpful, is being pitted against the nature of the dwarf, a thief and villain. We see that the girls must remain true to who they are for their magic to work.

Next, the dwarf is captured by a fish. The girls cut his beard once more, diminishing him further. The dwarf is full of curses and fury, another sign of his true nature.

Finally the dwarf is captured by an eagle. The girls rescue him, and again he is angry and ungrateful.

Notice that each element of the forest has taken a turn trying to kill the malicious dwarf: the tree is a creature of earth; the fish a being of water; and the eagle a bird of the air. Each elemental being sees the dwarf as a threat, and means to eliminate this danger from the forest. The girls, one of whom is fire (Rose-Red), and the other spiritual or heavenly (Snow-White, snow; each element—air, fire, water, earth and spirit—is represented here), save him each time. But now we see why they have done so.

The girls were waiting for circumstances to be perfect. In the end, it is so. The dwarf reveals his treasure, openly on a piece of flat ground: " . . . the dwarf, who had emptied out his bag of precious stones in a clean spot, and had not thought that anyone would come there so late." The girls come upon him, and call into play their lover and ally, the bear. The creature kills the dwarf, whom the sisters have weakened by cutting his beard. The sisters are now free to claim this treasure that Snow-White has seen in her Underworld visions.

The Grimms added the element of the "enchanted bear" who is returned to human form. (And happens to have a twin! What a surprise!) But in older versions of the tale, the bear is a bear. That is an important element for us, because the bear is a creature of the Underworld, of dreams and visions. Connecting with the bear as a spiritual animal, a totem animal, was the most important connection for the girls. It was the bear's Underworld wanderings that led the girls to their treasure. That they were lovers with the bear was natural to the original story, though the Grimms needed to rationalize this by creating an enchantment that, when broken, created a human lover.

By the way, in chapter 3, on "Hansel and Gretel," there's more about siblings and how they work together magically.

WHY CONNECT WITH A TOTEM ANIMAL?

In many traditions of magic, practitioners work to connect with animals as spirit guides or Underworld messengers. In Wicca, it is believed that the Gods and Goddesses express themselves through Nature, and will often appear in such animal forms as deer, birds, horses, and cattle, to name just a few. Examples are Mab, associated with ravens; Rhiannon, with horses; Diana and Artemis, with deer; Brigit, with the hare; Herne, with the stag; Odin, with ravens and horses; Mithra, with bulls; and Pan, with goats. It is through animals that these Gods reveal themselves to us and give us information. Witches and Druids often look to birds, hedgehogs, cattle, and hares to reveal future events or to inspire dreams. Gerald Gardner, founder of modern Witchcraft, wrote in his private journal that he had found evidence that the word *witch* comes from a term meaning "to foretell the future by the cries of animals."

In Finno-Siberian cultures, as broad a term as that may be, we find the consistent presence of spirit guide animals. Siberian peoples such as the Mansi and Khanti look to the bear for information on hunting and planting; the Inuit follow the movements of whales, bears, seals, and caribou for their connection to the Gods or spirits; the Saami and Lapps venerate seals and eagles. Each of these peoples believe that the Gods or spirits speak to them through these animals, and give omens and inspiration in trance and dreams in these forms.

In many of these cultures, a shaman, witch, or holy person will enter a trance state and contact the spirit of an animal as a guide. This animal will lead the spirit of the shaman (we'll use that term even though various cultures have their own names for this Underworld visionary) to visions that reveal information he or she needs, a plant that will cure a particular illness, the location of a herd that may be hunted, or a solution to a problem facing the community. When the shaman returns to the waking world, he or she has this knowledge and is ready to deal with the problem at hand. To be able to do this, the shaman must spend years forging a relationship with totem animals of the Underworld.

In monotheistic religions, animals are also seen as signs from the Heavens. In Ezekiel's dream, the Universe is revealed as the four creatures forming the Heavens: the bull, the eagle, the lion, and the angel (Ezekiel 1:10). Noah is guided to land by a raven and a dove (Genesis 8:7–8). In the Hebrew Midrash Mishle, a bird foretells to Solomon the arrival of the Queen of Sheba. And Jesus assumes the role of the lamb, the sacrifice to God. Jesus was also born in a barn, signifying his relationship to the animals there as well as to humans.

Every culture has stories of creatures of the natural world speaking to us and giving knowledge through their connection to dreams and the Underworld. The bear and raven are especially connected to that world, and appear in the myths of many Underworld Gods. It is the bear that often contacts developing magicians and guides them to their visions, or to other animals who will serve as totem creatures.

So, for our first journeys to the Underworld, we will use the sisters' bear as our guide.

People in ancient cultures who use totem animals or spirit guides study for many years before connecting to their guides. Witches and Druids also study for many years; in Wicca, it is customary for a student to go through various initiations before doing serious trance work. While conventional wisdom says it takes "a year and a day" to be prepared for one's first initiation, truthfully a seeker should spend two or three years studying Wicca in a coven structure before taking the first-degree initiation.

What does all of this mean to us? It means that doing this ritual once or twice may not connect you to your spirit animal. Rituals by their very nature are meant to be done again and again the same way, and it is a mistake to create a new "ritual" each time you celebrate or get together as a group. Rituals are powerful when they become second nature, and practitioners should strive to perform their rituals in much the same way each time, and to memorize the words and steps of ritual to drive these into the unconscious mind. This process of "waking up" the unconscious by performing the same ritual time after time is what allows us to access the powers hidden in our psyche and utilize these subconscious powers to "do magic."

Take a look at the High Priestess card of a traditional Tarot deck, such as the Rider-Waite deck. We see a woman shrouded in blue robes, with a river flowing from the robes outward. The river and her blue shrouded robes represent the unconscious mind, emotions, and dreams. On her chest we see a cross of equal arms—not the Christian cross, but a cross of sun and moon, masculine and feminine, night and day—pointing us to the joining of conscious and unconscious mind, or id and ego to use Freudian terms. She holds the Torah in her lap, partly hidden; the Torah is the basis of Jewish and Christian ritual and worship, and forms the core of mystic Hebrew Qabalah. It is hidden because only a devoted seeker, willing to study and strive upon the very difficult path of spiritual learning, may come to a revelation of the deep mysteries of the Qabalah and the Torah (or the deep revelations of any spiritual path).

Behind the High Priestess is a curtain, held aloft between two pillars. These are the Qabalistic pillars of Boaz and Jachin, or male and female, day and night, light and dark, sun and moon, life and death: the outer columns of the Qabalistic Tree of Life that Hebrew mystics use as a diagram to show the powers by which Yahweh (God) created the universe. Behind this veil is the flowing river, leading the seeker to the deepest mysteries of spirit and purpose. Only a seeker who has the patience, courage, and learning to pierce the veil may proceed down the river of darkness, the unconscious, dreams, and intuition to learn the inner mysteries.

One meaning of this card is that a seeker must be willing to immerse himself or herself in ritual and self-focus in order to achieve these goals of magic and trance. One cannot expect this to be done in one ritual, or even in a week or a month. It is important when connecting with totem animals to understand that years of trance work, ritual, and study might be necessary. One must do the ritual again and again, each time delving deeper into dreams and the unconscious.

The ritual here will carry you to the threshold. You must be willing to perform the ritual over months or even years to journey deeply into the realm of the bear, where your trance visions will show you dreams, inspiration, art, and knowledge. If you are willing to do this, then you will achieve your goal.

THE ROSE-RED RITUAL

This ritual may best be done indoors for focus and concentration, or outdoors in moonlight in a very quiet area. Remember that Snow-White hibernated with her bear indoors by a comfortable fire. A cozy room at night is the best setting for this magical working.

You will need:

- A broom (witches call the magical broom a *besom*, pronounced BESS-*um*)
- A rug or mat to sit or lie on comfortably; an animal fur (or faux fur) would be perfect, while a wool rug or cloth mat would be just fine
- An altar with the following upon it:
  - A wand
  - An athame or ritual knife
  - A single candle

• A chalice (cup or goblet) of juice or wine, and a small plate
of cakes or slices of bread (any baked good will do)

The circle is cast very simply, like this:

First gather around the altar, sitting quietly. This is a very calm,
introspective ritual, so a very quiet mood should be set. When all are
ready, the circle is swept three times around (this is best done by a
female, though if no female is in your circle, the youngest male will
do), with everyone chanting:

> "Sweep the circle thrice around,
> wake the bear below the ground
> Sweep the circle thrice around,
> wake the bear below the ground
> Sweep the circle thrice around,
> wake the bear below the ground."

(Repeat until the entire circle is swept three times.)

Now the circle is cast three times around using the wand. The person casting should say:

> "Cast the circle three times round
> For the sleeper underground
> A second time the circle spin
> The sleeper wakens well within
> Cast the circle go times three
> Sleeper come, appear to me."

Now turn to the east, and say:

"East, air, clouds above, guide our desires, join us in this circle."

Facing south: "South, fire, warmth in winter, heat our hearth, join
us in this circle."

Facing west: "West, water, blood, and seas, flow in our dreams."

Facing north: "North, earth, night, and darkness, guide us to the
realm of the ancient ones."

Return to face east. Then face the altar, and say:

"Nyx, Goddess of darkness, join us in our circle. Bring us night and dream, moon, and silence. Hail Nyx!

"Morpheus, God of the inner world, God of trance and vision, be with us in our rite. Bring us mist and wonder. Hail Morpheus!"

Now light the single candle.

At this time, all sit facing the altar in a meditative position. Lying down is fine, but don't get so comfortable that you fall asleep. If you are doing this ritual alone, you should read the meditation below, and know it well enough to move through the steps in your mind. If the ritual is being done by a group, one person should be chosen to speak for the group and read the meditation to the circle. That person begins the meditation, saying:

"We meet tonight to call upon a spirit animal, the bear, to guide us in trance as he once guided Snow-White and Rose-Red to their treasure and their destiny. Visualize your own treasure, whatever it may be. A career, a better job, an education, a beautiful love, a close friend, a sweet child to love and care for. Whatever you wish for, whatever your treasure is, we will ask this spirit ally to lead you to it, in dreams and visions. We will relax our conscious minds, quiet the voices that speak to us day after day, and walk the moonlit road to the spirit world, the deep night, and the forest where Rose-Red first saw the bear that guided her to her treasure.

"We go within on the road of breath. As you breathe, feel your breath, flowing in and out. Follow your breath, through your nose, deep into your body. You follow your breath into the darkness, feeling your breathing as a cool breeze against your skin.

"Now you are traveling farther, feeling your breath. You walk forward, into the dark, into the long cavern of yourself. You feel the cool breeze against your skin. You move into trance and dream. Now you are in the long dark tunnel, following the cold breeze, trusting the darkness to lead you where it will.

"Far ahead you see light, faint and unsteady. You walk on toward this small speck of light that now guides you. A tiny glowing ember, like the first star in the twilight sky. You feel the damp beneath you, and the surface steadies you in this place of night and mist. You draw toward the light. You feel the cold and damp on your skin, and you long to be warm.

"Now the light seems to be the glimmer of fire. It is brighter now, and you can make out shadowy shapes dancing in the glowing light. It is firelight, and you can make out trees and brush nearby. You smell pine and cedar, and feel the crunch of leaves and needles beneath your feet. Snow and ice are still here. You hear the cry of an owl, the rustle of branches as some creature stirs.

"The fire light peeks through a window ahead, in a wooden door set into a cottage, and a tiny path just barely seen in moonlight leads you closer. It is a small cottage and you feel you have seen it before, perhaps in dreams. You peer through the window and see the glow of a hearth fire.

"You knock and wait. It is so cold and damp here, but within that door it is warm and dry.

"You hear movement inside the cottage. The door opens, and a girl's face peers out. She is bright and beautiful, and she seems eager to meet you. Her hair is thick black, like night, and her eyes are such a deep blue you are startled. But wait. Her hair is deep red now, like autumn leaves. And her eyes are green. The girl changes before you, and you watch with amusement and surprise.

"She wears a long red gown, and holds a candle on a silver holder, lighting your way as you step into her house. She bids you welcome, first with blue eyes warming as she peers at you, then with gray eyes watching you closely.

"You enter.

"Before you there is a hearth fire, casting flickering light and shadow through the room. There is a huge beast beside the fire: it is a sleeping bear. The girl motions to you with an agile finger. She lies down beside the huge creature and curls into a nook between the bear's shoulder and paw. Her hair is black now, and her eyes blue. She smiles, the most beautiful, irresistible smile you have ever known.

"'Lie down with me,' she smiles.

"And you lie down beside the bear. You relax against the creature. Feel the fur of the bear upon your skin, and smell the gamy smell of him. He shuffles, moves, gathers you gently toward him. You are surrounded by fur and muscle. Lie here, feeling the power of this creature, but be careful not to sleep.

"You have not come here to sleep. You will call to this great creature and wake his spirit, so that he might speak to you and lead you in dreams to a treasure. You prepare yourself, for he may be calm or furious when he wakes.

"Run your hand on the bear's coarse fur. Feel the fur in the webbing of your fingers. Rub your cheek against his warm face. Tug his fur, lightly, and sing in the bear's ear. Sing in his ear, to waken him."

(All may join this chant, singing very softly)

> "Wake bear, wake, and hear me sing
> That you may lead me to my dreams
> Wake bear, wake, and hear me sing
> That you may lead me to my dreams."

(Chant continues)

"The bear opens one sleepy eye, and faces you. The girl stirs near you, for she is awake now, too. The bear pulls you near him with velvet paws. He will speak to you. Feel his warm breath. Softly bid the bear hail. Watch the bear carefully, and listen to him speak."

(All may continue to chant. Each visualizes the bear, and waits, asking the bear to speak to her or him. This may take some time.

Allow at least five minutes, maybe more, for members of the circle to have their vision.)

"We thank the bear for his wisdom. It is time to return from the forest. Stand now, and take in this room, where the bear sleeps and a warm fire glows. Commit this place to memory, for you may visit it many times and come to regard it as a sort of home.

"The strange girl has risen now. She wants you to stay, but she knows you must go. Promise her you will return. Ask her if she wishes you to bring her any gift upon your next visit." (The speaker pauses.)

"The girl takes up her little candle, and motions toward the door of the cottage. You bid the girl goodbye, and prepare to face the night. Open the door and step outside, into the cold and damp. Walk forward, into the dark of the forest.

"Walk upon the road of night. Feel the cold breeze against your skin. Walk forward, feeling the damp, the cold of wind, through the darkness. Stretch out your hand to feel the wall along which you walk. It is damp, but it comforts you to have a path for your journey.

"The night is much colder after you have been in the warmth of the cottage, against the bear's deep fur. But you walk ahead, guided by the wall beside you and the breeze. Hear my voice, and move toward it. Let it guide you home.

"Now you sense a small light, the light of a single candle. You see the light flicker and dance. You feel your own breath, in and out. You feel the place around you that you are in now, and sense through closed eyelids the light of the candle dancing.

"You are home again. Warm in the candlelit place, your body safe here after your journey. The candle burns on our altar. Your friends are here, waiting, each with their own story to tell.

"When you are ready, open your eyes and see the candle, your friends, this place that is your own place.

"Breathe deeply, and rest here. Carry with you the wisdom of the bear!"

All now sit for a moment. When they are ready, they can speak of what they saw during their vision. Then a speaker continues:

"Now let us share food and drink, and thank Nix and Morpheus for their dreams and visions. Let us bless the wine (juice) we are about to share.

"Mother of night, father of dreams
Walkers on the starlit way
Bring us vision, bring us wisdom
Bless the food we share this day."

All share a drink from the chalice, and eat the cakes. This is a good time to relax, joke, and laugh together. Leave a small portion of the food and drink to give to the Gods later.

When you are ready, extinguish the single candle:

"Nyx, we thank you for your darkness this night. Morpheus, we thank you for dreams and visions. We carry the things you have shown us into our lives, and into the world. Magic will change our world, and make us strong and wise. For this, we thank you!"

Facing east: "East, air, clouds above, we thank you for joining us in this circle."

Facing south: "South, fire, warmth in winter, we thank you for joining us in this circle."

Facing west: "West, water, blood and seas, we thank you for joining us in this circle."

Facing north: "North, earth, night and darkness, we thank you for joining us in this circle."

One person walks counterclockwise (widdershins) around the circle, saying:

"We return this circle to the night
Reverently we douse its light

Ever may it light our heart,
Merry meet, and merry part!"

Be sure to offer some of your food and drink to the Gods by pouring it into a garden, forest, grassy area—or into moving water, such as a stream, river, or lake.

Do not be discouraged if it takes some time. Repeat this circle as needed until you feel the bear responds to you and begins a dialogue with you in this astral place, or place of trance. It may take practice to do this. Investing time and patience into anything valuable is important. While we may live in a world where things like information and warm food come instantly to us through technology and microwave ovens, ritual is a place where magic, trance, and vision develop slowly and fully over time. Like learning to play a sport or a musical instrument, or coming to understand art or literature, ritual and trance must be constantly honed and refined. Skills come with practice and experience.

HANSEL AND GRETEL: FAERIE MIRROR MAGIC

In "Hansel and Gretel," the Grimms tell the story of a brother and sister abandoned by their family during a time of famine. Following a prophetic bird, they venture deep into the forest, which in fairy tales often represents a magical Underworld where visions wait and danger lurks. We will use their visions to learn scrying, a form of magic using mirrors and reflections. Again, the story quotes are from the Margaret Hunt translation of the 1812 Children's and Household Tales.

"H ard by a great forest dwelt a poor wood-cutter with his wife and his two children. The boy was called Hansel and the girl Gretel." So begins this odd tale of famine, siblings, prophetic birds, and an evil woman.

Let's recount the story as it appears in the Grimms' collection. Most of it is well known, but there are some details you may not have noticed when you were young.

The family on the edge of the forest is desperately poor. The story says of the woodcutter: "He had little to bite and to break, and once when great dearth fell on the land, he could no longer procure even daily bread." The father talks over the situation with his wife (who the Grimms waffle between calling the children's mother and step-mother), and Mom decides that they need to lose the kids or all four will starve.

But the children are so hungry they can't sleep, so they are awake to overhear their mother's plans. Hansel takes quick action, stepping outside and filling his pockets with "white pebbles which lay in front of the house glittered like real silver pennies." In the morning the children follow their parents into the forest, but Hansel leaves a trail of glittering stones. That night, the two are able to follow the pebbles home.

Hard times fall again, and Mom is dead set on getting rid of these two little burdens. She is cunning, too, and has locked the door so that Hansel cannot sneak out to get more stones. When they set off into the woods she gives the children a bit of bread, and Hansel uses this to mark the trail. But as we know, birds eat the bread crumbs, stranding the children in the forest.

The children wander for three days, and fear they will die of hunger. But at noon on the third day, they spy a snow-white bird in a tree, which sings to them. The bird flies off, and they follow; the bird leads them to a house made of food in the forest. At once, the two hungry children begin eating the dwelling.

A voice challenges them, asking who is eating her house, and the children respond, "The wind, the wind, the heaven-born wind" and continue eating. But when the woman appears, the children are terrified. She calms them, feeds them a meal, and makes up little beds for them.

The storyteller now informs us that the woman is a "wicked witch," whose edible house is simply meant to draw hungry children to her so that she can eat them. The storyteller also informs us that witches of this sort have red eyes and rely on their sense of smell. (Really?) The witch immediately begins to prepare Hansel for eating, fattening him up while she sets Gretel to work in the kitchen. But clever Hansel, knowing that the woman does not see well, tricks her: when she checks to see if he's been fattened up, he sticks a bone out of his cage for her to feel. Thinking the bone is Hansel's finger, she laments that the boy is too thin, and waits weeks for him to plump up, giving both children time to gain strength.

The woman decides that, fat or thin, Hansel will make a delicious meal. She decides to have Gretel as an appetizer, and asks the girl to climb into the oven to make sure it is lit. But the clever girl tricks the woman into crawling into her own oven, and locks her inside the oven to bake. Gretel frees Hansel, and the two discover that the woman's house is full of treasure. They help themselves to it, and head home.

They come to an expanse of water, which they cannot cross. But Gretel calls out to a passing duck to ferry them across one at a time, and the bird does. When they arrive home, their mother has died, and they share their wealth with their father. Now all may live happily.

THE FOREST: NOT ALWAYS WHAT IT SEEMS

The story's opening is an interesting one: "Hard by a great forest dwelt a poor wood-cutter with his wife and his two children." In folklore, myth, and fairy tales, the forest represents the dark and unknown. It is the Underworld, where magic lurks and where the commonplace of our waking world is mirrored, inverted, turned upside down—a theme we will explore often in discussing these stories. The fact that the woodcutter and his children live "hard by" the forest means they straddle the two worlds. They have a life in our sunlit world, but they are ever close to the Underworld of the tangled forest.

It is an analogy to the human condition. Though we live our lives in the waking world of what we deem reality, every time we sleep and dream, daydream, or experience the deeply spiritual, we cross that threshold into this other world, the forest, the world of Faerie magic, visions, and prophecy, and of nightmare.

The two children grew up here on this border. They know the forest, and know that if they are brought there and abandoned, they will be lost. It is a lurking fear for Hansel, so much so that when he overhears his mother's intention to do just that, he has a plan already in place. He knows that the silver pebbles outside his home can guide him back, and he does not waste time in stuffing his pockets with them. Hansel has thought about this!

The Grimms' version is very clear about motive: the threat of starvation. The population of Europe suffered through several centuries of rampant plague, decades of war, and agonizing crop failures. The so-called Little Ice Age occurred during the Renaissance in northern Europe, and erratic climate shifts continued into the nineteenth century. In the wake of the devastation of the Napoleonic wars, for instance, 1816, the "Year Without a Summer," saw snow in mid-June. Crops were destroyed by the frost, and the aftermath was a year of starvation and disease. German readers would have been very familiar with the motive of Hansel and Gretel's mother.

What the Grimms waffle on is the relationship between mother and children. They begin the tale by calling her the siblings' mother, then use the term stepmother, then go back to mother. The Grimms were notorious for changing characters around to suit their morality and that of their audience: in the earliest forms of this story, Hansel and Gretel were turned away to starve by their birth mother.

So the children are abandoned in the forest, lulled into sleep by Mom setting a branch to sound like the sawing of wood nearby. But clever Hansel lays his stones behind him, guaranteeing the children a path home. They return in the middle of the night, and evil Mom turns her own blame on them, saying, "You naughty children, why have you slept so long in the forest? We thought you were never coming back at all." This and the sawing branch are our first clues at the deviousness of the mother. We'll see more of it soon.

Famine returns to the land, and once again Mom plans to abandon the children in the deep forest. This time she takes the precaution of locking the doors so Hansel cannot collect his pebbles. Mom takes the children into the forest, with Hansel using bread to mark the trail.

THE CHILDREN IN THE UNDERWORLD

Now we see a start to the relationship of the sister and brother with the birds of the forest. First the birds eat Hansel's bread crumbs, trapping the children in their Underworld realm. The siblings wander the forest for three days, hungry and tired.

On the third day they see "a beautiful snow-white bird sitting on a bough," which sings to them. They are lulled by the song, and follow the bird, who leads them to a house made of food.

We've already seen that birds are prophetic creatures, and are creatures who travel between our world and the Underworld. While black birds are often seen in this office, completely white birds are also seen as travelers between the worlds. White birds are considered angelic, and they resemble snow, which falls from the heavens, uniting Heaven and Earth. It is no wonder that in folklore the white stork brings babies, for this white bird is seen as carrying the souls of the Underworld to their rebirth in our world.

This white bird leads the two children to this amazing discovery: lost and starving, they are now confronted by a fortress of candy. Hansel tells his sister, "We will set to work on that . . . and have a good meal. I will eat a bit of the roof, and you, Gretel, can eat some of the window, it will taste sweet." Grounded Hansel is planning to eat the part of the house made of bread, while angelic Gretel gets the sugary sweet areas.

But the forest is a place of enchantment, and a place where there is ever reversal of the roles we assume in our world. Hansel and Gretel have been raised by a devious woman who has repeatedly tried to starve them. Now the children are confronted by a devious woman intent on overfeeding them in her efforts to kill them. The "wicked witch" appears, lulling them with sweetness and offering food and beds. The children fall into her trap, and spend a delightful evening feasting and sleeping.

The listener is now told in an aside from the storyteller that "the old woman had only pretended to be so kind. She was in reality a wicked witch, who lay in wait for children, and had only built the little house of bread in order to entice them there. When a child fell into her power, she killed it, cooked and ate it, and that was a feast day with her." The storyteller also phrases something in a very interesting way: "When Hansel and Gretel came into her neighborhood, she laughed with malice, and said mockingly, 'I have them, they shall not escape me again.'" This is a strange phrase. The listener perceives that the "witch" has never encountered these particular children before. Is this a strange slip of the tongue accidentally used by the storyteller and transcribed carelessly by the Grimms? Hang on to that thought; we'll get back to it in just a moment.

Now for the siblings who were starving, abundant food is the enemy. The woman cages Hansel and attempts to fatten him so that she may devour him. She sets Gretel to preparing the oven that she will use.

Throughout the record of Faerie lore, we see Faerie creatures who seduce and devour their human prey. I've already mentioned a few: Reynardine, the fox-man who seduces young women in the Scottish mountains, then eats their flesh; Lorelei, the Rhine Nymph who drowns young men as they attempt to caress her; the Glastig, seducer-devourer of strapping young hunters. The "witch" is just this type of creature. She seduces the children with cravings, namely food and comfort. While other Faeries offer the comforts of a lover, warmth and sexual caresses, the woman here offers the comforts of a mother: nourishment and safety. As with all of these seducer-murderer Faeries, these are a lure, and the mothering role is reversed when the children are trapped by what should be a loving, motherly relationship with this woman.

The Grimms were notorious for changing characters, and often turned "fee" or *Faerie* into *witch*, the popular villain of eighteenth- and nineteenth-century Europe. While the great witch hunts of the Renaissance were mostly over by this time, they were still firmly within memory. Stories were still told, especially in the German cities of Fulda and Trier, where just a century earlier hundreds of women had been tortured and killed, most of them burned alive (as our "wicked witch" will be).

In this atmosphere of witch hysteria, the Grimms probably felt a witch would make a better villain: it is very possible that the original villain of "Hansel and Gretel" was a seducer-murderer Faerie, whom the Grimms saw as just not scary enough. They've obviously never actually met one.

In the midst of the evil the children find themselves in, another Faerie world reversal takes place. Up to this point it has always been clever Hansel who leads the two, strong in his decisions and comforting when things look bad. When Gretel despaired at the story's start, it was Hansel who assured her: "Gretel wept bitter tears, and said to Hansel, 'Now all is over with us.' 'Be quiet, Gretel,' said Hansel, 'do not distress yourself, I will soon find a way to help us.'"

It was Hansel who thought to drop pebbles in the path, and who established the children's relationship with the birds when he dropped bread. In the midst of this, he assured Gretel again: "Hansel comforted his little sister and said, 'Just wait, Gretel, until the moon rises, and then we shall see the crumbs of bread which I have strewn about, they will show us our way home again.'" And it was Hansel who gloated over how sweet their meal of the house in the forest would taste when Gretel was cautious about eating.

But here in the mirror world of Faerie, it is Gretel who takes action. Waiting until the time is right, Gretel tricks the "witch" into climbing into the oven, locking her in so that she will be burned alive. Gretel then frees Hansel, crying, "Hansel, we are saved. The old witch is dead."

The language at that moment is interesting: "Then Hansel sprang like a bird from its cage when the door is opened." It was a bird that led the children to this place, and now Hansel is likened to a bird when he sees his fortune shifting.

The two children now search the house and find treasure. As we have seen, and will see again, when humans enter the enchanted house in the forest the denizens there—be they dwarfs, robbers, dragons or "witches"—are hoarders of treasure. Part of this represents the gifts of the Underworld: prophecy, intuition, the Faerie sight. Those who make this perilous journey return with some great advantage, if they return at all. In fairy tales, this is often shown as more tangible treasure, like gold, silver, and jewels.

The children stuff their pockets with these gifts, and set out to return home.

Coming to the house of food they had wandered in the forest for three days. Yet the journey home is quite different: "When they had walked for two hours, they came to a great stretch of water." There was, of course, no stretch of water on the way in. But in folklore, the journey to and from Faerie always involves crossing water. The children were led into the forest by the white bird, who symbolized the journey of the soul between the worlds. To get back, the children must cross this expanse of enchanted water. And just as a bird led them in, it is a bird who will get them out. Again it is Gretel here in the Faerie forest who takes charge, knowing the exact spell that will cause the duck to respond: "'And there is also no ferry,' answered Gretel, 'but a white duck is swimming there. If I ask her, she will help us over.' Then she cried, 'Little duck, little duck, dost thou see, Hansel and Gretel are waiting for thee. There's never a plank, or bridge in sight, take us across on thy back so white.'"

Hansel wants the duck to take them both, but again Gretel must intervene and insist that they would be too heavy. Though they have traveled together into the magic forest and through their initiation ordeal, they will cross alone, seeing only what each is meant to see of the passage. That is the very personal nature of the initiatory experience.

Freed now from the enchantment of the tangled forest, they only walk for a short time, and are back at their father's threshold.

Now we read something a little odd: "The man had not known one happy hour since he had left the children in the forest. The woman, however, was dead." No explanation is given for the mother's death. It is simply stated as fact. But let us remember the odd turn of phrase used by the storyteller in describing the actions of the "wicked witch": "I have them, they shall not escape me again." Why "again"?

In the deep enchanted forest, the mother, who in our world attempted to starve the children, takes the form of the deceiving witch-mother, offering nurture and comfort to the children, then attempting to kill them with food and plenty. The witch uses the word *again* because the children have already escaped her in the physical world. She has lured them here to the Underworld, where she will try again to kill them in a very different way, a mirror of the starvation she employs in our world. And though they were unable to fight her in our world, here in the mirror world of Faerie, Gretel has the strength to destroy the devious woman. The woman is burned alive, a punishment for witches: but more profoundly, she is baked like food, the lure she herself tried to use to trap and kill the children.

THE MIRROR OF FAERIE

This idea of the Faerie mirror, an Underworld where roles are reversed, is not only seen in the mother figure, who starves and abandons the children in our world, and overfeeds them in the Faerie forest; it is seen in the children themselves. The mythic brother and sister, male and female who mirror each other, is seen throughout folklore. Across this lore, we see sibling abilities that complement each other, and may be used to gain insight and prophecy.

Perhaps the best-known mythic brother and sister are the Roman Apollo and Diana. God of the sun, Apollo was also seen as a God of divination. The Oracles at Delphi were thought to derive their visions from the Sun God. He is also a God of music and artistic inspiration.

Apollo's powers are rooted in his relationship with his sister Diana, chaste moon Goddess, whose dark powers the God is able to tap for his dream visions and insights (in some myths, Apollo is brother to Artemis or to Selene, also chaste moon Goddesses). It is Diana's dominion over the night that allows bright Apollo to dwell in the dream kingdom, culling visions and musical inspiration.

We see a very similar relationship in British myth between the Goddess Mab and the God Mabon. Mab is a dark Underworld Goddess who haunts the night, riding a great white mare. Her brother Mabon is the young God of the grain, who grows in the crops and is cut down in the harvest. (Pagans call their harvest holiday at autumn equinox by this God's name.) When Mabon is cut down by the scythe, it is his sister Mab who will gather his spirit up in a wild ride through the autumn forest, carrying him to her Underworld where he will rest, waiting to be reborn into the spring crops. His Underworld visit, like Apollo's, gives him dreams and visions, and the ability to bring life into the world as spring arrives.

The brother God–sister Goddess relationship is seen in a much older culture, the Sumerian culture of the ancient Middle East. In the Gilgamesh epic, we find Utu and his sister Inanna. The Underworld Goddess Inanna is able to use the World Tree, Huluppu, to see between our world and the Underworld, and she shares her visions with Utu so that he may take action in a great war that creates the world.

Eastern European folklore sees a brother-sister pair who have these same complementary roles, though their functions are not as clear-cut as in some mythologies. In Estonian songs, like the one here, the brother has traveled to the Underworld, and is now invisible to all but his sister: she must thaw him from the frozen Underworld so that he can resume his earthly life (just as Mab rules the seasons that allow spring to thaw the earth so that Mabon may grow within the crops).

> Come to the ground, lovely brother
> Step on the ground, dear brother!
> My sister, sweet birdie,
> Swallow with golden crown!
> My fingers are frozen to reins,
> My feet are frozen to stirrups
> My dear young brother,
> Honey of my mind
> I shall heat the hot sauna

And foment you with the birch whisk,
Defrost your fingers from reins,
Release your feet from stirrups.[5]

Notice that the brother here calls his sister his *sweet birdie*, implying that his sister may take the form of a bird to travel to the Underworld to search for him, very much like Hansel and Gretel's bird.

All of these brother-sister elements are here in this tale. Hansel is the young God of grains and food: he uses the bread to track their path into the forest, and diminishes in the forest's winter world. There Gretel, Goddess of dreams and visions, guided to her Underworld destination by a bird, takes the strong lead. She waits until her intuition tells her the time is right to bring spring (balance) back to our world. At that moment she destroys the "witch," ending the power of winter and famine. She must now lead Hansel over the water, back to our world where the mirror image will be of our reality. Here, instead of famine and want, Hansel may produce prosperity (the growth of crops) for his father, the old God: Apollo is son of Zeus, the thunder-wielding sky-father God; we assume Hansel's father is the same sky God.

This mirror duality of male and female, Underworld and Overworld, dream and waking, produces balance in our world and in our mythic consciousness. This union of male and female also produces life. Life-producers in myth can be brother and sister as well. In Genesis, Adam and Eve are brother and sister and are the parents of all humans. This is also true of the Egyptian brother and sister Isis and Osiris, who represent life and death, night and day, and earth and sky.

Magically, the energies of male and female mirror each other in abilities. Male energy is positive, light (as in the day), active, and intellectual; female energy is negative (not in a bad sense, but in the

---

5. Lintrop, "The Great Oak and Brother-Sister," 49.

sense of electrical current), dark (as in the night), reflective, and intuitive. Both must be used to achieve a successful magical working.

So it is with our little Hansel and Gretel. To prevail over their mother, and to create prosperity in their world, Hansel must take the active, intellectual role of planning for their journey into the dark forest. Once he leads them there, it is Gretel's intuition and clarity that reverse their reality, ending their starvation and want. Hansel must be led from the dark Underworld by Gretel, who can communicate with the water birds to cross her brother back over the mirror-lake to our world. Once back, it is Hansel who leads, showering his sky-father God with gifts of prosperity.

Hansel and Gretel are mirrors of each other, as male and female and as magical entities. They can see into the Faerie world of the dark forest, and come out whole and with the gift of prosperity, by using their mirror magic.

MIRROR MAGIC

Glass Mirrors

In "Hansel and Gretel," we see how the water-mirror of Faerie affects events in our world. Mirrors figure heavily into Faerie lore. Mermaids and Sirens are seen peering into their mirrors, and while sailors construe this as vanity, it is actually because these creatures can use their mirrors to foretell a shipwreck or a drowning. Because mirrors hold Faerie enchantment, Scottish legend warns never to pick up a mirror one finds on the ground, especially near the sea.

In these tales the mirrors are just as we think they should be, made of reflective glass. Magicians use reflective mirrors to "scry," or peer through the mists of the Otherworld, in order to prophesy, or see the truth of a situation.

If you'd like to try scrying, your best bet is to use a black glass scrying mirror. These can be bought at occult shops or ordered on the

Internet. They are made of colored glass, are very dark, and are reflective like a standard mirror.

If you do not have a black glass mirror, you may use a dark-blue cobalt glass plate or tray, which are very easy to find in vintage shops or secondhand stores.

To work with a scrying mirror, you need to be in a quiet place where you will not be disturbed. Light a single candle, and use the light of the candle to shed sparse light on the mirror surface. Sit quietly with your eyes closed and feel the surface of the mirror. It's best to begin with a question or to hold a situation in your mind. When you are ready to begin, say: "Faerie sight, Faerie sight, allow me to see through the veil this night!" and look into the mirror.

Do not expect too much: allow your vision to become hazy and allow the mirror's surface to show you what it will, rather than trying to see particular images. You may simply get a feeling or a fleeting thought from peering into the mirror: that's okay, trust your instinct. The mirror is giving you information; allow yourself to believe it.

Do not try for too long your first time. A few minutes is plenty (and will seem like a lot longer!). When you are done, put the mirror down, close your eyes, and reflect on what the mirror has shown you. Allow your intuition to interpret for you, but do not fall back on a result you came into the ritual hoping for. Let your intuition tell you what the mirror truly shows you.

This may take a few tries before you feel like you are getting anywhere. Do not give up. Magic is a gradual process and takes time to master. No one does it perfectly on their very first try.

Water Mirrors

In some tales, water is used as a mirror into the Faerie world. Water is always crossed when a human travels to Faerie. We see Hansel and Gretel cross water to return to our world from the Faerie forest. The theme is echoed throughout the mythic record: many Faerie stories show a human crossing rivers or an ocean to reach an enchanted land.

Faeries will often use the water to foretell the future. Ireland's very famous Banshee is always associated with water: she spends her days washing clothing by the waterside, and can foretell death as she peers into the water.

History does not tell us how the famous soothsayer Thomas of Ercildoune, who received his gift of prophecy from the Queen of Elfland, was able to see through the veil of time. But based on one of his prophecies, we have a small clue. Thomas predicted that the Haig family would eternally control the country estate of Bemersyde on the Scottish border. The prophecy held even when the Haig family seemed to have died out in the late nineteenth century; the British crown gave the estate to World War I hero Douglas Haig.

What makes the prediction interesting to us is that Thomas very specifically references water as he prophesies:

Tide, tide, whate'er betide, There'll aye be Haigs at Bemersyde[6]

Tide, tide is certainly a reference to the sea, and it is quite possible that Thomas used the rhythms of the sea to peer into the future. He did, after all, cross a sea of water and a river of blood to reach the Faerie Land, according to folklore.

Tolkien knew the tradition of water scrying well, and in *The Lord of the Rings* his elf queen Galadriel scries using a fountain of water deep in the elven forest.

Scrying into water is very much like scrying into a black glass mirror. Use a dark container, like a black glass or ceramic bowl, filled about half full with water. You may want to infuse a small amount of India ink into the water to make it very dark. You can use a candle or, better yet, reflected moonlight to create a little reflection on the water, and look deeply at the reflection, noticing fleeting shapes and

---

6. Eyre-Todd, *Byways of the Scottish Border*, 141.

pictures. Let your eyes go a bit blurry, and accept whatever thoughts or images that may come.

Here is a scrying ritual to be done by one person or a small group. This ritual should be done when the moon is shining brightly.

You will need:

- A small altar (a stone or blanket outdoors will do nicely)

- A wand

- A black glass scrying mirror or a bowl of water for scrying

Gather in your circle quietly and with great reverence. This is a very sedate ritual, and should be approached with stillness.

Cast your circle, saying one line each time around:

> "Cast the circle neath the stars
> in the still of night
> Let the moon and zodiac
> guide us in our sight
> Dream and intuition
> draw our inner light!"

Now greet each of the elementals this way, facing each direction as you speak to that elemental:

> "Spirits of east! Creatures of air!
> You of thought and care
> Guide us in our search for truth
> Spirits of south! Creatures of fire!
> Yearning and desire
> Draw us to the moon's pale light
> Spirits of west! Creatures of water!
> Bring from chaos art and order
> That we may know your sooth

Spirits of north! Creatures of earth!
Give our intuition birth
That we may know true fortune's sight!"

Always return to the east and bow when you cast the elemental directions to ascribe a full circle.

Now sit quietly for a time, focusing on the matter you wish to see clearly. If you are in a group, you might each take a turn saying what matter you wish to have clarified. If you are alone, speak aloud and say what you are focused upon.

Now pick up your scrying tool (mirror or bowl), and hold it up, presenting it to the moon and the elements. "Bright moon, our Mother's face, spirits of air, fire, water, and earth: speed my vision this night!"

Hold the bowl so that it catches some light of the moon or the altar candle, and peer into it. Allow any images to form and simply take them in; you will interpret later on. When you have seen all you feel you will see, pass the bowl on. Each member of the circle should be patient, and allow each to take their time peering into the tool. Use the time you spend waiting to focus on your question or concern.

When all have gazed, hold up the bowl in thanks: "Moon, air, fire, water, earth, we thank you for the vision you have given us! Blessed Be!"

Now each should share what images they have seen, and what they feel those images mean. Each member of the circle may offer interpretations in a respectful way.

When each person has spoken, end the circle by thanking the elementals:

"Spirits of air, thank you for joining us in this circle. Hail and farewell!"

Repeat this in each direction, returning to the east to form a full circle.

Now walk widdershins around the circle, saying: "We cast this circle into the earth until we have need to call upon its energies again. Blessed Be!"

Perform this ritual as often as desired.

RUNNING WATER

In the Wiccan Rede, there is a line that states:

Where the rippling waters flow

Cast a stone and truth ye'll know

Scrying into running water, such as a river or stream, is an ancient Faerie magic. Irish bards would sleep next to flowing streams so that the Faerie spirits of the stream would teach them new songs.

Here is a spell for learning the truth of a situation:

Find a round stone. A stone with a hole in it made by natural forces is the best type of stone to use here. Go to a river, stream, or brook.

Focus for a moment on the matter you wish to see truthfully, and close your eyes for a short time. Say:

> "Tide, tide,
> Grant me sooth,
> Reveal to me what stands as truth!"

Throw the stone into the water. In about two weeks, the truth will reveal itself.

There are many other ways of scrying into mirrors or reflections. Use your imagination. Know that whatever works best for you is fine, and there is no "wrong way."

Chapter 4

BRIAR ROSE (SLEEPING BEAUTY): SEEKING INSPIRATION AND DIVINATION IN DREAMS

In this story, a young woman is cursed at birth: she will be pricked by a spinning wheel and fall into a deathlike sleep. Despite her parents' precautions, the prophecy comes about, and the girl sleeps for a hundred years. We will use the experience of trance and dream states presented in this story to create a ritual for receiving inspiration and guidance from your own dreams. Unless otherwise indicated, story quotes are from the Margaret Hunt translation of the Grimms' 1812 Children's and Household Tales.

L egend tells of King Arthur, who sleeps in the Isle of Apples, and will awaken in Britain's time of greatest need. The same is said of the French Charlemagne and the Welsh Bran, both asleep for centuries, expected to wake when they are somehow called. The sleeper who will wake someday is a story seen across cultures and across centuries, from the Dutch-American Rip Van Winkle to Ossian, the Irish hero who journeyed to the Underworld for three hundred years. Here our heroine is Briar Rose, or Sleeping Beauty as most of us know her, asleep in a tower in the forest, forgotten by the world as a century passes by her.

At its heart, "Briar Rose" is the quintessential story of a Faerie enchantment. But time and the clumsy hand of storytellers, including the Grimms, have fleshed this simple story out with details that range from awkward and silly to creepy and perverted. Elements woven into the tale over its long history include rape, torture, and murder. Very heavy burdens to bear for such a small, pretty story!

The Grimms' telling begins with a king and queen lamenting that they cannot conceive a child, a common fairy tale motif, and one we see in such other Grimms' tales as "Hans the Hedgehog" and "Rapunzel." As Maria Tatar points out, "the inability to conceive often leads fairy tale couples to make reckless promises or to engage in outlandish bargains."[7] In this case, it is not until after the child is born that the couple decides carelessly, and they are punished for their lack of manners.

What happens between the lamenting and the birthing in this tale is interesting. We are told that "once when the queen was bathing, a frog crept out of the water on to the land, and said to her, 'Your wish shall be fulfilled; before a year has gone by, you shall have a daughter.'" The queen is bathing in a pool, someplace where a frog would live. She is nude and vulnerable in a natural place, a common situation in folklore and myth for a tale of sex, love, and tragedy. Remember that Hades first saw Persephone while she was bathing in a stream (some tellings say while she was picking flowers by a pool), and David began his deadly obsession with Bathsheba after seeing her at her bath. Here the queen, nude and sensual in some forest

---

7. Tatar, "Introduction. Snow White," in *Children's Stories and Household Tales* (2004 edition), 232.

glade, is approached by a frog, who divines that she will have a child (the outcome of her overt sexuality).

In this story, the frog is a symbol of fertility and birth. The little critters appear in early spring, when the earth is greening after the deathlike sleep of winter, and frogs go through an amazing metamorphosis from egg to tadpole to leggy amphibian. So it seems appropriate for a frog to deliver the strange news that the queen is pregnant.

But before you get all excited by the symbolism, be mindful that in earlier tellings of the tale it is not a frog but a crab that crawls out of the primal, watery depths to deliver the prophecy. While this may sound strange, it makes perfect sense. The water represents emotion and dream, and the crab is a creature in a shell, representing a contained unit of dream and desire. In the Tarot, the Moon card displays just such a scene: a wolf (wild desire) and a dog (controlled social interactions) stand on either side of a lake, like the one in which the queen might have bathed. Above them is the full moon, pulling at their emotions, casting a net of dreams over the wild wolf hunter and the domesticated dog, man's best friend with his still-wild instincts. From the depths, a crab crawls between them, indicating the deepest urges and nightmare visions both have lurking deep within. Each will respond as is his nature: with the wild violence of the wolf, or the careful containment of the dog.

The crab in the Tarot also represents speech: a word is a unit of sound (a shell) that contains a meaning (the flesh of a crab). Words are our basic unit of communication, but each word, with its many shades of meaning and intent, can be used for good or bad, for healing or for hurt. Throughout this tale, words will be used to bless and to curse. In fact, here the crab does both: blesses the queen with a wish fulfilled that will lead to a hundred and fifteen years of trouble.

So the crab appears before the naked queen to say that her deepest desires, the urge to bear life, will come to fruit. She is joyous, and upon returning home shares the joy with the king. Soon a girl is born. In the Grimms' story she is named *Dornröschen*, literally "Little Thorn Rose." In older tales her name is Talia, meaning "blossoming girl."

Now the problems begin. In a strange series of backpedaling explanations and uncommonly clumsy storytelling, the Grimms inform us that the royal couple hold a celebration at the girl's birth. They wish to invite "the wise women, in order that they might be kind and well-disposed towards the child." This is a fairly obvious euphemism for witches, and there are thirteen witches or "wise women" in this kingdom. But apparently the king only owns twelve gold plates. Rather than have another gold plate made, or buy a set of thirteen silver plates, the king invites twelve of the wise women to dinner but tells the thirteenth to simply stay home.

The wise women are asked to bless the newborn with magical gifts, and each imbues her with some desirable virtue or physical trait: "One gave virtue, another beauty, a third riches, and so on with everything in the world that one can wish for." (Beauty, wealth, and virtue are traits that fit the era's model of a perfect young woman.) But suddenly the snubbed witch appears, and curses the girl: on her fifteenth birthday, she will be pricked by the needle of a spinning wheel and fall dead. Luckily, the last of the invited witches has not yet given her blessing, and in our second instance of awkward backpedaling, this witch may now alter (but not undo) the curse: the girl will not die, but sleep for a hundred years. Is it me, or is it odd that the uninvited witch couldn't wait until the twelve invited guests were finished before magically appearing? Timing is everything.

This portion of the story, piled high with awkward storytelling and the Grimms' strange tidying, appears in older versions in a much more consistent form. The gift-givers are Faeries (in Perrault's 1697 version we see "the Princess had for her godmothers all the fairies they could find in the whole kingdom"), and in return for their gifts, the girl is held in thrall by the Faerie world, where she must journey when she reaches sexual maturity. Throughout mythology, a journey to Faerie that seems to last one night turns out to have taken a hundred years when the traveler returns to our world, and time does not seem to affect the sleeper here during her journeys through enchanted realms. We'll talk more about this soon. For now, back to the story the way the Grimms tell it.

The king is very concerned about the curse and orders that all spindles in the kingdom be burned. We wonder how anyone had clothes for the next fifteen years, but that is never explained. Instead, the narrative jumps fifteen years ahead, with this improbable sentence: "It happened that on the very day when she was fifteen years old, the king and queen were not at home, and the maiden was left in the palace quite alone."

I'm not sure about you, but if my daughter was under a curse that she would die on her fifteenth birthday, I would not leave her alone in the castle on that very day. It's like a horror movie where the girl says, "I'm going outside!" and the whole audience is thinking, "Don't go outside!" Well, our little Briar Rose is now alone in the castle on her fifteenth birthday and decides to go exploring. And what does she find? Why, a locked room she's never seen before. And what is in there? Of course, an old woman with a spindle!

Briar Rose is curious, having never seen a spindle, and touches the machine. Immediately she pricks her finger and falls into sleep. In the Grimms' version we are told "she fell down upon the bed that stood there," which is just very convenient. I imagine the king issuing orders that say, "Burn every spindle, but just in case a spindle manages to get into the secret locked upper room, make sure there's a bed in there for my daughter to fall down upon."

So Briar Rose falls into a deep sleep, and just at that moment the king and queen return from their oddly timed trip, and also fall into the same sleep, as does everyone in the castle. The Grimms added what they meant to be a funny pastiche of courtly sleepers, including various animals and a cook about to box a child's ears.

Time goes on, and various princes attempt to rescue the Sleeping Beauty in the Forest (which is actually the title of the French version), but each would-be suitor is consumed by the thorns that grow about the castle. The Grimms' original tale had a morbid description of the hideous death of each suitor, but this was edited out of later editions (what a surprise). The journey through the thorns calls to mind the suitors of Rapunzel, who were killed or blinded by thorns. In that story, the true love, blinded, actually healed and returned to claim his prize (as we'll see in just a few chapters).

After hearing all the warnings, a king's son decides he is not afraid and enters the forest. His fearlessness, however, is never put to the test, as the day he approaches the castle is the exact day the hundred years are done. "But by this time the hundred years had just passed, and the day had come when Briar Rose was to awake again. When the king's son came near to the thorn-hedge, it was nothing but large and beautiful flowers, which parted from each other of their own accord, and let him pass unhurt, then they closed again behind him like a hedge."

Again, this is an odd bit of storytelling. But the young man enters the castle, and finds the girl asleep in the tower. He kneels before her, and she wakes at that moment. The Grimms tidy up the ending by allowing the cook to box the boy's ears, and the couple are married in royal splendor.

THE OLDER TALE: FLAX AND RAPE

This pretty story is very different in older versions, and has a very different outcome in those tellings. Written versions go back to the fourteenth century, where Briar Rose was called Talia (Thaleia), which means "The Blossoming One" in Greek (reminiscent of the term *Nymph*). In that much older telling of the story, Talia is born to a king who asks wise men and astrologers to foretell her future. They grieve that she will come to some great harm over a tiny piece of flax. The king orders all spindles to be destroyed, as flax is the grain used to spin linen thread.

When Talia becomes fifteen, she happens to see a woman walking by, spinning flax. The girl is curious about a process she has never seen and asks the woman if she might try it. A tiny splinter of flax is caught under Talia's fingernail, and the girl falls into a sleep, seemingly dead.

The brokenhearted king cannot bear to bury his daughter, and instead places her in a room in his country estate (very much like Snow White in her glass coffin in the forest).

A young king riding through the countryside comes upon the estate and, exploring there, sees the sleeping girl. Unable to wake her, he has sex with her: "As he looked at her, and tried to wake her, she seemed so incredibly lovely to him that he could not help desiring her, and he began to grow hot with lust. He gathered her in his arms and carried her to a bed, where he made love to her. Leaving her on the bed, he left the palace and returned to his own city, where pressing business for a long time made him think no more about the incident."[8]

Still asleep, Talia gives birth to twins, a boy and a girl. As the twins grow and suckle their mother, the boy cannot find her breast, and suckles Talia's finger. He dislodges the flax splinter, and she wakes.

In time the king returns to Talia, and finds her awake and caring for his children, whom she has named Sun and Moon. We now learn that this necrophiliac king is an adulterer as well: "Now the young king already had a wife, who had become suspicious when he did not return for several days from the hunt, and hearing him call strange names in his sleep, she was overcome with anger and jealousy."[9]

---

8. Basile, "Sun, Moon and Talia," *Il Pentamerone* (story 29).
9. Ibid.

The wife learns of Talia and her children. In a jealous rage, she orders Talia to be tortured and killed, and the children to be cooked and served to her husband in a stew. But a goodhearted cook saves the children, and while the queen is torturing Talia, the king hears her cries and rescues his lover. The queen herself is burned to ashes in the fire that is meant to burn Talia. His jealous wife conveniently out of the way, the king marries Talia and raises their children.

Now if you thought Briar Rose was a little weird and creepy, how about this version of the story? This is a very different look at Sleeping Beauty, in which the "blossoming" girl is raped while she sleeps, then tortured by a justifiably jealous queen, and narrowly escapes death. She is only saved by her philandering lover, who murders his own wife out of his love for Talia. Not exactly Disney fare, is it?

In 1911, seventeenth-century Italian fairy-tale collector Giambattista Basile's telling of "Sun, Moon and Talia" was re-edited in English by E. F. Strange for publication by Macmillan and Company. Interestingly, Strange omits the rape, and has the twins wander in and find Talia sleeping: "Meanwhile, two little twins, one a boy and the other a girl, who looked like two little jewels, wandered, from I know not where, into the palace and found Talia in a trance. At first they were afraid because they tried in vain to awaken her; but, becoming bolder, the girl gently took Talia's finger into her mouth, to bite it and wake her up by this means; and so it happened that the splinter of flax came out."[10] This is, like the Grimms', a bit of creative tidying to cover the nastier elements of this creepy little tale.

THE GIRL ASLEEP

At the core of each of these narratives, we have a few basic elements: a girl is born to royal parents who are afraid they are barren, so she is very special, and represents all that is cherished and beautiful in girl children; at her birth, a group of enchanted beings, originally Faer-

---

10. Basile, "Sun, Moon and Talia," *Stories from the Pentamerone.*

ies, bless her or divine her future, creating or portending an element of trial, death, and barrenness; the girl reaches maturity at fifteen years old and falls into a trance or enchanted sleep; it is during this sleep that we see the signs that the girl has blossomed into a sexual being. In the older tale, she is so appealing in sleep that a king who is already married rapes her, desiring her beyond any other (including his own wife). In the more modern tale, young men are willing to brave death and despair to find the girl, because she is so desirable.

In both tales, a young man of position and power, a king or prince, finds the girl and is able to possess her sexually. In the end, after a bit of rape and torture in one version, she becomes his lover and wife, bearing his children.

Just before our heroine is born, and just after, we see the element of prophecy. In the Grimms' tale, a frog tells the bathing queen she is pregnant. In older tales it is a crab. And as soon as the girl is born, enchanted beings—whether Faeries, witches, or astrologers—are able to predict the infant's destiny. We know from this that "Briar Rose" is a tale of dreams and divination, things that connect us to the unconscious, that deepest wellspring of the mind that produces unexplained images, premonition, and instinct.

Looking again at the Moon card of the Tarot, we see the crab rising from the water under the full moon, the wolf and dog responding to the unbidden, often surprising visions and feelings the creature carries from these murky, uncharted depths. We all experience this. We all have dreams that puzzle us, feelings of portending harm that make our hair stand on end and that we cannot shake. We all have emotions that we'd rather not feel, that carry with them desperate sadness or sudden anger. Like the dog in the card, we learn to function in society despite these deepest impulses, not allowing ourselves to act out inappropriately when these feelings arise. Sure, you'd like to throttle your boss or your teacher, scream at your absent parent that he or she abandoned you, tell your former lover that she or he destroyed your confidence by leaving you and moving on successfully with his or her life—but we don't. Unlike the wolf, who is allowed to howl at the full moon and rend the throat of its prey, we must live among "civilized" people, so we train ourselves from the youngest age to get along, mask our feelings, and be pleasant and productive. Those who do not learn to do this are ostracized, shunned, or jailed.

But those urges haunt us. We carry on our normal life with those dark impulses, dreams, and visions lurking, like the crab, just beneath the surface of our consciousness. This duality is seen in the archetype of Briar Rose: these opposites of dark and light live constantly within her. As much as she represents the era's model of the perfect girl, blessed with wealth, beauty, and virtue, our heroine lives with impending doom every day of her life: the prophecy that she will be destroyed by her "blooming" womanhood. Beneath the calm, normal-seeming surface is the constant knowledge that at the age of fifteen she will experience desolation and death. We know that dream and the Underworld will loom large in this tale right from the start.

So the crab's (or frog's) prediction is made. When the baby arrives, she is named Thaleia or Talia in the older stories, Briar Rose in Germany, Sleeping Beauty in the Forest in France. All of these names have something in common: they are a paradox. Talia, "The Blossoming One," speaks of the girl as a flower, blooming in the prime of her life. Yet we know from the second paragraph of the tale that the girl will be cut down the moment her bloom takes hold. Basile's name for the story, "Sun, Moon and Talia," also clues us in to the notion that the girl is both day and night, lightness and darkness, and that these disparate virtues will be brought forth from one girl's blossoming loins in the course of the tale. Like sun and moon, our sleeping girl is also summer and winter—the blossoming one of summer, and the ghastly, sleepy pallor of winter when all things die in our world. She carries within her both life and death.

That notion of both light and dark, summer and winter, thorn and flower, is reflected in the German name *Dornröschen*, "Little Thorn Rose," or Briar Rose. Here we see that the girl has the beauty and joy of a flower, the rose; yet deep within her lurks the briar, that thorny branch that tangles the forest, pierces the skin, and is quite visible in winter when flowers and leaves have died. This is again echoed in her French name, *La Belle au Bois Dormant* (literally, "The Beauty in the Woods Asleep"), which may mean either the sleeping beauty in the woods, or the beauty in the sleeping woods, implying that the lovely girl lies in the forest during its dark winter dormancy. In fact, in the Grimms' version we see her dual nature reflected in the forest around her. Her namesake briars, which grew while she was in the dark Underworld, have become beautiful flowers when she wakes and is ready for a sexual relationship. ("When the king's son came near to the thorn-hedge, it was nothing but large and beautiful flowers.")

So, like the dog and the wolf in the Tarot card, this beauty has both dark and light, summer and winter, growth and death within her. While the world at large cannot see this, the enchanted ones, Faeries, astrologers, and witches can plainly see it and express this to the girl's parents. When she reaches her sexual maturity, at fifteen, she will realize the darkness inside her: she will journey to the Underworld, appearing dead to all the world, for one hundred years.

THE HUNDRED YEARS' SLEEP

Fifteen would be a very typical age of sexual maturity a few centuries ago in the French or German forests. Girls married soon after the onset of menses, which would have come later then than it does in young American women now. While Judaism celebrates maturity at thirteen, Hispanics celebrate the maturity of women at fifteen. The *quinceañera*, or "sweet fifteen" ceremony, can be traced back to the early Aztecs, who considered a fifteen-year-old girl ready for motherhood. The same type of ritual, with various levels of sexual overtones, is practiced throughout South and Central America, and in Spanish-speaking communities in the United States. The Mexican form of the ritual was influenced by French culture during the nineteenth century, when for several years France governed Mexico (showing that our little Briar Rose would have been seen as mature at fifteen by the French storyteller). One of the most important elements of the Mexican quinceañera celebration is that the father of the fifteen-year-old girl replaces her flat shoes with high heels, which traditionally shows that he understands that his daughter is now sexually attractive to young men and will willingly allow her to pursue a sexual relationship with her intended lover, once she is married.

At fifteen, Briar Rose would have assumed the role of a mature woman, and beside sexual maturity, that would mean taking on the work of an adult woman. This is symbolized by the spindle, or the flax that would be spun into linen. The very tool that Briar Rose would have used to assume her place at the head of a family turned against her, and pricked her finger, or lodged in her nail bed, throwing the girl into a period of sleep.

In chapter 1, on Snow White, we spoke about sleep as a symbol for winter, dormancy, and death. The element of the hundred years' sleep in fairy tales is very meaningful: the notion that the physical world goes on around us while we search the Underworld, or the unconscious world of dream, for some vision that will complete us. It calls to mind rituals that have been held for many centuries by native peoples such as American Indian tribes and Indigenous Australians. For the latter group, such a ritual is the famous Walkabout, a period when adolescents entering adulthood separate themselves from the rest of the group and wander off alone to "find themselves" by fending for themselves for several months (up to a year). This is very like the dream quest, a time when the physical world of the community's daily life goes on unseen while the adolescent experiences themselves only, and must struggle, in a sense, with whether he or she will be the dog or the wolf when the crab crawls up from the murky depths.

While we know about the initiation of young men in the Walkabout (and for more information on these types of male initiations, see my book *The Flowering Rod*), young women in indigenous cultures also undergo the same types of ritual dream quests. Navajo girls go through the *Kinaaldá*, a rite of passage, at age thirteen: "A Navajo girl, upon reaching the age of thirteen and experiencing her first menstrual period, becomes initiated into womanhood by a beautiful four-day ritual entitled the Kinaaldá, which is part of the Navajo Blessing Way Ceremony. The Kinaaldá literally translates as 'puberty ceremony,' and this term is interchangeable with both the girl and the ceremony."[11]

This type of ritual was seen in other tribes, such as the Quinault Indians of Washington. There, girls who have experienced their bleeding time are sequestered for five months, after which "the girl's ... long stay in the dark cell was now over. She was now regarded as eligible for marriage, and ordinarily did marry within a short time."[12]

These rituals are common for both boys and girls among most indigenous peoples, and have been handed down to us in the form of rituals like the quinceañera, the bar mitzvah, and even the heavily commercialized sweet-sixteen party. While most of these rituals have been stripped of their elements of sexuality and seclusion, many young people still feel these rituals are a signpost that they have matured. They give the teen a feeling of confidence as she or he enters a new phase of life.

Briar Rose's sleep represents this type of ritual of seclusion before adulthood. In her case, it is a dream quest, a time of seclusion like

---

11. Amrani, "The Kinaalda Ceremony—A Dance into Womanhood."
12. Olson, *The Quinault Indians*, 105–6.

the one the Navajo or Quinault girls would have undertaken. Briar Rose is wandering the Underworld of dream, where the crab resides, searching for a dream sign that will allow her to mature and take on the role of an adult woman. In fact, in the older tale, her vision allows her to actually become an adult woman by bearing twin children. Creepy as that tale is, the names of the children give us a clue that they are born of her dream experience: Moon is the child of a dream realm, a realm of night; Sun is the child who has led Talia back into the daylight world, the waking world where reality will return.

The names also represent the sister and brother Diana and Apollo, who as we have seen give her intuition and prophecy. In Basile's version of the tale, Talia wakes but stays sequestered for some time, raising the twins, until the world comes for her in the form of the philandering king. She must then undergo an initiatory trial by defeating the jealous queen, thereby gaining her rightful place as adult woman and queen of her world. The jealous queen takes the place of the evil stepmother who must challenge the girl's self-identity and force her to mature. In a sense, she is the priestess who grants Talia her initiation in a trial by fire. Literally!

THE BRIAR ROSE RITUAL

This ritual is a little different from any we have done so far. It is a very introspective ritual and is meant to be done alone, or perhaps with one other person with whom you are so close that you may sleep in the same bed. The only way to do the ritual with more than two people would be to time the ritual so that several people perform it in separate places at the same moment, and later compare their experience.

You will need a Tarot deck, and it's best if it is a deck with classic Tarot imagery, such as the Rider-Waite deck, the Thoth deck, the Royal Fez Moroccan deck, or the Marseilles deck. Other decks are fine for divination, but here we want the very specific images that appear on classic Tarot cards.

You will also need:

- A wand
- A white candle in a glass holder
- A blank book (to use as a journal)
- Incense, salt, oils, and rainwater or melted-snow water (used for purifying the ritual bath)

You will do this ritual on the night of a new moon, at the time you would normally prepare for bed (there will be follow-up work until the next new moon).

You might prepare for the ritual by taking a cleansing bath: in a candle-lit bathroom, run your bath water. Bless the bath by pouring in salts and oils (rose oil would work perfectly). Then ask the elementals to join you this way:

Wave incense over the bath, saying: "Spirits of air, bless this bath and give me deep thoughts and intuition."

Wave a candle over the water: "Spirits of fire, light in me the spark of inspiration."

Place some rainwater or melted-snow water into the tub: "Spirits of water, allow me to see visions in dreams."

Place salt into the tub: "Spirits of earth, keep me safe and warm in my sleep."

Now get into the bath, relax, and say: "Briar Rose, walker in the dream worlds, come to me! I wish to follow your path into the Underworld of dream and emotion. Briar Rose, be with me this night, and wander with me on the path of moonlight."

Stay in the bath and relax for as long as you like. When you are done, ask the elementals to follow you into your bed.

Once you are ready to lie in bed, place the white candle in its holder on your bedside table or a safe surface near the bed. (Make sure nothing is close enough to catch fire if you fall asleep while the candle is burning, and that the candle is on a flat surface so it will not tip over. Trust me, I speak from bitter experience.)

Next, shuffle through the Tarot deck to find three cards. The middle card will be the Moon, card number eighteen. The first card should represent you before your dream quest: for a woman, it might be the High Priestess, card two, a young woman who seeks secrets in the Underworld, hidden behind the sheet before which she sits. For a man, it might be the Magician, card one, who wishes to learn magic and prophecy. The third card will be you fulfilled: for a woman, the World, twenty-one, a female dancer who is sure and confident. For a man, the Hermit, nine, a sturdy climber who carried with him up the mountain the light of knowledge.

Light the white candle in a glass holder so it can burn all night without worry of anything catching fire. Now get comfortable in bed, the way you will sleep.

Lay the three Tarot cards you have chosen out on the blankets before you. Study the first card: you are on a dream quest, seeking intuition and knowledge from your journey into the dark Underworld. Look into the eyes of the High Priestess or Magician. The figure is you, ready and strong, but not yet knowing the deepest mysteries of yourself and your dreams. Study this card for a few minutes, and when you feel you have some understanding or insight into the card, write it down in your journal (use a short phrase; do not spend a long time writing).

Now take up the Moon card. Look at the full moon, which guides dreams. The crab at the bottom of the card is your guide, and will carry you with it down into the murky depths of sleep and oblivion. You want to tell the crab something, ask it to guide you, ask for its divination. Write down in your journal what you would ask the crab.

Now take up the final card, the World or the Hermit. You wish to know, as this character does, the deepest mysteries, to divine where your path might lead you. Hold this card's image in your mind for a few moments, then settle yourself into sleep. As you drift off, repeat this chant in your mind:

> Briar Rose, Talia, sleeping one
> Take me on the road where you have gone
> Show me secrets in my dreams
> Let me see what you have seen

Now it's up to your dreams. But when you first wake up, in those seconds before you are truly awake, write in your journal anything that is in your mind, no matter how weird, trivial, or half-remembered it seems.

Keep this dream journal every day until the following new moon. Then put it away for another month, new moon to new moon. Now read it over (if you have done this timed with a friend or friends, read your dream journals together). When you have read it over, write in it your observations or intuitions about the dreams and visions you saw.

Repeat this ritual cycle every few months. You will begin having very vivid dreams, and divining useful visions from them.

LITTLE BROOMSTICK (BEAUTY AND THE BEAST): BROOMS AND BROOM MAGIC

"Beauty and the Beast" might be the most popular fairy tale in our culture (at least it runs neck and neck with "Little Red Riding Hood"). There have been movies, television shows, Broadway plays, and even a comic-book character. In this tale, a man makes a bargain with a hideous enchanted creature: his daughter for his own life. The man's beautiful daughter must live with the beast, who visits her each night as she sleeps in his majestic castle. The girl is torn between her duty to her father and her relationship with the monstrous creature. In this chapter, we will compare the Grimms' 1812 version from Children's and Household Tales to a version collected by Ludwig Bechstein, another German folklore collector, and published in 1845 in the book Deutsches Märchenbuch (German Folktale Book). We will then talk about a very little understood magical tool, the broom, and learn some spells and uses for that handy instrument.

Beauty and the Beast. It's probably safe to say that every American child grew up on this tale of love, intrigue, and divided loyalties. Young adults of the 1980s loved the television series setting the tale in a modern, squalid city, and children of the '90s thrilled to the Disney movie and its various offshoots (including a Christmas "midquel").

The Grimms collected the tale as "The Summer and Winter Garden," which was a very old tale in their time, and had been told and collected across Europe. We'll look at their version, and compare it to a version collected by another German, Ludwig Bechstein. Bechstein collected tales at about the same time as the Grimms, the first half of the nineteenth century, and he was the more popular collector among the common people in his day. Unlike the Grimms, he kept the tales pretty much the way he'd collected them: no changing characters or making mothers into stepmothers. So the tale may be a little more convoluted and make a bit less sense in places. That's just the way it was told. We'll figure it out later on.

Bechstein's version has a strange title, "Little Broomstick." The title refers to a minor character in the tale; we'll try to figure that one out, too.

The tale begins very much like the one Disney used. A merchant has three daughters—the older two pretty rude and self-centered, the younger daughter beautiful, modest, and pious. In this version, the youngest girl is named Nettchen. Nettchen is a German variant of the Hebrew name Anna; the name means "God was gracious," so we see the girl's goodness and piety right there in her name. In other variations, the girl is named Belle or Bella, which are French and Italian for "beautiful," from which the tale gets its better-known title.

A little deviation from the Grimms' tale comes right here in the second paragraph, when we are told that "Nettchen . . . had a dear girlfriend who was very poor, but equally beautiful and virtuous. She was a broom binder's daughter, and was for this reason called Little

Broomstick by young and old alike. Both girls were of one heart and one soul. They entrusted one another with their little secrets, and between them all class distinctions fell by the wayside. This angered the older sisters greatly, but Nettchen let them scold, and loved her Little Broomstick nonetheless."[13]

The story goes on like the Grimms' version now: the dad is leaving for a business trip and asks each daughter what she'd like him to bring home to her. The two older girls want the bling, but little Nettchen assures her dad she has everything she needs. Dad presses her, and she finally asks for "three roses growing on one stem," sure that her dad will not be able to find this in the dead of winter.

The father is returning from his trip when he sees a walled garden abutting a castle, in which roses are growing in winter. Dad finds three roses on one stem, and picks them. At once, a beast—described as having a long snout, a "shaggy coat," and several other unpleasant qualities—appears before him. The Beast tells the man he will be killed for picking the rose. The man begs for his life, telling the Beast why he picked the flower. The Beast surmises that the man's youngest daughter must be quite a babe, and exacts a promise that in return for his life, Dad must hand the girl over to the Beast as a wife "in seven months."

The man returns home and says nothing to Nettchen, but he tells the two older daughters about the Beast and his promise. The two older sisters, we are told, took pleasure in the situation.

The time to fulfill the bargain arrives. The Beast's carriage pulls up, but the merchant decides to pull a fast one: he sends Little Broomstick in Nettchen's place. But the Beast immediately recognizes the deception. He returns Little Broomstick in his carriage, and his servants leave the peasant girl and take Nettchen.

---

13. Ashliman, trans. Original title: "Besenstielchen." ©1998 by D. L. Ashliman. Used here with permission. Please see the bibliography for more complete information on this source.

Nettchen is understandably frightened, but she is brave and holds it together. The girl is ushered into a lovely castle, where she is served a sumptuous meal. She is shown by silent servants to a beautiful bed-chamber, where she says her prayers and lies down to sleep. But when she wakes, there is the Beast lying beside her. The Beast rises and leaves quietly, giving Nettchen time to consider what is going on.

She doesn't seem to be very concerned about her situation. In fact, the Beast sleeps with her each night, and she becomes less and less afraid. The Beast cuddles her, "and she stroked his shaggy coat and even allowed him to touch her lips with his long, cold snout." Compare this to the treatment of the bear by Snow-White and Rose-Red.

Now this version of the tale condenses events that take a good deal more time to tell in the Grimms' version: One night the Beast fails to appear, and Nettchen is quite concerned. She finds herself unable to sleep without him, and realizes she has grown quite fond of him.

In "The Summer and Winter Garden," the Grimms' version, there are weeks or months of courtship, until Beauty receives word that her father is dying from his yearning for her. The Beast allows the girl to return home to see her father, with the promise that she will return. She returns to the Beast, whom she finds dying in his cab-bage garden. Here is how the Grimms tell this passage of the tale: "She looked for the beast, but he was not there. She looked every-where, but could not find him . . . Then she was doubly sad, and did not know how to console herself. She sadly went into the garden where she saw a pile of cabbage heads. They were old and rotten, and she pushed them aside. After turning over a few of them she saw her dear beast. He was lying beneath them and was dead." In this version, Beauty revives the beast with water, and at that moment he transforms into a handsome prince.

But in Bechstein's "Little Broomstick" we are spared a few details: the Beast simply doesn't show up at bedtime. The girl wanders to a lush garden, where she finds the Beast lying half dead by a pool. Her breast is referenced ("A bitter pain penetrated her breast, and she cried over the death of the poor beast"), but her tears wake the Beast and transform him into the usual handsome youth.

The Beast then explains that Nettchen has redeemed him from a curse: "My father wanted me to marry a woman whom I did not love. I refused steadfastly, and in his anger, my father had a sorceress transform me into a monster. The transformation was to last until an innocent virgin would fall in love with me in spite of my ugly form ..." Nettchen has freed the Beast, and he asks her to marry him.

Here we see the Beast's piousness: he refuses to marry without love, and prefers to face a horrible fate rather than compromise his morals. The reader is meant to forgive his act of threatening a man with death, and then kidnapping and raping a young woman, when his motivation becomes evident.

BUT WAIT, THERE'S MORE

The Grimms' tale ends here. But "Little Broomstick" is only half over.

Nettchen was not to return to her father's house for a year. But now we are told that she obtained a (very convenient) mirror in which she could see events at home. In it, she sees that her sisters are just fine, but that her father is heartbroken over her absence. She also sees Little Broomstick missing her desperately. Finally, the mirror reveals her father dying, while her sisters seem not to care.

The former Beast tells the girl that there is a life-saving herb in his garden, and as the year is almost up, she can go gather her father, her friend, and her evil sisters and bring them to the castle where Dad will be nursed back to health. The girl brings everyone back. Her father is cured, and she and Little Broomstick resume their friendship. But with her sisters it's a different story: "Nettchen had a forgiving heart, and however much she had been hurt by her sisters, she wanted to share her good fortune with them. Therefore she invited them to visit her, and showed them all her wealth. However, the splendor angered the sisters, and they resolved to kill their happy sister. Once when they were in the bath, they forced Nettchen under the water, and she drowned."

Nice, huh? But now a "tall female figure" rises from the water and brings Nettchen back to life. This is the sorceress who first enchanted the young man, and she is pissed off. She asks Nettchen what the girl would like done with the sisters. Nettchen begs for their lives, but the sorceress isn't having it. She tells the girl that her sisters must be punished: "Let them be transformed into columns and remain such until a man falls in love with them, and that will never happen."

The two sisters are transformed, and we are told they remain stone columns in the garden to this day, for no one will fall in love with a girl who has a heart of stone.

The tale ends this way: "The good Little Broomstick remained Nettchen's most faithful girlfriend. She still shares her good fortune with her, if in the meantime the two of them have not died."

BEASTLY BUSINESS

We have a number of riddles in this tale; first, there is simply the basic Beauty and the Beast story: who is the Beast that is summoned by the plucking of a rose, and why can only Nettchen (or Belle, or Bella) transform him to a princely young man? And why the further developments in this version, like Nettchen's drowning and the sisters being turned to stone? And finally, who is Little Broomstick, and what is she doing in this tale? In fact, why is the entire tale named for her, when she is a minor character who hardly appears at all?

I know what you're thinking: stop asking me so many questions. All right, let's try to answer a few.

First, let's look at the Beast. He is obviously an enchanted being, living in a castle surrounded by a walled garden and summoned by the plucking of a rose. We see the same story in the song "Tam Lin," a traditional Scottish ballad of a Faerie changeling who was summoned by a beautiful maiden, Janet, picking a rose, and who then became her lover (back to that in a moment or two). In other versions of "Beauty and the Beast," it is not a rose that Dad is sent to bring back as a gift: in one version it is a "little nut twig," but as we'll see in "Cinderella," hazelnuts are enchanted and can call forth Faerie spirits. So this Beast is a Faerie or changeling, who haunts a secret or forbidden castle, and like Tam Lin is summoned by the plucking of a rose or some other enchanted flora.

Let's compare the Beast in this version to the creature in other versions. In this tale the Beast is simply described as a hairy monster with a big snout in an overcoat. In other versions he is a bear and a horse, and in a few versions the Beast is a snake (a snake with three heads, in one telling). That calls to mind Eve and the serpent: again, a walled or protected garden with a forbidden plant (the fruit of the tree); and again there is a monstrous lover, the serpent, and a handsome human lover, Adam. The bear version reminds us of "Snow-White and Rose-Red," in which the titular girls have a romance with a bear lover and a princely human lover. And the horse version is like the Turkish story of "The Horse-Dew and the Witch," in which a shah asks his three daughters to personally feed his prize horse while he is away for a time. The two older daughters try to feed the horse, but he will not accept food from them (calling to mind the two older daughters in this tale). The youngest daughter feeds the horse with no difficulty. Upon his return, the shah learns of this, and marries his youngest daughter to the horse. Each night, the stable is transformed to a rose garden (another secret walled garden), and the horse into a handsome young man.

All of the versions of this story owe a debt to much older myths and legends in which stunningly beautiful women are drawn to monstrous lovers. Right off the proverbial bat, the tale of "Beauty and the Beast" resembles an ancient Greek myth, that of Cupid and Psyche.

In that myth, Venus becomes terribly jealous of a mortal named Psyche who is stunningly beautiful (like our Nettchen or Belle). Venus sends her son Cupid to kill the girl, but Psyche is so beautiful that when Cupid enters her chamber and sees her asleep, he fumbles and sticks himself with his dart, and thus falls in love with the sleeping girl. He wishes to marry his lovely obsession, but insanely jealous Venus opposes the union, so Cupid secretly houses Psyche in a beautiful castle to protect her from his disapproving Goddess mother.

Cupid visits his lover each night, but warns her she must keep the lamps unlit so she cannot see him. Psyche assumes he is a horrible monster, and makes love with him but is also terrified of him. This goes on for a good deal of time: Cupid visiting the girl by night, in utter darkness, and Psyche believing she is having sex with a loathsome beast.

In the end, Psyche cannot resist the temptation to light a candle in the midst of their passions. She does so and discovers Cupid's true identity. To marry her lover, Psyche must visit Hades, ending her mortal life so that she can become immortal. Finally, Zeus gives Psyche immortality, and she marries Cupid and gives birth to Voluptas, the curvy demi-Goddess from whose name we get the adjective voluptuous.

This is a tale of perception: first, Venus's perception of herself as the most beautiful creature in the universe is threatened when a mortal girl seems more beautiful than she. This is a page right out of "Snow White." Like Snow White's mother, the Goddess is willing to destroy the girl to maintain her own perception of being the icon of beauty.

Psyche is locked in a sheltering castle tower, sort of a love slave, and visited by Cupid only in utter darkness. Her perception is that

Cupid, the epitome of male beauty, must be a hideous monster. She makes love to him night after night, but imagines that if she looked upon him she would be terrified. Of course this thought eats at her until she must take the risk of lighting a candle: at that moment she sees a stunningly handsome God. What girl wouldn't want one of those?

BEASTS, GODS, AND FAERIES

The story of Cupid and Psyche shares its theme of monstrous lovers with a traditional British Faerie ballad, "King Henry." In that tune, a fictional King Henry is trapped in a hunting hall by a monstrous Faerie woman who demands first that he kill all of his hunting animals, horses, dogs, and hawks, in order to sate her hunger; then she demands that he lie down and pleasure her. But when he does, she becomes the "fairest lady that ever was seen." Again, Henry's perception changes drastically when he beds the Faerie monstrosity.

There is certainly a Faerie presence in the tale at hand. The Beast fits every condition of a Faerie changeling: he governs a haunted castle; he is summoned at the plucking of a rose or a twig of nuts; and he seduces chaste young beauties. In this version, we also have the "sorceress" at the end who rises from the water with her enchanted wand, controlling life and death. It's certain that the German storyteller used the word equivalent to *sorceress*, because as we discussed in chapter 3, on "Hansel and Gretel," witches were the go-to villain of the day. But this enchanted female seems to be a Nixie, a water Faerie often mentioned in the Grimms' tales. Rising from the water, taking humans as changelings, and able to heal the drowning Nettchen, this is a classic Nixie. The "sorceress" also fills the role of Venus, who must be appeased before Cupid can marry Psyche.

But wait. Nettchen herself is a bit of a changeling, too, isn't she? In pretty much every version of the story, she is exchanged for her father's life. In all classic stories of changelings, they are humans

taken into the Faerie world and secluded there. Often there is an exchange, and a Faerie is left in exchange for the human. In this case,
Dad has entered the Faerie world of the walled garden, and so is in
the domain of Faerie: now another human life must be offered if he
wants to return. Beauty nearly always goes willingly, eager to save
her father: in this tale she is snatched when Little Broomstick won't
do as a substitute. Little Broomstick is not of her father's blood, and
so probably won't do as a trade.

It is what happens each night that Nettchen/Beauty is in the castle that is fascinating: "After saying her prayers, she surrendered to
the arms of sleep. When she awoke she saw to her fright that a dis-
gusting shaggy monster lay next to her. But it was lying there still
and quiet, so she left it alone." This is exactly what happens to Psyche
in the castle of Cupid, to Snow-White and Rose-Red with their bear,
and to the youngest daughter in "The Horse-Dew and the Witch": in
each of these tales, the girl lives a relatively normal life each day, but
by night, while in bed, asleep, she is visited by her demon lover.

In chapter 1, on "Snow White," we spoke of sleep, dreams, and
our connection through these to the Underworld. For Snow White
and for Nettchen, the nightly visit to the Underworld involves situations that the girl would not allow herself by day. Not only does she
have sex, but she has sex with a beastly, hideous creature (certainly
not something a sweet, pious girl would do, but perhaps something
she might dream of doing). She seems to enjoy it, enough to repeat
the experience night after night; and she wakes each day without
trauma, living her waking life by day as if nothing abnormal were
happening at all.

In our culture we use the term "dream lover." The Beast is literally
a dream lover, invading Nettchen's dreams each night, where he is
made manifest, able to sleep with her, hold her, enter her. This is the
door the Faerie Beast/horse/bear/serpent uses to enter the girl's living world and become her mortal lover.

THE FAERIE MIRROR, AGAIN

As listeners who have heard this tale since infancy, we know something that Nettchen doesn't know: that the Beast is really a handsome prince. We know that the dew-horse will become a human gentleman by night, that the bear will lead Rose-Red and Snow-White to a treasure before taking his lovely human form, and that the serpent in the garden will give Eve the knowledge of her sexuality so that she may take her brother Adam as a husband, creating humanity. We know these tales so well by now (or tales like them) that we are completely confident that the Beast will disappear, and the girl will get her handsome prince.

But what if he didn't? Or put another way, what if these Faerie creatures, furry and slithery and coarse and taut, are the real form of the lover? What if the "handsome prince" is just the dream shape, the ruse, a glamour formed to make the listener more comfortable? Remember how, in our discussion of "Snow-White and Rose-Red," we said that in many versions the bear is simply a bear (that speaks, and sleeps with humans)?

We see a threshold in these tales, where myth, in the form of dream, may cross into reality. Does Nettchen's love for the Beast allow him to revert back to a prior human form? Or is it that he agrees to assume that shape by day, returning by night to his true form to sate his lust and adoration for his lover?

While Nettchen is asleep, she lives in the Faerie world, where she can see her lover's true form. In this state she is comfortable and accepting of his beastliness, growing intimate with her unsavory paramour.

But if Nettchen and the Beast wish to re-enter the waking world, things must change.

We have often seen changeling tales in which the changeling lives in our world for some time, but must return to her or his own world, Faerie or the Underworld, to make the transition permanent, to take a shape that is of the mortal world. One place we see this clearly is in the tale of Rhiannon from the *Mabinogion*. You'll re-member that in that tale, Rhiannon has entered our world as a hu-man-seeming woman to marry the mortal Pwyll. But after her son is taken by a Faerie in a changeling exchange for a foal, Rhiannon, a horse Faerie, must carry riders on her back and wear a harness and saddle: she must live as a horse, her Underworld shape.

It is this return to her Underworld character that allows her son to be returned to her, and allows her to live as a human woman fi-nally. We see this in a tale closer to "Little Broomstick," when Psyche, who has made love to what she believes is a hideous monster, dis-covers Cupid's true form; she must venture into the Underworld of Hades in order to come out as an immortal and have Cupid in his handsome, God of Love form. (We have to wonder what Cupid looks like there.)

Here is where we see the strange extended version of Little Broomstick starts to make a bit of sense. Like Psyche, Nettchen must journey to the Underworld and give up her mortal life to be with her Beast husband. While the Beast may now look like a handsome prince, he is still an enchanted creature living in a secluded castle. Nettchen's sisters serve the function of giving the girl the push, again literally and figuratively, to revisit the enchanted world she has lived in during her dream state, where she may have sex with her enchanted lover; now through death she journeys to Faerie, return-ing with the help of the river Nixie who revives her (and who is like Venus in the Greek myth).

But the Nixie must take a life in the exchange. She takes the two sisters, who are painted as so devious and manipulative that the lis-tener doesn't mind the bargain. After all, one human life is like an-other to a Faerie. So two sisters for a Beast and a cute girl? It's a fair trade.

THE FINAL RIDDLE

We're left with one final riddle: what is Little Broomstick doing in the story? In fact, why is the tale named for her?

Little Broomstick is a peasant girl, living more closely to Nature than the more well-to-do Nettchen and her sisters. We read in the tale: "She was a broom binder's daughter, and was for this reason called Little Broomstick by young and old alike. Both girls were of one heart and one soul. They entrusted one another with their little secrets, and between them all class distinctions fell by the wayside. This angered the older sisters greatly, but Nettchen let them scold, and loved her Little Broomstick nonetheless."

The girl's father is a broom-maker (and as such, the girl herself would work in his shop and make brooms, too). To do this, he must grow broom corn, cut the wood used for the handles, and use the secret ingredient: the acorn that hides inside the join of the broom and the wood.

In Wicca and other traditional Pagan religions, there is a magical connection between young women and the broom. Witches call this tool the *besom*, and are so connected to this magical tool that they are typically depicted riding it.

The honor of using the besom to sweep the magical circle is traditionally given to the youngest female in a group of Wiccans. Little Broomstick would be viewed as a very magical young woman, the youngest female who is keeper of the mysteries of the broom. Little Broomstick would have this incredible power inside her, the spark of fertility that the broom represents in the youngest women of the coven, who because they have not yet lost many of their eggs through menstruation, have the greatest ability to create life. This is an ancient magic, an awesome power that only young women have. Listeners in medieval Europe would have understood this on some level.

We are also told that the two girls "were of one heart and one soul." Nettchen shares this ancient magic, and what's more, through her love of Little Broomstick is aware of it. It allows her to venture into the Faerie world knowing she will come to no harm.

In most versions of "Beauty and the Beast," it appears to us, the reader, that Dad's life is traded for Beauty's. After all, the Beast is quite insistent that he will only spare Dad if Nettchen/Beauty is brought to his castle instead. But remember Tam Lin and his rose? (I told you we'd get back to that.) The rose may have summoned Tam Lin for pretty much anyone, but it was Janet, and Janet alone, who could carry Tam Lin's child, and save him from his fate of being a sacrifice to Hell at the hands of the Faerie Queen.

Now let's imagine that the Beast, like Hades viewing Persephone, had cast his dream-eye on Nettchen, and desired her and her alone. He knew the father would be wandering by, so he set that rose out there in the dead of winter (hence the Grimms' title, "The Summer and Winter Garden"). Dad fell for the trap, but the trap was set for Nettchen, not Dad.

Now the Beast must leave an enchanted girl in Nettchen's place. Well, Little Broomstick, the magical kid with the innate life-creating broom mysteries locked within her, is just the girl! A creature of the magical world already, she is whisked off by Dad, thinking no one will miss a lowly broom-maker's kid (in the Grimms' version, by the way, they send the miller's girl). But the Beast sends her back, and takes Nettchen.

In Faerie exchanges, a life from the Faerie world is usually left in our world. The clever Beast has foreseen that Dad will send the kid who already has a foot in the enchanted world. Great! The Beast returns Little Broomstick, making the exchange that frees him to take Nettchen with no Underworldly repercussions. The Underworld is satisfied. Magical Little Broomstick may dwell in our mortal world while Nettchen is held in the secluded castle.

At the end of the tale, Little Broomstick accompanies her friend to the dream castle. The Underworld is, after all, her home away from home. And she may now share with Nettchen a magical bond that might not have been possible before. While we hear very little about the girl, she is mentioned prominently in the final paragraph: "The good Little Broomstick remained Nettchen's most faithful girl-friend. She still shares her good fortune with her, if in the meantime the two of them have not died." Death? For these girls? Hardly likely in the Faerie world of the secluded castle.

BROOMS AND BROOM MAGIC

In "Little Broomstick," we see that Nettchen (Beauty) is led to the Beast by a rose in a walled garden. But there are actually two magical plants in the story: the other is broom corn, used by the story's title character, whose magic is expressed through her broom-making abilities.

In many systems, the broom is seen as a powerful magical tool. The broom carries so much magic in folklore that mythical witches are seen as flying on a broom through the air. Modern witches are thought to use the broom as well: Harry Potter fans know the image of Harry playing quiddich on his Nimbus 2000.

How did the broom, or besom, become such a fabled tool, and how can we use the broom in ritual and magic?

Let's take a look at the construction of a broom, and at what the parts represent, to figure that out.

First off, there are actually a few different kinds of brooms. The traditional "witches' broom" is a hearth broom, made of broom-corn bristles and an ash handle. The broom corn is technically *Sorghum vulgare*, and is a type of grassy plant used to make molasses. Broom corn looks like eatable corn when it grows, and is harvested the same way, so it represents the harvest, a sacred rite in Paganism and Witchcraft. The harvest is presided over by such Gods as Bacchus and Dionysus, Saturn, and Mabon; and Goddesses such as Ceres, Pomona, Demeter, and Mab. So the broom corn is sacred to each of these deities.

The ash used in the handle is European ash, *Fraxinus*, a family that includes the rowan tree or mountain ash. Rowan in Ireland is called the "May Tree," because it is the first white flowering tree to bloom in May, signaling the beginning of spring and the planting season. While modern Pagans celebrate the spring holiday of Beltane on May first, in Ireland it is celebrated whenever the rowan gets its first bloom. In times past, the ash was used to make spears for hunting, so the tree is sacred to such Gods as Herne, Cernunnos, and Lugh, and to Goddesses such as Artemis and the Irish Flidais.

When a traditional broom is made, the broom-corn bristles are bound with willow and sewn onto the ash handle. Buried in the join, where the broom meets the ash, is an acorn. Magically, the corn bristles of the broom represent the sexual part of a woman, and the ash handle that of a man. The union creates life, and the fertile ovum inside a woman is represented by the hidden acorn. So in Wiccan traditions, the broom is often used by a girl or very young woman (called the handmaiden or simply the maiden), because it is felt by traditional Wiccans that she has the most potential to bear life.

Especially for a woman, sweeping the circle and feeling the broom's fertile energy can bring an amazing feeling of magic and power, though I speak from experience in saying that a man can feel that energy as well. Many modern Pagans may feel that sweeping a ritual area with the broom clears away negative energy, but among traditional Wiccans this is not the purpose of sweeping: sweeping the circle spreads fertility energy that will be used by the group to create magic.

In a Wiccan ritual, it is the right of the maiden to sweep the circle, but an older woman or a man may do so, especially if no young woman dedicated into the group is present. In other Pagan traditions, any member of the group may sweep. Sweeping is one of the first ritual actions, and helps bond circlegoers who concentrate their focus as the sweeping defines the ritual area. The circle is swept three times in a slow, circular motion around the outside. Those inside the circle will chant a blessing or sing a song while the action of sweeping is going on. Below is the song my group sings. Notice that the words relate to the materials of the broom, and to how they will be used magically:

> Corn of golden broom
> Tied beneath the moon
> Ashen handle, oak seed charm
> Dance in magic, ward off harm
> Weave the circle well
> Weave the enchantment well
> Sweep the circle well
> Sweep the circle well
> (Kenny Klein, from the CD *Oak and Ash*, 2006)

After the circle is swept, the broom is laid across the floor or the ground at the east edge of the circle, the place that represents youth and birth. There may also be times when the maiden will hold the broom for certain workings that require raising magical energy for a spell: this is usually done by chanting and dancing, and the maiden will chant and dance with the broom, which helps direct the energy of the group. This is one practice that might have helped to form the stereotype of witches riding their broomsticks.

GETTING A BROOM

If you want to try some broom magic, or simply want a broom in your magical arsenal, you'll need to get one, either by buying one or making it. If you are crafty, you can make your own broom. There are some very good guides on the Internet, and some good print guides.

I highly recommend *Broom-Corn and Brooms*, an 1887 treatise recently reprinted by Algrove Publishing's Classic Reprint Series.

If you are not so crafty, there are excellent sources for traditional hearth brooms on the Internet or at craft fairs and festivals. I personally have bought several brooms at Renaissance Faires. You can also find crafters making hearth brooms in the American South, where broom-making is still very much alive. If you are able to speak to the crafter personally, make sure the bristles are made from broom corn, and if you can get an ash handle, so much the better. If the crafter will make you a custom broom (and most will), ask her or him to place an acorn in the join. You may want to find an acorn that feels special to you and bring it along when you speak to the crafter.

One final word on buying a broom: Wiccans believe that when you purchase a magical tool, you must pay exactly what is asked fairly in price, and never try to haggle. Negotiating to get a "deal" will negate the magic of the tool and devalue the craftsmanship of the maker. It is best if you can pay the asking price in exact change (of course, a plastic purchase will do just that).

BLESSING YOUR BROOM

Once you have your beautiful new besom, you will want to consecrate (bless) it. Here is a ritual for broom blessing. We will call on our story's title character, Little Broomstick, whose intense magic and travel between our world and the Underworld you should hold in mind while preparing to bring your broom into ritual.

You will need:

- A white candle
- A red candle
- A small dish of salt
- Water (preferably rain water or melted snow) in a small dish or bowl

- Incense

- Your wand

Set your tools on the altar, with the incense in the east, the red candle in the south, the dish of water in the west, and the dish of salt in the north. Place the white candle in the center of the altar. Light both candles and the incense.

Hold your new broom to your chest, close your eyes, and feel the tool's energy. Think about the materials that made your broom, and where they came from: the broom corn growing in the ground, the ash handle when it was a tree in the forest; think of the workers and crafters who harvested the materials and prepared them.

Now hold the broom up to the east, and say:

"Like Little Broomstick, I seek to use the magic of the broom. Hear me, spirit of Little Broomstick, you whose broom carried you between the worlds. I now hold this broom, and ask for a blessing!"

Hold your broom over the incense:

"Spirits of east, I ask for your energy and youthful delight in blessing this broom. May it ever bring me joy."

Walk to the south part of the altar and hold your broom above the red candle (not so close that it will catch fire). Say:

"Spirits of south, I ask for your passion and swift decision in blessing this broom. May it ever bring me thoughts of that which I desire."

Walk to the west, and touch a drop of water to your broom:

"Spirits of west, I ask for your empathy and depth of emotion in blessing this broom. May it ever bring me sympathy and satisfaction."

Walk to the north, and touch a few grains of salt to your broom:

"Spirits of north, I ask for your firmness and deep wisdom in blessing this broom. May it ever bring me rest and peace."

Walk back to the east and silently present the broom by holding it up to the east. Then face the center of the altar. Hold the broom above the white center candle (again, being careful not to set the broom or yourself on fire):

"Goddess and God of corn and grain, Lord and Lady of the growing things of the Earth. Demeter and Dionysus, Saturn and Pomona, Mab and Mabon, bless this broom that I may use it to work only the magic that is right, good, and true for me to use! Let this tool bring me insight, inspiration, and joy! So Mote It Be."

Now sweep three times around the circle deosil (clockwise), repeating this chant as you go:

> "Weave the circle well
> Weave the circle well
> Sweep the circle well"

When you are done, sit down in the east and lay the broom on your lap. Feel its energy, and try to feel whether the energy of the broom has changed now that it has been consecrated. Try to determine how it feels different; being sensitive to changing energy is a very important part of working magic.

When you are done, thank the Gods and Goddesses, and extinguish the center candle flame. Now walk around the circle with your broom and thank the spirits of east, south, west, and north. When you return to the east, lay the broom down and say:

"The circle is ended, my will is done."

BROOM LORE

Besides being used to sweep a ritual circle, the broom is an age-old fertility charm. In parts of Europe and Africa, brooms have long been used as a symbol of marriage and as a tool in marriage ceremonies.

In Ghana, brooms are waved over the heads of a marrying couple for fertility in marriage. Throughout Europe, marriage ceremonies involved jumping over a broomstick, a custom that was carried to the American South. In fact, "jumping the broomstick" is a term meaning getting married, and among European Gypsies, Welsh, and Irish communities of the nineteenth century, it appears a couple needed only to jump over a broom to be considered legally married. One custom says that whichever newlywed lands on the ground first as the broom is jumped will be the head of the household.

Once married, the couple would mount the broom above their bed as a charm to bring on children. In time, if a couple had had all the children they wished for, they would take the broom down (though these communities treasured large families, so it was probably a rare occurrence to remove the broom).

While fertility for farm families meant lots of children, for us it may also mean creative flow, ideas that can be used in our job or studies, inspiration, or divination. Now that you have your broom, place a couple of hooks or long nails above the head of your bed and lay the broom there when you are not using it in ritual. If you are struggling with any problem, like coming up with an idea at work, a topic for a paper or report, a decision about your situation or your relationship, or you need inspiration or guidance, touch the broom before you get into bed at night. Ask the broom for its guidance and wisdom. As you drift off to sleep, feel the broom's energy above you. Allow the tool to help you find answers while you sleep; you should wake with the perfect idea or the right decision.

LOOKING FOR MR. GOODBROOM

Brooms are a tool that represent fertility, and that can mean sex, love, and romance. If you are seriously seeking a romantic relationship, here is a simple spell.

Many of us, when we were younger, lay in bed and held our pillow like it was an imagined lover. Sure, no one likes to admit that they've done this, but we all have. Well, in this spell you will do this with your broom.

Prepare for this spell by imagining you are meeting your ideal lover in your bedroom. Wear what you might wear to do so: a robe, exciting undies, or nothing at all. The more you act like you are truly meeting a person who loves you and desires you, the better the spell will work.

Next, lie in your bed with your broom beside you. Hold your broom tenderly, as you would hold a lover (other descriptions than tenderly are at your own risk). Speak to your broom, and tell it what you would like in a partner:

"I will that rather than you, broom, I have a strong, handsome, caring lover here beside me." Or, "I will that rather than you, broom, I have a curvy, sensuous, passionate lover here beside me." (You get the idea.) Now say, "Broom, help me work my will. Loose your fertility into my life, and draw to me the person for whom I am just right! As I will, broom, So Mote It Be!"

Touch your broom and feel its energy (anything more involved is between you and your broom). When you are done, hang the broom back above your bed (or lay the broom beneath it) and sleep knowing that the broom is guiding the right person to you.

Sweet dreams!

Chapter 6

CINDERELLA: A RITUAL FOR MANIFESTING WISHES

A girl's mother dies, and her father remarries a horrid woman with two horrid daughters. The orphaned girl is reduced to the status of a household servant, but she never loses hope. Guided by her mother's spirit, she enlists the help of an enchanted tree and a wish-granting bird. In the end she becomes the person she was meant to be, and marries a prince. We'll explore a ritual for manifesting wishes based on the magical theme of the tree and the bird. The story quotes are from the Margaret Hunt translation of the Grimms' 1812 Children's and Household Tales.

Say the title *Cinderella* to almost anyone who grew up on Disney, and that person will immediately think of the two best-known themes of the tale: a wish-granting fairy godmother and a magical pumpkin that becomes a carriage, driven by coachmen mice and foot-men frogs. But if you take a look at the tale as the Grimms collected it, you might notice that neither of those are actually in the story!

The fairy godmother came into the Disney version from other traditional sources. In the very similar Irish story "Fair, Brown and Trembling," there is a hen-wife who grants Trembling her wish to go to the feast; and in the Norwegian and Georgian tales, it is a magical cow who grants the girl her wish. It is Charles Perrault—whose collection of French tales wound up in the fairy books edited by Andrew Lang (and who created a moral ending for each tale)—who has Cinderella aided by a godmother (though no mention is made of her being a Faerie).

But the Grimms' Cinderella gives us two much more ancient elements: the wise hazel tree and the prophetic bird that will guide the pious heroine to justice and love.

"Cinderella" begins with a dying mother's promise. The woman promises her daughter that she will be protected, even from beyond the grave. But the girl's father takes a new wife, and the daughter must accept two new siblings. The stepsisters cast the girl into the role of servant. She has no proper bed and must sleep in the cinders by the fire; always covered in ash, she is called Cinderella. The sisters also have a habit of throwing the girl's peas and lentils into the hearth fire, which sounds odd but may make sense later on. Bear with me.

The girl's father prepares to go to market one day, and asks what each girl would like. The stepsisters want expensive clothing and jewels. But Cinderella asks, oddly, for a tree branch. The father brings each girl her requested prize, and Cinderella plants the tree branch by her mother's grave, watering it with her tears.

Now we see a strange scene: Cinderella sits each day by the tree, and a bird appears, to tell the girl he will give her whatever she wishes for.

As in the Disney version, the king's son holds a ball and the step-sisters are invited. They tell Cinderella she must stay home because she is dirty and has nothing to wear. Cinderella pleads, and her step-mother sets up a series of seemingly impossible tasks, again involving peas thrown in the hearth fire. Cinderella completes the tasks by asking the help of the birds that live in her garden. These doves are glad to aid the girl in a series of ever more difficult tasks, but the stepmother goes back on her word each time, denying Cinderella her opportunity to attend the ball.

The resourceful girl asks the bird in the hazel tree for a dress, and manages to make herself look beautiful. As in the movie, the prince notices the girl above all others, and is charmed by her. Unlike the movie version, Cinderella must find cunning ways to hide herself each night as she leaves the ball; one night she hides in a pigeon house, another night in a large pear tree. Finally, on the third night of celebration, the prince lays a trap for the girl by putting tar on the steps. Her shoe comes away as she runs, and the prince begins his storied quest to find the maid whose foot will fit the shoe.

Coming to the home of the three girls, he allows the stepdaughters to try on the shoe. Each of the stepdaughters hopes to marry the prince, but the shoe is too small for each of them. Each must cut off a part of her foot to fit the shoe, and each fills the shoe with blood. Nevertheless, the prince rides off in turn with each girl, thinking he has found his true love. Each time they must ride past the hazel tree. It is the bird in the hazel tree that points out that each of these are the wrong girl. The bird insists to the prince that he has not yet discovered the right sister: "There's blood within the shoe, the shoe it is too small for her, the true bride waits for you."

Returning to the house of the girls, the prince asks about a third daughter. The father denies having one, except for "a little stunted kitchen-wench." The prince insists that this girl try on the shoe, and when she fits the shoe perfectly, the prince recognizes her as the girl from the ball.

As Cinderella and the prince ride away, the birds in the hazel tree assure the prince he has chosen correctly: "No blood is in the shoe, the shoe is not too small for her, the true bride rides with you," and they alight on Cinderella's shoulder. There they perch at the wedding, and when the stepsisters come alongside Cinderella, the birds peck out the girls' eyes.

In looking at the Grimms' version of "Cinderella," there is a wealth of older Faerie lore and myth. Let's take a moment to look at each of these sometimes complex elements.

ORPHANED AND ABANDONED

Just as in many of the Grimms' tales, this story begins with a child left orphaned. The orphaned or abandoned child is a familiar character whom we see in the Grimms' "Snow White," whose mother dies soon after she is born; and in tales like "Hansel and Gretel," or the lesser-known tale of "Brother and Sister," which begins very much like "Hansel and Gretel." The motif is so universal in the Grimms' tales that it goes beyond human orphans: in "The Bremen Town Musicians," it is four animals who have been abandoned and must make their way in the world.

Stories of abandoned children are common for a few good reasons. One is that it really happens. In the Middle Ages, Europeans suffered catastrophic starvation and gruesome wars, and children were often left with no parents and no home. This continued throughout the centuries. Dickens's Oliver Twist and Victor Hugo's Cosette were orphaned victims of war and poverty less than two centuries ago. (And wars in Afghanistan, Iraq, and Somalia create real orphans as this book is written.) Our hearts go out to these children. We feel sympathy for the heroine or hero—a poor, defenseless child left alone. We long to see these characters rise above their circumstances and prove their resourcefulness and courage, as all of these heroes and heroines do. We want these children to succeed, to overcome their hardship, and to find justice for their misfortune.

Cinderella is not totally alone. She has a father, who the story tells us is wealthy. But once the action begins we see very little of him. In fact, he practically abandons her from the time he remarries. He does nothing to defend his daughter when she is abused by her new stepsisters. At one point in the story, he refers to Cinderella as "a little stunted kitchen-wench which my late wife left behind her." We sense that the father has no love for the girl (and from this statement, we might even imagine that he suspects that she is not his biological daughter). In fact, at the story's end when justice is meted out to the various evil-doers, the stepmother and stepsisters, Dad is not even mentioned.

Dad is a specter; poor Cinderella is a victim of circumstance, alone against very real abuse, with no one to protect or champion her. Except, that is, her dead mother, who made a promise upon her deathbed to cherish her daughter even from beyond the grave: "The wife of a rich man fell sick, and as she felt that her end was drawing near, she called her only daughter to her bedside and said, 'Dear child, be good and pious, and then the good God will always protect you, and I will look down on you from heaven and be near you.'"

One other fact about the story's opening: the tale never tells us Cinderella's actual name. We get very little information about her at all; unlike Snow White, who we know is "as white as snow, and as red as blood, and her hair was as black as ebony," or the Robber Bride, who we are told is "beautiful," or Red Riding Hood, whose wardrobe we know quite well, we learn almost nothing about Cinderella in the opening lines except that her father is wealthy, her mother has died, and that she is "pious." We are given an example of her piety in the fact that she visits her mother's grave each day, presumably while her father is off womanizing.

ENTER THE EVIL STEPMOTHER

Dad's womanizing pays off, for "by the time the spring sun had drawn [the snow] off again, the man had taken another wife." The wife brings her own two daughters into the marriage, and as we all know, the two stepsisters immediately begin to torment Cinderella.

Throughout folklore we see this motif of the (often abusive) false parent and siblings. Gwion Bach is chased and eaten by his surrogate mother, Cerridwen. In the Greek-Roman myth of Cupid and Psyche, Cupid's mother Venus (Aphrodite) despises Psyche for her beauty, and curses her. But Cupid (Eros) falls in love with the girl, and hides her in a fortress to protect her from his jealous mother. (Cupid's union with Psyche makes Venus the girl's mother-in-law.)

In folk ballads you do not have to look far to find the same evil-stepmother motif. In the Scottish ballad "Willie's Lady," Willie's mother does not like her son's new bride, and casts a spell so that the pregnant bride will always be in labor but never give birth. Willie must find a way to undo the spell before his wife dies of her labor pains. In another Scottish ballad, "The Famous Flower of Serving Men," a noble young woman's mother does not like her husband, and sends cutthroats to her home in the middle of the night to kill her family:

> My mother did me deadly spite
> For she sent thieves in the dead of night
> They killed my lord, they slew my babe
> They made their sport and went their way
> (Traditional)

In the aftermath of this trauma, the young woman cuts off her hair and poses as a man:

> I cut my locks and I changed my name
> From Fair Eleanor to Sweet William

I went to court to serve my king
As the famous flower of serving men

She becomes a favorite of the king. Being a beautiful young soldier, she is given the song's title as her moniker. In time, the king learns that she is a woman and falls in love with her. She is then able to tell him her story, and she asks that he give the order to kill her mother for her wicked deeds.

Of course, fairy tales are full of these distrustful, neglectful, horrible parents: parents who starve their children ("Hansel and Gretel," "Brother and Sister"), parents who allow their children to wander unprotected in the forest ("Little Red Cap," which we know as "Red Riding Hood"), and of course parents or stepparents who try to kill their child ("Snow White").

Why do we find this so often in these tales? What makes us respond to a story about a neglectful or homicidal parent? What exactly are we getting out of it?

For starters, lurking inside every child is the deep, primal fear that their parents will someday abandon them or stop serving their needs. Children are wholly dependent on their parents' care, and the fear that they might lose their parents' love and nurturing is the fear of death that is part of our basic survival instinct. All children know deep inside that if their parents suddenly gave up caring for them, they would die. And while rationally most children know their parents love them, this irrational fear surfaces now and again, as all irrational fears do.

Children also have the fear that their parents will leave them in the care of a distrustful caregiver (an "evil stepmother"). A babysitter or family member might not attend their needs as diligently as their own parent would. Or they might not attend to their needs at all. We all sit on the edge of our seat at the movie portrayal of the oblivious babysitter who listens to headphones or makes out with her boyfriend while the child's life is threatened just a room away.

And what if the parent died? Who would care for the child then?

Children can process these anxieties by hearing them expressed in folklore, and empathizing with child heroes who are able to conquer these situations and ultimately triumph. The fact that Snow White or Hansel and Gretel made it through their ordeals comforts a kid. Maybe, just maybe, if it ever happened to them, they could make it through as well.

Throughout these tales is the idea that the hero or heroine has somehow switched places, fallen out of their rightful situation and through no fault of their own become a victim of fate. Cinderella should have been the happy, spoiled daughter of a loving mother and a wealthy father, but fate robbed her of her mother's presence and of her father's love. Her position in life went to her undeserving stepsisters. The same can be said of Snow White: she should have been her father's beloved daughter, but her mother's jealousy prevented that. Her mother became obsessed with taking Snow White's place in her father's affections, and Snow White was cast out and left to the ravishes of Dame Fortune.

The evil stepparent or stepsibling is more than just a bad person: she is the agent of cruel fate, acting out her small role in a larger tragedy in which a person cries out, "This is a mistake, this wasn't supposed to happen," but because of the role they've been cast into by the stepparent (orphan, servant, derelict), no one will believe them. Their cries go unheeded, and the world goes on despite this horrible turn of fortune.

To correct this cosmic error, the heroine must defeat the usurper—in Cinderella's case, her usurping stepsisters—and in doing so, reclaim her birthright. This is played out in mythology again and again. Each hero must defeat or destroy the false heir to his or her own legitimate position. Zeus must kill his father Cronus to claim his place as king of the Gods of Olympus; Arthur must prove himself by freeing the sword from the stone so that he may replace Uther Pendragon as king of Britain. Moses must abandon his adopted father the Pharaoh in favor of his true father, Jehovah, in order to become king of the Hebrew people. In more modern myth, Luke Skywalker must face off with his evil father, Darth Vader, to bring peace to the galaxy and become the rightful heir to the title of Jedi Knight.

In each story, a character is denied her or his rightful entitlement and must reclaim it by displacing the person who is usurping it. Children may have this fear, especially when a new child is born into the family. A child may ask: Will my parents still love me after the new baby is here? Will they stop caring for me? Young siblings argue over toys, space in the home, and attention from parents, grandparents, and friends; older siblings may compete for romantic attention, or for resources (food, friends, the car, the television channel). In each case, each child feels he or she deserves what the sibling has usurped.

In a mythic sense, the heroine must struggle against fate to reclaim what is rightfully her own. That's something we all feel deeply. Ask any accountant or legal secretary, and she'll tell you that she was truly destined to be an astronaut, rock star, or race car driver. And even astronauts, rock stars, and race car drivers struggle against the "slings and arrows of outrageous fortune." Illness, fortune, and war haunt even the most successful life, these things we seem to have no control over. Just look at Lance Armstrong's battle with cancer, or looking back a bit in history, the often horrific life of Charles Lindbergh, the "rock star" of adventurers whose child was kidnapped and killed. We respect the hero who can rise above the bitter roadblocks fate lays in his path. We're rooting for Cinderella, because we know we could easily be in her place.

PEAS AND LENTILS

We begin to see Cinderella's day-to-day struggle. We are told that she must sleep in the cinders of the hearth, and this is how she gets her name: since we never knew her real name, we define Cinderella by the evidence of her torment. As the story develops, we see her in a desperate cycle of abuse: she is slovenly and dirty because she is forced to sleep in the ashes, and each time she'd like to participate in the family's doings, she is told she cannot because she is so slovenly and dirty.

One of the tricks each member of the new family seems to play on her is to destroy her peas and lentils, both eatable seeds. It's interesting how the Grimms' version of the tale keeps taking the reader back to these peas; early in the story we are told that "the sisters did her every imaginable injury—they mocked her and emptied her peas and lentils into the ashes, so that she was forced to sit and pick them out again." Later she must appease her stepmother by again picking peas out of the fire: "As, however, Cinderella went on asking, the stepmother said at last, 'I have emptied a dish of lentils into the ashes for you, if you have picked them out again in two hours, you shall go with us.'" This scene is repeated a second time as the stepmother denies Cinderella's request to attend the feast.

The reason for this strange scenario is hinted at in an early part of the narrative, when we see the father setting off for market. He asks each child what she wants. The sisters want clothes and jewelry. But Cinderella says, "Father, break off for me the first branch which knocks against your hat on your way home." It's a strange thing to ask for, until we learn that the first thing that knocks against Dad on his return trip is a hazel branch. This he brings to his neglected daughter, and she plants it at her mother's grave, watering it with her tears.

. . . AND HAZEL

According to European folklore, the hazel is a very powerful tree, used for wisdom and prophecy. One legend says that if you make a wish wearing a "nut cap" of hazel branches on your head, your wish will be granted. Hazel branches are used for dowsing or "water-witching," a method very successfully used to find underground springs of water. Halloween is sometimes called "nutcrack night" in England. Hazelnuts are used on this night in a spell to foretell one's future lover (much like the magic employed by the maid in Keats' "The Eve of Saint Agnes").

The hazel is also a powerful protection from Faeries. In an Irish tale of a young woman abducted by the Faeries, the changeling woman tells her husband to bring a hazel stick and use it to beat upon the horse she rides during the Faeries' Wild Ride over a river crossing. She will fall from the horse, and be free from the Faeries' hold upon her.

In Druid lore hazel is called *coll*, the tree of wisdom. According to Irish myth, a salmon that lived in a lake ate nine hazelnuts that had fallen into the water from a tree on the shore. Each nut became a spot on the salmon's sides. A hermit wished to eat the salmon in order to gain the tree's wisdom, and he set the boy Finn McCool to cook the fish for him. But Finn accidentally burnt his finger on the salmon as he cooked it, and instinctively licked his finger. He, not the hermit, obtained the salmon's wisdom (another myth in which a child defeats a false heir, the hermit, to gain his rightful entitlement, the wisdom of the hazel tree). This may be why Finn is named Mc-Cool, or Mac (son) of Coll (the hazel).

Over time the Pagan elements of hazel lore were replaced by Christian elements, as storytellers of Germany were universally Christian in the Grimms' time. Here is a tale the Grimms themselves collected in the German forest concerning the hazel tree:

One afternoon the Christ-child had laid himself in his cradle-bed and had fallen asleep. Then his mother came to him, looked at him full of gladness, and said, have you laid yourself down to sleep, my child. Sleep sweetly, and in the meantime, I will go into the wood, and fetch you a handful of strawberries, for I know that you will be pleased with them when you awake. In the wood outside, she found a spot with the most beautiful strawberries, but as she was stooping to gather one, an adder sprang up out of the grass. She was alarmed, left the strawberries where they were, and hastened away. The adder darted after her, but our lady, as you can readily understand, knew what it was best to do. She hid herself behind a hazel-bush, and stood there until the adder had crept away again. Then she gathered the strawberries, and as she set out on her way home she said, as the hazel-bush has been my protection this time, it shall in future protect others also. Therefore, from the most remote times, a green hazel-branch has been the safest protection against adders, snakes, and everything else which creeps on the earth."[14]

Another hazel story involving biblical figures tells that after the fall, Adam was told he could create any animal he liked by striking the sea with a hazel branch. Adam created a sheep. In her turn, Eve created a wolf that devoured Adam's sheep. Adam then created a dog, which kept the wolf at bay so that order was restored. This story again has a theme of false inheritance and entitlement: Adam strives to create animals that may live in harmony with humans; to do so, he must thwart Eve's attempts to create animals that will eat domesticated stock. Through the dog, Adam takes his place as master of livestock. Tied to this, hazel wood is traditionally used to make the shepherd's crook.

Cinderella somehow knows that her father will bring her home a hazel tree, and she also knows to plant this on her mother's grave. The nuts of the hazel will give her wisdom; this is tied into the other seeds she must gather, peas and lentils. Each is a symbol of the potential Cinderella has for breaking out of her fated misery and "blossoming" into the life she was destined to have. In *The White Goddess*, Robert Graves writes: "The nut in Celtic legend is always an emblem of concentrated wisdom: something sweet, compact, and sustaining

---

14. Grimms (Hunt, trans.), *Grimm's Household Tales*, tale 148.

enclosed in a hard shell."[15] This type of meaning is associated with the nut throughout European lore.

All three seeds—peas, lentils, and hazelnuts—refer to the potential inside of Cinderella, or the seed of her being, which must grow into her rightful place in life. Seeds rest beneath the earth, in the Underworld, and grow up through the ground into our world: each year we see the world reborn after winter (death), when plants grow and bring life. The image of the peas in the fire alludes to Cinderella suffering to make her more determined and more capable. It is also the image of the phoenix, rising from its fiery ashes.

THIS PLACE IS FOR THE BIRDS

Once the hazel tree is planted at her mother's graveside, birds fly into it and begin granting Cinderella wishes. The number of birds in the tree seems to change constantly; at first it is one particular bird: "a little white bird always came on the tree, and if Cinderella expressed a wish, the bird threw down to her what she had wished for." Later, various doves help Cinderella pick peas from the fire. However once Cinderella is restored to her true position, and rides to the prince's castle, we read: "As they passed by the hazel tree, the two white doves cried . . . the two came flying down and placed themselves on Cinderella's shoulders, one on the right, the other on the left, and remained sitting there." So we are left to wonder how many birds are really in this tree.

The reason the number is inconsistent is because of the type of birds at work here. These are not ordinary birds, but enchanted creatures.

Enchanted birds appear across European folklore. We saw one in "Hansel and Gretel." Russian tales talk of an enchanted bird called a Sirin. These tales say that only saints may understand the song of the Sirin: others will be driven mad by it and ultimately die. This

---

15. Graves, *The White Goddess*, 181.

echoes pious Cinderella's ability to communicate with her birds. In the French tale of "Little White Thorn," the title character wanders naked into a field on May Morning, and steps on a certain plant (reminiscent of Cinderella's hazel tree). From that moment she can understand the speech of an enchanted bird who leads her to reclaim the fortune that has been denied to her family (very similar circumstances to the story here).

Like Eden or Avalon, Cinderella has created a haven for herself at her mother's grave, shaded by the hazel that gives her wisdom and guarded by the magical bird, who grants the girl her wishes. We are told she goes to this Eden-like grove three times a day to pray (a reference to her piety). This is Cinderella's refuge, but it also represents the Underworld. In this enchanted place, Cinderella is not a "little stunted kitchen-wench." Here she is recognized by the birds, her mother, the tree, and her God as the true heir to her mother's place in the world. Here she may commune with the Underworld (represented by the hazelnuts and her peas and lentils), which will aid her in regaining her place.

In the very same paragraph we learn of the prince's ball, which we all know will be the opportunity to do just that, regain her rightful place. The sisters receive their invitation, but as we later learn, the prince does not even know of Cinderella's existence, so she receives no invite. Undaunted, she asks to be allowed to go, but her stepmother chides her: "'You go, Cinderella,' said she, 'covered in dust and dirt as you are, to the festival. You have no clothes and shoes, and yet would dance.'" Here we see the oppressor's circular logic: Cinderella is covered in dust and dirt because her mother and sisters have made her that way to deny her of her birthright; they use her plight, which they have caused, as their very logical excuse to exclude her.

But like the peas in the fire, Cinderella has been tempered. This is shown in the trial her stepmother sets for her: if she can pick out the peas her mother has thrown into the fire in a certain amount of time, she may join her sisters at the ball.

We see the sort of interaction the saints are said to have with the Sirin, as Cinderella calls the enchanted birds to her aid, and they pick the peas from the ashes in plenty of time. The Faerie nature of the birds is further stressed by the fact that they don't eat the peas, as any normal bird would. They are on task, knowing the peas are Cinderella's means of salvation.

But the stepmom is not to be trusted and, as we know she will, reneges on her promise. The righteous Cinderella has proved herself, but is denied her just reward.

The stepmother's actions here may be a veiled allusion to the biblical story of Peter, who in John 13 is warned by Christ that he will deny his savior three times. Peter assures Jesus he will not, but when he is surrounded by Roman guards he does just as Jesus predicted. When Peter denies Jesus the third time, a rooster crows, stressing the prophetic nature of birds that we see in the story here. The stepmother denies the biblical God by promising a reward to the pious Cinderella and then, like Peter, denying it. Like the biblical rooster, the doves are witness to Mom's betrayal.

When the stepmother finally denies Cinderella several times (we imagine it was three times in the most pristine versions of the story), the hapless girl goes to her Eden-like grove. This is a very different scenario than the Disney version we were raised on: in that telling, Cinderella gives up, sits down, and cries. Her tears bring on a Faerie, a godmother who offers to help the girl. The moral seems to be that if you are not successful, sit and cry and someone will help you.

GOING TO THE BALL: PIGEONS AND PEARS

But our true heroine is no quitter. She has faithfully cultivated her mother's gravesite, and planted her hazel garden there. She takes action, knowing the enchanted birds are her allies:

"As no one was now at home, Cinderella went to her mother's grave beneath the hazel tree, and cried, 'Shiver and quiver, little tree, silver and gold throw down over me.' Then the bird threw a gold and silver dress down to her, and slippers embroidered with silk and silver."

Notice that she does not actually address the bird, but speaks to the tree. Fables often warn of the risks of wishing for something on a whim. Cinderella's wishes must be tempered with wisdom, so she asks the wise hazel tree for "silver and gold," and receives a beautiful dress and slippers from her ally the enchanted bird, each containing the silver and gold she'd asked for. There is a complex interaction here between Cinderella, the tree, and the bird, guided over by the mother.

The story here calls the ball a wedding, and the festivities last several days (three to be exact, that magic number that often appears in myth and fable). Cinderella must hide her true identity until the wise hazel allows her to reveal herself: she dances with the prince that first night, and then escapes into a pigeon house, again calling upon her avian allies to hide her so that the prince will not know her humble station. In any story of this type, it is important that the hero prove his or her merit before revealing their plight. That way no one will love them or care for them out of pity, but out of pride and gratitude. Cinderella must win the prince's true love before she can reveal herself fully to him. In a sense, she must keep her chastity until she has his promise of commitment; then she may give herself fully, sexually to him.

We already know the birds are Cinderella's allies, and the pigeon is a close relative of the dove (technically a pigeon is a rock dove). The pigeons hide Cinderella from the prince, allowing her to escape. The birds also represent flight; Cinderella has made no commitment to the prince yet, and may fly from his company as she must to retain her chastity.

The second night the entire scenario is played out again. The bird gives Cinderella a dress even more lovely than the first one, and she dances with the prince again. When it is time to leave, she eludes him by hiding in a pear tree.

The pear is a soft, supple fruit, shaped a bit like a woman. We often say a particular type of woman is "pear shaped," a phrase used often in media and fashion, and while this may carry an (undeserved) unpleasant connotation now, it was considered a very lovely shape in Europe at various times. Look at paintings such as Ingres's *La Grande Odalisque*, the 1482 portrayal of Eve by Hugo van der Goes, Titian's *Venus of Urbino*, or any of Renoir's models. Each of these women of exquisite beauty can be compared to the delicate fruit of the pear tree, with its gentle curves and lush bottom.

The pears in "Cinderella" are even described in detail, as "the most magnificent pears." There's no mistake that as lovely as the pears are, they allude to the loveliness of Cinderella's supple form. While the first evening Cinderella gave the prince the slip by hiding in a bird house, representing flight or escape, she now shows him that she wishes him to spend the long, lonely night dreaming of her curves and of the promise hidden under that beautiful dress. She is described as climbing the tree nimbly, like a squirrel: we can only imagine Cinderella's subtle beauty, her lithe form and soft step, as she bounds up the pear tree in her glittering dress.

Something very unusual happens here; Cinderella's father appears in the story, and oddly, the prince seems to know he is her father: "He waited until her father came, and said to him, the unknown maiden has escaped from me, and I believe she has climbed up the pear tree. The father thought, can it be Cinderella. And had an axe brought and cut the tree down, but no one was on it." Dad has been completely absent from the girl's life up to this point, allowing her to be tortured and bullied. Now he cuts down the tree she has hidden in. This may symbolize cutting all of his ties to her, so that she is free to marry. Or he may be trying to quell her sexual allure, represented by the pears; he cannot, for she has eluded him and escaped the tree.

Notice that both nights, the object that hides Cinderella is destroyed; the pigeon house is "hewed to pieces" with an ax, and the pear tree is likewise cut down. We are shown that Cinderella's old life as a servant is being destroyed, and if she plays her cards right, she will begin a new life.

THE SISTERHOOD OF THE TRAVELING SHOE

The third night of the ball, the scenario is played out again, but this time the prince is prepared:

"The king's son, however, had employed a ruse, and had caused the whole staircase to be smeared with pitch, and there, when she ran down, had the maiden's left slipper remained stuck. The king's son picked it up, and it was small and dainty, and all golden. Next morning, he went with it to the father, and said to him, no one shall be my wife but she whose foot this golden slipper fits. Then were the two sisters glad, for they had pretty feet."

Again the prince seems to know whose daughter Cinderella is, while her own family has no clue. Also, remember that the Grimms' story refers to the ball as a wedding; it is very possible that the prince is forsaking an intended wife because he has seen Cinderella, and will now have no one but her. This would be another instance of Cinderella reclaiming her rightful place from a usurper.

At this point in the story, we see a major shift in focus, and perhaps a bit of a sexual fetish.

As for shifting focus, how old is Cinderella anyway? Like many of the Grimms' characters, Cinderella's age seems to be a bit of a question. At the story's opening, we are plainly told that Cinderella is a child. Through the story, we see the girl and her stepsisters as children dependent on their mother and their absentee father. No age is assigned to any of the girls. But suddenly the story becomes extremely romantic, with each girl competing for the prince's attention. And how do they compete? Not with their faces or figures, or even their feminine charm: the sexuality of each girl is epitomized by her feet!

Feet are sexy, make no mistake about that. There is a huge genre of erotica that emphasizes these shapely extremities, and this genre has existed from time beyond memory. It is a shapely part of a woman that can be shown publicly, adorned sensuously, pointed and arched gracefully, without breaking any social or moral taboo.

Feet can play an important role in public display of a young woman's budding sexuality. In the celebration of the quinceañera, a father slips his daughter's flat shoes from her feet and replaces them with heels, signifying that he sees his daughter as a sexual being, old enough to seduce a man whom she might marry. This public display of foot adoration is a ritualized coming of age in Hispanic communities in many countries. In Western cultures, many post-pubescent girls stop wearing child-oriented shoes, like saddle shoes or loafers, and begin wearing stockings and high heels as they explore their newfound womanhood. The ritual of painting one's toenails is also a rite of womanhood in many American cultures.

The fetishistic bend of Cinderella's tale begins with the pear tree: Cinderella must nimbly climb the pear tree in golden slippers. The storyteller draws us to no other thought than Cinderella's tiny, shapely feet in her delicate slippers, stepping lithely among the pears with their feminine shape. Perhaps when her own father cuts the tree down, like a quinceañera rite, he severs his claim on her by destroying the place where her feet have been: he shows that her sexuality is not his—but her lover's, the prince.

The next night the prince, filled with thoughts of Cinderella nimbly stepping from branch to branch, lays pitch, a sticky tar-like resin, on the stairs. When Cinderella runs daintily away from him, her shoe becomes stuck, and she must run barefoot through the paths and lawns to her home. The prince takes up the shoe, described as "small and dainty, and all golden," a fetishist's dream. He goes directly to Cinderella's home, and asks that all the girls there try on the shoe. The sisters are pleased, "for they had pretty feet." This is again a very different vision than the Disney telling we grew up on. There the sisters are a bit grotesque, and we know all along that no prince could ever choose them. But here we see that the sisters have a beauty, expressed in the narrative by their pretty feet. If we did not know their secret, that these girls abuse their sister, we might simply see them as two beautiful girls. The prince sees them this way, and believes this to be the home of his future bride.

Each sister tries on the shoe, but each has to cut off a part of her foot to make it fit. Just like the archaic phrase "cut off your nose to spite your face," these girls are marring their beauty (their pretty feet) to gain the prince's love. By marring their beauty, each sister is showing us, the reader, that she is unlovable. Only Cinderella, whose facial beauty may be hidden under ashes, has the pretty feet that will truly fit this shoe.

As I mentioned earlier, the prince is content with each of the sisters once she has tried on the shoe. Unlike the Disney telling, these girls are pretty enough, and the prince believes the shoe fits. It is the enchanted bird in the hazel tree that alerts the prince to the mistake he's making: "They were obliged, however, to pass the grave, and there, on the hazel tree, sat the two pigeons and cried, 'Turn and peep, turn and peep, there's blood within the shoe, the shoe it is too small for her, the true bride waits for you.'" The prince and his false bride must pass the grave, where Cinderella's mother may protect her from the Underworld. Her agent the Sirin bird turns the prince's attention to his companion's foot, her place of beauty, and he sees she is not beautiful, but marred. Each time he returns to the house, and asks another girl to try the shoe on.

On the third try, the prince asks if there is another daughter. Here the father shows his utter abandonment of Cinderella when he makes his comment about her being "a little stunted kitchen-wench." But the prince understands that the orphaned girl is his prize, and that beneath her shame she is beautiful. He calls for her to try the shoe, but the stepmother emphasizes her outward appearance, saying, "Oh, no, she is much too dirty, she cannot show herself." The prince insists, and Cinderella is brought out.

But now the prince is ready to commit. Cinderella has washed her face and hands, and her beauty is now almost fully revealed. The final step is in the very ritualized trying of the shoe: "Then she seated herself on a stool, drew her foot out of the heavy wooden shoe, and put it into the slipper, which fitted like a glove."

Notice that each of the two sisters put on the shoe in a separate room of the house, out of view of the prince. It was like they were undressing in a private room, then showing themselves fully dressed, in a way that only revealed what they wanted the prince to see. But Cinderella sits right in front of the prince, unafraid for the prince to see her "naked," as it were. She removes the wooden shoe, which hid her pretty foot from the world. She extends her bare foot, revealing her naked beauty. The heavy wooden shoe represents her oppression: in a practical sense because it is a work shoe, not the shoe of a wealthy heiress, and because its bulk hid the beauty of her foot—though it also represents her secret beauty that none but the bird and her mother has seen until now, because the shoe protected that beauty from being scarred by the ash and fire. But the lovely, form-fitting slipper shows Cinderella's true beauty, and the promise of her sexuality. By denuding her foot in front of the prince, not in a private room, she expresses that she will give herself sexually to him.

When she takes off the wooden shoe; shows her graceful, lovely foot; and fits the slipper; the prince is sold: "And when she rose up and the king's son looked at her face he recognized the beautiful maiden who had danced with him and cried, that is the true bride. The stepmother and the two sisters were horrified and became pale with rage, he, however, took Cinderella on his horse and rode away with her."

You'll notice that even though Cinderella had washed her face, the prince did not recognize her until she'd bared her foot and tried on the shoe. At that point the picture is complete: this is the rightful heir to the prince's love (and a bit of the Grimms' awkward storytelling).

A HAPPY ENDING . . . WELL, FOR SOME

The righteousness of Cinderella's place in life is echoed as the prince rides a third time past the grave, an act that each time reminded us that Mom was protecting her daughter: "As they passed by the hazel tree, the two white doves [pigeons] cried, 'Turn and peep, turn and peep, no blood is in the shoe, the shoe is not too small for her, the true bride rides with you,' and when they had cried that, the two came flying down and placed themselves on Cinderella's shoulders, one on the right, the other on the left, and remained sitting there."

Notice that there are two birds. This might signify that the bird that was called by Cinderella's mother no longer needs to watch over her daughter, and two birds, representing Cinderella and the prince, may now leave the hazel tree and the graveside, and bless the marriage.

These birds are not sweet little things; they peck the stepsisters' eyes out, one side while coming, and the other side while going. You'd think that after walking down the aisle and having your eye pecked out, you'd resist the urge to walk up the aisle, but the sisters seem a little less wary than they ought to be, and they end up blind. Their blindness represents their failure to see Cinderella's true place as heir to her father's fortunes and to her mother's love. In a sense the sisters were always blind to Cinderella's true form. Rather than use their sense of sight to perceive Cinderella's royal birthright, they tried to steal it from her, and the punishment now fits the crime.

In this telling, the stepmother goes unpunished, though in other tellings, she is burned alive or eaten by birds. Dad simply disappears from the narrative altogether. His role seems a tenuous one; he is only in the tale to give Cinderella a horrible new family, and to provide her with the magical tool she will need, the hazel branch. Oh, and he gets to chop stuff.

An orphan displaced from her legitimate claim, an evil surrogate parent, a guiding prophet, a tree of wisdom, a foot fetish, and a deadbeat dad: Cinderella suddenly seems like a very complex myth. It is, having derived from the most ancient Faerie lore and sacred tales. Like many of the Grimms' stories, it carries the hazelnut of myth, magic, and wisdom deep inside its Disneyesque prettiness.

THE CINDERELLA RITUAL

This is a ritual to effect change in the physical world—meaning, to change the way things are. Internal change comes when you change the way you act or behave. We wish to change our place in the world around us. Whether what you wish for is a new job, a house, a promotion, a lover, or spouse, this ritual will change the way the world sees you, and the way the world works for you.

Many people say this can be accomplished through prayer. Technically speaking, that is not true. True prayer, in the form of the Catholic Mass or the saying of the Rosary, Protestant prayer meetings, Wiccan ritual, Pagan circles, or Jewish services, is meant as worship. In prayer, whatever form it takes in your own life, you want nothing more than to connect with the Divine, whether you see that as the Gods, God, Jesus, Allah, the Universe, the Force, a Higher Power, or the Common Good. Whichever of these you call the Divine influence, prayer means allowing yourself to feel the presence of the Divine in your life.

When you feel the Divine, and then ask the Divine to help you in achieving a goal, that is called petition (or simply put, a wish).

You are petitioning, or requesting, that a force greater than yourself offer help in creating a new reality. For you to have some positive result, other elements in the world must change. For instance, for you to receive a promotion, someone in a position above you in the company structure must recognize you as worthy. Often it means someone must leave their position and create a vacancy. Many things must change for you to reap the reward. For this reason, a petition is a complex thing, and should be approached with reverence and care.

The branch of magic that works with effecting change through magical ritual is called Ceremonial Magic. Ceremonial Magicians (shortened to CMs among Pagans) might be Pagan, Christian, Jewish, or of some other spiritual study, but each conducts rituals to create change in the world. A Ceremonial Magician believes he or she is working through a universal magical energy, and is doing what CMs call "The Great Work," a term for working universal good through personal and group ritual. One of the most notable groups practicing Ceremonial Magic today is the Order of the Golden Dawn. Their ranks have included many of the greatest ritual magicians of the past century, and many good books are available focusing on the magic and rituals performed by this order.

There is an old saying: be careful what you wish for, because you might get it! Any Ceremonial Magician will tell you that when you petition, you should be very sure that the thing you are projecting for is what you truly want. In the story of "Cinderella," the hazel tree counsels Cinderella using its wisdom, and the bird represents the Divine force aiding Cinderella in changing the world around her. Cinderella must also put in the work of attending the ball, and of escaping until the time is perfect for her identity to be revealed. Like Cinderella, you must be prepared to do the work. If your wish is to be promoted, you must be prepared to handle the responsibility and the harder work; if your wish is to get better grades, you must do the schoolwork; if your wish is to have more friends, or a faithful lover, you must keep up your end of the relationship and be a true friend and a trusted paramour. If you end up not wanting to do these things, perhaps you were not careful in what you wished for!

For this reason, you should spend some time in working up to doing this ritual. You need to think carefully about the things you want. Keep a journal over at least three months (or more). In it, write daily about the thing you want in as much detail as possible. How will you react when you get it? What will your day-to-day life be like when it happens? For instance, Cinderella probably lived quite differently as the prince's wife than she did as a servant to her sisters. Was she prepared for her responsibilities as a wife and mistress of a household? She would have commanded a staff of servants. Did her experience as a servant prepare her for this? In short, doing magic is serious business, and should be approached that way. If you want to change your life, be prepared for the consequences.

In the story of Cinderella, the girl is guided by the wisdom of the hazel tree, which represents Divine guidance. We will use hazelnuts, also called filberts, to represent the tree and its wisdom. We'll also represent this Divine wisdom with the number three Tarot card, the Empress.

Cinderella called upon the enchanted bird as her magical aid in the story. The bird, like the Magician with his baton, was able to transform the natural energies around Cinderella into the things she needed—in her case, beautiful gowns. We will use the Tarot card number one, the Magician, to represent this aiding force. The Magician uses his will along with the Divine universal forces (pictured in the card as roses) to change the world around him. This is what we will strive to do in this ritual. In our ritual we will call the Divine force the Gods, or the Lord and Lady. You may substitute whatever expression of the Divine you are comfortable with; if you are not Pagan or Wiccan, you may say God, Jesus, Allah, the Universe, the

Force, my Higher Power, or the Great Work wherever the ritual uses the Gods or the Lord and Lady. If you are not sure what you believe, say, "That Which Is Greater Than Me."

This ritual should be done on the full moon. We will set up a standard altar, with twelve candles, a taper (a small candle for lighting the other candles), and a wand. You will also need nine hazelnuts, also called filbert nuts; the Tarot card number three, the Empress; and the Tarot card number one, The Magician, on the altar. You will need a dish placed on the altar; a simple household dish is fine, but you may prefer an ornate dish, such as an antique china dish or a silver plate. Finally, you should have a cup or chalice of wine, or fruit juice if you do not drink wine. (While wine is a powerful magical tool, drinking wine in ritual if you are too young or you have experienced substance abuse issues can violate the magic of this drink! Respect all of your magical tools, and they will work for you.)

This is a powerful but joyful ritual, and you may perform it alone or with others. Having other people working with you can increase the energy you use to change your world, and may make the ritual more powerful (though performing it alone is also fine, and the more seriously you take the ceremony, the more power you will find it has).

Prepare your altar either indoors or out, with a white altar cloth if possible. Arrange nine candles around the outside edge in a circle, with the nine hazelnuts each beside a candle; then arrange the three remaining candles in a triangle at the center of the altar. The center candle may be lit before beginning the ritual. Lay the two Tarot cards near the center candles, and have your wand wherever you can reach it. The dish should be somewhere near the altar's center. The journal in which you wrote about what you want should also be handy, perhaps under the altar.

Begin by lighting the center candle and closing your eyes. Imagine the thing you are asking for, as vividly as you can. If, for instance, it is a promotion, vividly see yourself sitting at your new desk, doing the tasks you would do in this position; if it is better friends, see yourself in a daily activity with these people. (Though never, never name specific people when doing magic! You may say, "People with the qualities I see in so-and-so.") If you would like a better home, visualize yourself living in your new place.

Now light your taper, and face the center of the circle, saying:

"Hazel tree, guide me in your wisdom as you guided Cinderella in fable. Empress, shadow of the Lady, give me the wisdom to gain what I wish for!"

Light the candle to the left of the lit center candle.

"Bird of magic, enchanted creature. You who sang to the wise ones, and gave Cinderella her treasured gifts, help me create magic this day! Magician, aid me, and as I will, so may it be!"

Light the candle to the right of the center candle.

Now take up your wand. Walk three times around the circle, saying:

> "Cast the circle three times round,
> once for seed beneath the ground
> A second time the circle tread
> for sun and raincloud overhead
> Cast the circle, go times three,
> with wisdom of the hazel tree!"

Return to your place in the circle. Take out your journal and read a passage or two you've written about what you are petitioning for. The more detail, passion, and descriptive words you use, the more powerful your ritual will be. If you are in the circle with friends, have each read a portion of your wish journal (if it's not too personal, and if they can read your writing).

Now explain in unrehearsed words why you want this thing. Say in your own words what you want, why you want it, and what you will do with it. If you have others with you, have each one say why they want this for you, and ask their blessing on your hope of getting it. Go around the circle, and let each participant take as much time as they need.

Now pick up the hazelnut nearest to you. Hold it on your hand, and as you do, use the taper to light the first candle (if you are in ritual with others, someone else may light each candle as you hold the seed). Hold the seed to your chest, and close your eyes.

"I stand in the garden now as it first was, before time began. Nothing is here but myself, and the roses of life and creation. Deep inside me those roses grow. I ask the hazel tree to help me feel the power inside me, as you helped Cinderella."

Now place this hazelnut in the dish on the altar.

Pick up the next hazelnut, going clockwise (in magic we call this deosil, or in the direction of the sun). Hold it to your chest, lighting the candle above it.

"Now I feel the power of creation surge inside me. Like the magician, I know I am a part of the universal energy, the magic of time and space. The Lord and the Lady work through me, as they have worked through all life since time began. I claim this power as my own!"

Place this seed in the dish, and move to the next seed and candle. Holding the seed, lighting the candle:

"I hold the seed, my wand, in the air, as Cinderella held the hazel branch. My energy flows into it, through it, into the world. Lord and Lady, create through me!"

Place this seed in the dish, and go to the next, holding the seed and lighting the candle.

"I call the spirit of the elements: wind and sun, water and earth, to aid me. As Cinderella sat upon soil and flower, in air and dew at her mother's grave, so I call on air, water, fire, and earth. Aid me, and as I will so may it be!"

Place this seed in the dish, and go to the next, holding the seed and lighting the candle.

"I call the Lord and the Lady to aid me, as Cinderella called her bird ally. Powers that created the universe, female and male of the true Divine, flow within me! As I will so may it be!"

Place this seed in the dish, and go to the next, holding the seed and lighting the candle.

"Now I ask that I be granted this wish, as Cinderella was granted her golden gown: [state your wish in about one or two sentences]. Lord and Lady, elemental spirits, hear my voice, and know my will!"

Place this seed in the dish, and go to the next, holding the seed and lighting the candle.

"I see in the very center of myself that I will have this thing I wish for! I can see myself with it now, happy and passionate, my heart filled with the joy of it. As I will so may it be!" Take a moment to visualize what you wish for.

Place this seed in the dish, and go to the next, holding the seed and lighting the candle.

"I thank the Lord and Lady for hearing me. I thank the elements— air, fire, water, and earth—for your aid. I feel your power course through me, and I am thankful for your presence in my life. I carry you with me as Cinderella carried the birds on her shoulders into her new life. Blessed Be!"

Place this seed in the dish and go to the last seed, holding the seed and lighting the candle.

"I thank all in this circle (say this even if it is only yourself; after all, the Gods, elements, and spirits are with you). I lay the seed down now, and allow the magic to take form. My will is sent into the world, so may it bring me happiness, love, and freedom. Blessed Be!"

Next, take up the cup or chalice of drink, and hold it to the Gods.

"To the gifts you have given me this day, and every day, as Cinderella never faltered but strove for freedom and joy, I strive, too. Blessed Be. I drink to the Gods!"

Drink, and share the drink with all in the ritual.

Now face the center of the circle. Take up the Empress card, laying it face down:

"I thank you, hazel tree, the Divine Female Wisdom, that guides me in life. Blessed Be!"

Snuff the candle above this card. Take the Magician card, placing it face down.

"I thank the enchanted bird, and the energy of magic made manifest in my life, the Divine Will of male regeneration that renews me. Blessed Be!"

Snuff this candle.

Walk widdershins, or counterclockwise, around the circle once, saying:

"I cast this circle back into the earth until I have need to call upon its energies again. As Cinderella achieved her dearest wish, so may I achieve mine. Earth the energy, and set the magic to motion! Blessed Be!"

Relax, eat something, and feel the magic inside you begin to work. If you feel you need to do so, repeat this ritual over three full moons.

Chapter 7

LITTLE RED CAP (LITTLE RED RIDING HOOD): SPELLS FOR PREVENTING UNWANTED ATTENTION

On the surface this is a cautionary tale about a girl who strays from the path. We will look at the subtle subtext between Red Riding Hood (Little Red Cap) and the wolf. We'll use Red's experience with the wolf to look at spells for avoiding unwanted attention. Unless otherwise noted, the story quotes are from the Margaret Hunt translation.

She is the rock star of the fairy tale world. While Disney has never done a feature-length film about her as they have for Snow White, Cinderella, and Beauty, rockin' Red is the star of stories and books (Angela Carter's "The Company of Wolves" and Jane Yolen's *Touch Magic*, among many others), cartoons (*Red Hot Riding Hood* by Tex Avery, creator of Droopy, starring a Betty Grable–inspired Red), and song: "How Could Red Riding Hood (Have Been So Very Good)?" by A. P. Randolph was the first song ever to be banned from radio play in 1925; Julie London had a hit with the song "Daddy," which also appeared the Tex Avery cartoon; and "L'il Red Riding Hood" was a Top Ten hit for Sam the Sham and the Pharaohs in 1966.

Red was the focus of psychoanalysis by Bruno Bettelheim, while feminist writers Catherine Orenstein and Susan Brownmiller viewed her as an icon of feminism and a mirror of womanhood, one for her courage and cunning and the other for her suffering. She also won the heart of Charles Dickens, perhaps the greatest writer of the nineteenth century. Seductive in her naïveté (or deceptively cunning... or both), impeccably dressed, a lover of solar energy and flower power, and a keen observer of the physical world (especially eyes, ears, and teeth), Red is a woman of passion, mystery, and inspiration.

She has had several names in her long career. The Grimms called her Little Red Cap; Charles Perrault called her by the name we know, Little Red Riding Hood; and in Andrew Lang's *The Red Fairy Book* (1891), she is Little Golden-Cap, and her true name is given as Blanchette ("Little White One"). Artists have portrayed her as a Pullip-headed imp, a cherubic blond preteen, an unwitting vixen, and a voluptuous vamp. In the long centuries of her stardom, she has battled werewolves, ogres, and Faerie seducers, and through it confronted her own fears and sexual impulses. Red is nothing if not a truly remarkable girl.

Her tale is told worldwide. Versions exist in French, Italian, Polish, German, and even Chinese! Red is a universal heroine, a girl for all seasons. What is it that makes Red so appealing?

Each version of the story that has been recorded in the last two centuries agrees on the major details: a delightful girl in a distinctive hooded cape sets off for Grandma's house; a wolf stops her and engages in conversation; she naively tells him exactly where she is going; and he arrives ahead of the girl, devours Grandma, and takes the old woman's place in bed. Entering, the girl notices the wolf's various physical traits, inducing the well-known question-and-answer session ("What big eyes you have . . . "). In the most familiar versions, the wolf eats our heroine; a woodsman or hunter rescues both the girl and the grandma; and the wolf is killed.

As the Grimms recorded the story, it is a morality tale. A girl is told to go to her grandma's house with cake and wine. We imagine the wine being as red as the girl's cap, the color that symbolizes both curiosity and passion as well as shyness and embarrassment. The girl promises to be good, but she makes two fatal mistakes: first, she speaks to a stranger, the wolf. She should have some instinct that warns her that this stranger is not to be trusted, but she just blurts out every detail of her trip: how far it is to Grandma's, what food she carries, and even the types of trees growing around Grandma's yard. The wolf then manages to distract Red by pointing out the pretty, shiny flowers and golden rays of sun. At any moment you expect this ditzy Red to exclaim, "Like, oh my God! Flowers!"

With Red distracted, the wolf runs ahead to Grandma's, where he gains entry by pretending to be the girl. He quickly devours Grandma, and then climbs into her bed. Wearing Granny's nightcap, he waits for Red's arrival.

When Red gets there, the Grimms jump right into the familiar dialogue. This is Red's second mistake; she seems to realize that this creature in her granny's bed is not her grandma, but she sticks around and courts disaster, exclaiming, "What big eyes you have!" and noticing every other trait of the wolf. Finally, the wolf leaps out and devours the girl.

In this version, a hunter just happens to be walking by and hears snoring inside the house. Suspicious, he enters, and finds the wolf in Grandma's bed. He is about to shoot the wolf but reconsiders, thinking the granny might be in there. He cuts the wolf open, freeing both Red and Granny. Then, oddly, rather than simply killing the creature, he and Red line the wolf's belly with stones. The wolf wakes, but cannot move, and dies. The hunter skins the wolf, while Granny simply eats the cake and wine Red has brought, and Red swears never to be ditzy again.

The Grimms then continue the tale, alluding to a second version in which the girl tricks the wolf into falling to his death by baiting him with sausage. The brothers actually collected two tellings of the story and combined them into this one narrative.

Earlier than the Grimms, Charles Perrault had collected the tale in France in 1697 (the version included in Andrew Lang's *The Blue Fairy Book*). Perrault actually included a "moral" at the end of the story:

> "Little girls, this seems to say,
> Never stop upon your way.
> Never trust a stranger-friend;
> No one knows how it will end.
> As you're pretty so be wise;
> Wolves may lurk in every guise.
> Handsome they may be, and kind,
> Gay, or charming—never mind!
> Now, as then, 'tis simple truth—
> Sweetest tongue has sharpest tooth!"[16]

Perrault seems to have read the tale as a warning against seduction by "wolves," and indeed, in the French slang of the period, when a girl had lost her virginity it was said that *elle avoit vû le loup*—she had seen the wolf.[17]

The Grimms are not very explicit in their depiction of Red's behavior once she enters the house: "She called out, 'Good morning,'

---

16. In Lang, ed., *The Blue Fairy Book*, 53.
17. Orenstein, "Dances with Wolves."

but received no answer; so she went to the bed and drew back the curtains. There lay her grandmother with her cap pulled far over her face, and looking very strange."

But other printed versions are a good deal more explicit. In *The Blue Fairy Book*, we read:

"The wolf, seeing her come in, said to her, hiding himself under the bedclothes, 'Put the cake and the little pot of butter upon the stool, and come get into bed with me.' Little Red Riding Hood took off her clothes and got into bed. She was greatly amazed to see how her grandmother looked in her nightclothes, and said to her, 'Grandmother, what big arms you have!'"[18]

Here, as in several other versions, Red gets naked before getting into bed. Interesting, especially as she immediately remarks on the physical clues that this is not her grandmother. Is Red aware that the wolf is in the bed? Is her action one of naïveté, or is she a willing participant in this seduction?

To answer that question, let's take our eyes off of Red for a moment, and take a long, analytic look at the wolf.

HUNGRY LIKE THE WOLF

The wolf is a character in a myriad of fairy tales, folklore, stories, and songs. As mere infants, we all feared for the three little pigs as the wolf "huffed and puffed" at their houses. For many of us, this was our first exposure to a villain that, as modern people, we'd never actually seen in Nature. But our forebears knew wolves well. Europeans and the first white settlers on the American continent fought a genocidal war against wolves, mountain lions, and eagles: any animal that eats the food we eat. The wolf took on the persona of pure evil, representing the carnivore, the attacker (even though quite often we were the ones doing the attacking).

---

18. Lang, ed., *The Blue Fairy Book*, 51–52.

In England wolves were hunted, and their fur merited a reward. For this reason, a hunted outlaw was called a "wolf's head." Under the rule of the English king Athelstan, in the tenth century AD, criminals could buy their freedom by killing a certain number of wolves annually. Various European rulers created elite corps of huntsmen to exterminate wolves, and by the twentieth century the wolf was all but extinct in Europe.

Before that time, though, the wolf was not all bad. The parent species of dogs, the wolf was seen as an ally and as mythical, a God of death and rebirth. Herne the Hunter, Odin, and the Goddess Hecate all commanded the wolf. Odin's son was named Hildólfr, War Wolf. Several Turkish tribes say that they are descended from a wolf mother who mated with a human lover, and the Romans believed their founders, Remus and Romulus, were saved from death and nurtured by the wolf Rhea Silvia.

Yet as the Old Gods diminished in lore, and became the devils of Christianity, so the wolf became a devilish figure. Feared and loathed through history, the wolf found its way into literature. Dracula commanded wolves, and took the form of one when he attacked Lucy Westenra and her mother. And as children many of us watched Lon Chaney portray a man who is bitten by a wolf, only to turn into a wolf when the moon is full.

Modern culture continues the tradition of wolf references. The Grateful Dead sang in 1970 of the Dire Wolf, a bandit who terrorized hungry miners, and current vampire films like Underworld portray werewolves as hunters of humans and vampires. And let's not forget Twilight. I know, we couldn't forget it even if we tried.

In the Tarot, we see a depiction of the wolf in card number eighteen, the Moon. The creature is standing on the bank of a moonlit stream opposite a dog. In this complex card, the juxtaposition of wolf and dog represent the human tendencies toward both good and evil. The dog is the cultured human, raised with morals and a knowledge of righteousness, and aware of what would happen should he veer astray. The wolf is the human who has no morals, no conscience. It is the person who gives in to his impulses, his evil tendencies. It is the sociopath, who operates without regard for his fellows. The wolf asks, what would you do if you could get away with anything? What desires would you fulfill if you had ultimate power, with no consequences?

That question represents the wolf in this tale, the seducer-devourer. He exists in many other tales. In Britain, he is called Reynardine (Fox-man, or Mr. Fox), a werewolf-type character who seduces young women and then eats their flesh. The same is seen in werewolf legends of eastern Europe. The idea is that a normal man may, through succumbing to base desires, without his morals keeping him in check, become a wolf, a predator, a devourer. This wolf has no regard for Red, for her safety or her chastity. He wants only to sate himself upon her, to have his enjoyment of her ripe body (ripe like the red apple, the color of her garments), and then eat of her tender flesh.

You may have noticed certain things about our wolf that are a bit defiant of Nature. Like the fact that he can speak English? In the oldest French version, the wolf is referred to as a *bzou*, a werewolf; the Chinese story also calls the seducer a werewolf.

For us, werewolves are a subject of Saturday-afternoon television reruns. But this has not always been the case. The French of the seventeenth and eighteenth centuries took werewolves pretty seriously, and werewolf attacks were reported across the French countryside. In 1693 one hundred people were said to have been killed by a large bzou in the French town of Benais. Between 1765 and 1767 the French village of Gévaudan was terrorized by a series of attacks that claimed at least one hundred victims, and survivors consistently described a werewolf. These attacks were taken so seriously that King Louis XV sent soldiers to hunt the beast, who was called *La Bête du Gévaudan*. Oh, and the nineteenth century had its share of French werewolves as well: from 1875 to 1879, more attacks occurred in the town of L'Indre. Almost all of the victims of these various attacks were women and children, and it is possible that the tale of Red and her wolf was influenced by these accounts.

The wolf could be a dog. That is, he could pass for a gentleman in polite society. But when alone with the girl, his wolf-like animal barbarity takes over. He becomes the wolf of the Tarot, unfettered by morality, ready to seduce and destroy.

So why doesn't the wolf simply devour Red there on the road?

It could be that the wolf wishes to catch Red at her grandmother's house because he does not want to be seen by other gentlemen as he attempts to seduce her. Perrault implies this: "As she was going through the wood, she met with Gaffer Wolf, who had a very great mind to eat her up, but he dared not, because of some faggot-makers [woodcutters] hard by in the forest."[19] Bruno Bettelheim suggests that Wolfie is an older, suave seducer, who keeps up the appearance among his peers of being a well-heeled fellow but who secretly lusts for and preys upon naïve young women. He must do this behind closed doors, partly so he is not found out and partly because he fears others might interfere, and protect the young women from his seductive cunning. In his mind, he is merely giving these girls what they secretly want, but are too shy or inexperienced to ask for (remember that red is the color of shyness and embarrassment). After all, the seducer ponders, why would Red tell the wolf the way to Grandma's house if she did not want to dally with him there?

WHAT WAS RED THINKING?

It is possible that Red knows this is the wolf in Granny's bed. After all, she told him how to get there! And now is it possible that she is well aware that she is crawling into bed naked with a seducer who

19. Lang, ed. *The Blue Fairy Book*, 47.

has charmed her in every way up to this moment, and is about to fulfill his deviant desires with poor, innocent Red?

What? Sweet, innocent Red? No way! That's what you're saying, isn't it? Let's turn our attention back to sweet Red and see if we can decipher this puzzle.

The Grimms never give us a proper name for Red. Our little beauty is defined by the garment she wears: a red riding hood, or red cap. The red riding hood is an interesting garment: the name says it all. It is meant to cover the head and shoulders when one rides a horse. At once the garment is both seductive (red, the color of passion and lust) and modest (covering the breasts, hair, and neck, and perhaps part of the face). One can imagine Red's eye and a little wisp of dark hair peeking seductively out of that concealing garment. Red as a juicy, succulent apple, the fruit of biblical seduction. In one version of the story, you'll recall, she is called Golden-Cap. Gold, the color of the sun and of sweet tangy honey. Peeping out of the folds of that honey-hued hood, we can only imagine how the girl's red lips and blushing cheek might have tempted.

In the Grimms' tale, Red is devoured. She must be. After all, unlike a proper girl of her time, she has played into the wolf's trap. As Catherine Orenstein points out, in the Grimm Brothers' day, "chastity was the feminine ideal, demanded by the prevailing institution of marriage."[20] The listener of the day would have perhaps expected Red to be devoured by her own lusts.

But is this really what it seems? Some writers feel that this is not a true death, but an initiatory experience. All true initiations invoke the experience of death; some have suggested that Red's acceptance of her sexuality represents her maturity, and that after she is eaten, being cut from the wolf's belly represents her rebirth as a woman. Remember that the wolf was once a God. Red may be like Persephone, lying with Hades in the Underworld, then rising so that spring may begin again.

---

20. Orenstein, "Dances with Wolves."

Mind you, though, the tale is not always told this way. In older forms, odd things happen, things that we did not hear in our comfortable homes when we were told this story straight out of Grimms.

Consider the Italian version, in which Red is seduced by an ogre rather than the wolf. First, she has a very strange conversation with her seducer, that begins like this:

"Little Red Hat tried to open the door, but when she noticed that she was pulling on something soft, she called out, 'Grandmother, this thing is so soft!'

'Just pull and keep quiet. It is your grandmother's intestine!'

'What did you say?'

'Just pull and keep quiet!'

From there, things just go from bad to worse:

"Little Red Hat opened the door, went inside, and said, 'Grandmother, I am hungry.'

The ogre replied, 'Go to the kitchen cupboard. There is still a little rice there.'

Little Red Hat went to the cupboard and took the teeth out. 'Grandmother, these things are very hard!'

'Eat and keep quiet. They are your grandmother's teeth!'

'What did you say?'

'Eat and keep quiet!'"[21]

The ogre continues to make Red eat Grandma, offering her Grandma's jaws and a drink of her blood. Finally, as we saw, he has her strip and join him in bed before devouring her. This is an interesting variation in the tale, because the ogre forces Red to devour grandma before he "devours" (ravishes) her. In a sense, the fiend is forcing Red to share in his sins of gluttony and lust. It is a demonstration of Red's naïveté, which makes her seem willing to go along with the ogre. In this version, Red is simply unaware of her fate until it's too late, and she's devoured, both euphemistically and quite literally.

---

21. Ashliman, trans. "Little Red Hat." ©2007 by D. L. Ashliman.

But Red is not always devoured. In older tellings, she often escapes, and in fact, triumphs over the wolf. In a French version of the tale, Red lies down naked with a bzou, but after the well-known conversation, tells the bzou she must "do it outside." The bzou tells her to do it in the bed, but she argues that it will smell bad. The "it," of course, is defecation: she tells the wolf she needs to go number two, and he offers that she may do so in the bed, attempting to strip Red of all the trappings of civilization and reduce her to a creature of lustful urges, like himself. Being a proper girl, she insists on going outside. The bzou ties a rope to her ankle so she will not be able to get away, and tugs it every few moments to be sure it is attached. But clever Red removes the rope from her ankle and ties it to a plum tree.

Red has lain nude with the bzou; whether through desire or naïveté, Red has given herself to the beast. Perhaps he binds her ankle in an attempt to show his sexual ownership of her. She wiggles free of him and ties the rope to a tree, to show he may not own her sexuality. She ties the rope to a plum tree, and fools the wolf. Red has run off, no bzou's possession. In a very allegorical fashion, she has left behind only her excrement.

While we often see Red as an innocent victim, this Red may be completely in control of her desires and of her sexuality. She chooses to go through with the seduction, and when it's time to leave, she does so at a time of her choosing. She shows the wolf that he does not own her, but instead that she owns herself. This Red will not be devoured! As for the Red who is devoured by the wolf, is she a victim or is this her initiation? We all live our lives the best we can, knowing full well (whether we like to think about it or not) that life is precious, and danger lurks around every corner. Devoured Red lives fearlessly, telling the wolf all: where she is coming from, where she is going, and who she is visiting. Of course in hindsight that's a big mistake. But don't we all make those big mistakes? And don't we all know that one of those mistakes can lead to our undoing? But even devoured Red gets out, cut from the wolf's belly by the huntsman (the Tarot dog to the wolf's, well, wolf). She has, we hope, learned a life lesson, and grown by it.

Maybe this is why Red is so universally loved. She shows us that we all make the big mistakes. But she also shows us that we can get through it, survive, and live to be wary of the next wolf we meet.

RED RIDING HOOD SPELLS

If, like Red, you are the object of unwanted attention, the first thing to do is take real-world action. Say no, tell people close to you that you are being harassed, report stalking to law enforcement officials.

That said, let's consider some spells you might use if someone is bugging you.

First, be very clear about what you want and don't want. Are you conflicted? Do you return the attention, but feel you shouldn't? Or is this someone to whom you once gave attention, then cut off, like an ex or a former steady date? Is it someone who is interested in you, but you've returned no interest? Is it someone who would like you to be interested, but you simply aren't? In any of these cases, once you start doing magic to get rid of the person, there's really no turning back. You cannot decide a few months down the road that you actually do enjoy this person's attention. If you believe there's some chance of having a healthy relationship, whether romantic or friendly, do not do magic to get them to leave you alone. If, however, you think the person's attention is truly unwanted, unwarranted, or malicious, here are some things you can do:

THE POPSICLE SPELL

A way to get a person to "cool off" their feelings for you is to do a little Sympathetic Magic.

In this case, to "cool someone off," we are going to actually cool them! You will need an ice cube tray or Popsicle tray. Using indelible ink, such as a Sharpie pen, write the person's name on a small scrap of paper. As you write, think of the person clearly in your mind. Visualize that person walking away from you, ignoring you, or otherwise leaving you alone.

Next, fill the ice cube tray with water and place the scrap of paper into the water. Place it at the very back of your freezer, and leave it there. It will freeze, and the person's attention toward you will freeze with it. Leave it there for as long as you like, and just forget it's there.

THE POSTAL SPELL

If you really want someone to move along, try this: write his or her name on a piece of paper. Visualize the person clearly as you write the name. You can even write the person's name a few times, saying it as you write, and visualizing the person leaving you, moving off to parts unknown for the foreseeable future. While it's usually not a good idea to name specific people in a spell, if someone is truly harassing you, this would be considered self-defense. Note that the spell does not harm the person, but merely draws their presence elsewhere. In any spell, you should mind the magical warning to "harm none!"

Place the paper in a standard mailing envelope. Look up the zip code of some remote place far from you, and send the letter to the person care of general delivery in that place.

For instance:

The Wolf
c/o General Delivery
Schmoeville, Alaska 99999

Mail the item and wait. If you put the proper energy and intent into the spell, the person will suddenly have some golden opportunity in Schmoeville, Alaska, that cannot be passed up! Off he or she will go.

Unlike this example, make sure you choose a real place with a real zip code. The person has to be in a position where he or she has some business or personal matter there that necessitates moving. This cannot happen with a fictitious place. (What? There isn't really a Schmoeville, Alaska?)

THE RED RIDING HOOD ROPE SPELL

In some versions, Red escapes the wolf. The wolf ties a rope around Red's ankle, but she ties it to a tree and runs off.

You can do a simple spell that simulates this story. Find some object that reminds you of the person you want to get rid of. It could be anything that makes you think of this person: a picture of the person, something he or she gave you, the person's favorite flower, an item of clothing similar to one he or she wears all the time. Take the object outdoors to a place where you will be undisturbed, and where there are trees (bushes, shrubs, or cacti will do). Now tie one end of a long cord or rope to the item. Tie the other end of the rope to your own ankle. Visualize the person as you do this, and see the rope as the unwanted connection between you two.

Now walk some distance away, maybe twenty feet, and take the rope off your ankle. Tie the rope to a tree. Leave the object and the rope there for three days. Then return to the spot, take the rope and the object, and properly throw them away. As you do so, visualize this person no longer in your life. You are free of this person, and always will be! (Leaving the symbolic offering Red left is completely up to you.)

THE RED RIDING HOOD REBIRTH SPELL

As I've mentioned, some authors see Red's time in the wolf's belly as an initiation. When the huntsman cuts Red out, she is reborn, more mature, ready to start a new life.

You can simulate this as a spell.

First, you will need a new garment you have never worn before. Any garment will do: a dress, pants, a shirt or blouse, shoes, even a scarf or bandanna. It does not have to be new from a store; it must simply be new to you.

You should do this spell on a new moon. You will need a closet, small room, or some other tight enclosed space that can be made very dark (a bathroom or laundry room, or if outdoors perhaps a cave or a copse of bushes in a very private area). You should be nude (skyclad). Since it will be you alone doing the spell, you should not be embarrassed.

First, meditate on the person or the situation you want to be rid of. Think specifically and carefully of the person. When you have meditated on the person for a really long time, do it some more.

Now undress, and enter the dark space. Close the door, and make the place as tight and dark as possible. You may wrap yourself in a blanket or some other fabric if you'd like, to simulate a tight, dark, womblike place.

Wait what seems like a very long time. If you feel it's been a long time, wait some more.

Now leap from the dark place into a lighted area, or into the outdoors. Feel the free, cool air around you. You are reborn, freed, open to new life!

As soon as you can, put on the new garment. Say:

"This new _____ (shirt, shoes, dress, apron, eye patch . . .) is mine alone, and each time I wear it, I will remember that I have been reborn, and I have freed myself!"

Wear the garment as much as you like (if it's underwear, make sure to wash it every now and then). Always remember the ritual when you wear it, and the spell you have cast.

Chapter 8

THE FROG KING, OR IRON HANS: A RITUAL FOR TRUE AND LOYAL FRIENDSHIPS

Better known as "The Frog Prince," and recently treated by Disney as The Princess and the Frog, *a girl makes a promise to a talking frog, breaks the promise, breaks the frog, and marries a prince who turns out to have a faithful servant. The servant has had metal bands placed upon his heart, and these burst as the wedded couple rides into the sunset. We'll examine the servant's relationship with his amphibious master as a role model for true and loyal friendships. As before, the story quotes are from the Margaret Hunt translation of the Grimms' 1812* Children's and Household Tales.

So, dad, I was, like, playing near the water, right? And, like, I lost my ball, and, like, a frog spoke to me! Is that normal?"

While the Grimms may not have encountered many California Valley Girls, there certainly must have been some German equivalent embodying the reluctant heroine in this heartwarming story of a girl and her frog.

Many of us grew up with this story, perhaps under one of its other names: "The Frog Prince," "Iron John," "The Queen Who Sought a Drink from a Certain Well," or "The Well of the World's End." Disney recently used the story as a model for its animated feature *The Princess and the Frog*. It is so cemented into our mindset that people exasperated by the dating scene often use the expression "You have to kiss a lot of frogs to find your prince." Let's take a look at the tale as the Grimms collected it.

We are given an enormous amount of information as the storyteller sets the scene for us. The story begins with the statement "In olden times when wishing still helped one . . . " Modern readers tend to think of the Grimms' day as "the olden times," but the Grimms collected this story from someone who set a scene of long-gone days, very unlike the times people lived in during the storyteller's life, when wishing apparently didn't do much good.

The story goes on to draw the listener in further: "There lived a king whose daughters were all beautiful, but the youngest was so beautiful that the sun itself, which has seen so much, was astonished whenever it shone in her face." We are given the notion that this girl, the youngest of several daughters, is so beautiful she has captured the attention of heavenly bodies. In a sense this equates the girl with Heaven and with warmth and comfort (qualities of the sun). It also equates her with the golden color of the sun, and, indeed, gold will be the start of the difficulty she finds herself in.

Finally the opening tells us: "Close by the king's castle lay a great dark forest, and under an old lime tree in the forest was a well, and when the day was very warm, the king's child went out into the forest and sat down by the side of the cool fountain, and when she was bored she took a golden ball, and threw it up on high and caught it, and this ball was her favorite plaything."

We have seen the great dark forest before. It is a wild place where the laws and morals of our civilized courts and castles do not exist. It is a place where animals speak, and where ancient magic drips from each branch and glistens on each leaf. The darkness of this forest calls to mind the eternal darkness of the Underworld. This unbelievably beautiful girl wanders daily into this chaotic place with her golden ball, which echoes the golden sun.

Centuries before "Iron Hans," the Greeks told the myth of Persephone. In it, Persephone, also an unbelievable beauty, is bathing in a stream in the dark forest. There she is spied by Hades, who falls in love with her. Hades rules the Underworld, and carries Persephone with him into that dark realm of death. She lives there with him for some time, until her mother Demeter grows worried and searches for her. After a long search, she discovers Persephone in the realm of Hades, and asks that her daughter be returned to our living world. At first Hades refuses: he loves the beauty too much. The Gods intervene, and Hades finally relents. But he says that if Persephone has eaten any food of his world, she must remain there. Persephone admits that she ate six pomegranate seeds. Her fate seems to be sealed. Demeter threatens Zeus that if her girl is not returned, she will cause all life on earth to die. In the end, an agreement is reached: Persephone may live with her mother six months of the year, and life will flourish; but for the six pomegranate seeds she has eaten, she must remain in the dark world of Hades for six months, and all life on earth will die.

The myth explains the seasonal change from winter to summer, and indeed, the pomegranate fruit partly represents the sun, dimmed to a cold light in frosty winter, bright and warm in summer.

In the first sentence of the Grimms' tale, we see the parallel. The beautiful king's daughter, a creature of life and light, enters the "great dark forest," a cold, eerie world much like that of Hades. She seeks out a well, a source of water and rejuvenation, just as Persephone sought out a bathing spot. The well lies beneath a lime tree, a fruit that informs that this well is a source of verdant life (and echoes the pomegranate in Persephone's tale). And she carries with her a golden ball: an image of the sun, an anomaly in this gray place, but representing the summer months, when life brings green to the forest.

Like the shifting sun, the golden ball does not stay in the bright sky where the girl has thrown it. It falls into the well, representing the days growing dark and cold in winter (and just like the endless seeming winter months, the well was "so deep that the bottom could not be seen").

So in only the first few sentences of the story, we see that this tale is based on an ancient myth of the Underworld, a beautiful Goddess, and the seasons of the year.

Just then, like Hades catching sight of lovely Persephone, a frog spies our girl crying for the lost ball.

In our discussion of "Briar Rose," we saw a frog and spoke of the frog as a symbol of life and rejuvenation. This frog is a bit different. Before life can begin, the way must be cleared by death. Death is the first step toward rebirth, and that's the kind of frog we have just met.

His first words to the girl are interesting: "What ails you, king's daughter? You weep so that even a stone would show pity." The Lord of the Underworld must be hard and cold, a dark God in a dark place. It's hard to imagine laughter and pity in the world of the dead. But the girl is so touching that he is moved by her. "A stone would show pity": perhaps he is equating his own heart to a stone?

She tells him she's lost her golden ball (that the sun has disappeared, making the world dark and wintry). The frog tells her he will retrieve the ball, but in return the girl must promise him something. She tells him she will give him her clothes, her jewels, or her crown. In many versions of the myth of Persephone, the Goddess must be stripped naked in order to enter Hades; the girl offers to denude herself, divest herself of her clothes, her jewels, and her crown before the Underworld lord. But the frog has other ideas. The girl must allow the frog to live with her, eat with her, and sleep in her "little bed." If she will do this, he will brave the depths of the well: just as Hades can brave the cold, somber Underworld as long as Persephone agrees to live with him there and share his bed.

The girl agrees enthusiastically, but her thoughts are "How the silly frog does talk. All he does is to sit in the water with the other frogs, and croak. He can be no companion to any human being." This idea will come up in our parallel to Persephone, so keep it handy for a moment.

Now the delighted frog retrieves the ball (the sun), and gives it to the princess. She runs off, leaving the poor frog behind, breaking her promise to him. But the frog is persistent. He comes sloshing into the castle that evening, and insists on seeing the girl.

Now we meet a new character in the story, King Dad. The girl explains her predicament to her royal father, and says she never expected the lowly frog to actually take her up on her promise. The king tells her in no uncertain terms that she must honor her promise to the frog: "That which you have promised must you perform. Go and let him in." And while this is good morality and kingly behavior, remember also that Zeus, King of the Gods, was forced to intervene when Demeter begged Hades to allow Persephone to return to the upper world. The king takes that role in the story here, making sure that the daylight world of the golden sun pays its dues to the dark Underworld.

"The king's daughter began to cry, for she was afraid of the cold frog which she did not like to touch, and which was now to sleep in her pretty, clean little bed." The frog is cold like the Underworld, and a life-giving Goddess would not enjoy the touch of an Underworld creature. But the king again insists that his daughter keep her promise. After the frog eats from her golden plate and drinks from her cup, off they go to the bedroom, where the girl places the frog in a cold corner (a dark Underworldly place in that golden castle of the sun).

In many of the Grimms' tales, as we've seen, girls go willingly, often eagerly to bed with gruesome animals. Rose-Red with her bear lover, Red Riding Hood with her bzou, and Nettchen with the Beast are all quite happy to accept the embrace of an Underworld varmint. But the princess is having none of it. When the frog insists on consummating the relationship, saying, "I am tired, I want to sleep as well as you, lift me up or I will tell your father," the girl has had enough. She "took him up and threw him with all her might against the wall. 'Now, will you be quiet, odious frog,' said she." Wow. Sweet, huh? And not the kiss we all somehow remember.

But this unseemly violence might not be as bad as it appears. Actually, it turns out that often in folklore a shapeshifting spell must be broken with death or violence. And being thrown against the wall is not as gruesome as some other shapeshifters' treatment. In the very similar Scottish tale "The Queen Who Sought a Drink from a Certain Well," the girl must behead the frog. Ew. In the Norwegian "Doll I' the Grass," a tiny bride who rides in a spoon drawn by mice (perhaps a motif behind the pumpkin carriage in Disney's version of "Cinderella") is thrown into a lake (representing drowning), and comes out a more average size.

MYTHIC TIES

Following the Goddess into our world is a form of rebirth for the Underworld God. That rebirth often involves a violent death first. In the legends of John Barleycorn or the Green Man, we often see portrayals of a gruesome death before the Green God will rise again. In the British folk song, we hear:

They hired men with crabtree sticks
To cut him skin from bone
And the miller he has served him worse than that
For he ground him between two stones
(Traditional)

But for all his agony, our hero the Green Man rises again:

But Little Sir John in the nut brown bowl
He's brandy in the glass
Little Sir John in the nut brown bowl
Proved the strongest man at last
For the hunter he can't hunt the fox
Or loudly blow his horn
And the tinker cannot mend his kettles or his pots
Without John Barleycorn

The God must often die a more violent death than that to be reborn. In *The Mabinogion*, Llew Llaw Gyffes, God of the Sun, must allow the winter God Gronw to chuck a spear at him. He is impaled by the spear, but he rises as an eagle, and in summer, comes back with the reborn sun. This is another seasonal tale; Llew Llaw Gyffes is the sun that shines in summer, and Gronw is death in winter.

Another myth of violence and the seasons is that of Dionysus, who inspires his Maenads, beautiful maidens, to rip him apart in their ecstasy. In various myths the Maenads also rip apart the God Orpheus and King Pentheus of Thebes. Like Llew, Dionysus is ripped apart to be reborn, as grapes are squished to make wine.

Like all of these mythic figures, the frog must die to be reborn. Here in the golden castle of the sun, he is thrown against the wall by the beautiful, Maenad-like Goddess, the princess. He is squished, but he rises again as a handsome prince, the incarnate God of the Green Places. Now the princess may love him, and the two agree to be married. The princess learns "he had been bewitched by a wicked witch, and how no one could have delivered him from the well but herself, and that tomorrow they would go together into his kingdom." Notice he could not be freed from his Underworld form by any old hottie, but only by this particular princess: in other words, only Persephone could transform Hades.

THE FAITHFUL SERVANT

Now we come to an odd point in the story. Unlike the Scottish title for the tale, "The Queen Who Sought a Drink from a Certain Well," in the Grimms' version our golden princess is not even mentioned in the title. The character who is mentioned does not even appear in the story until this point: Iron Hans. Called Iron John in some versions, this is the prince's faithful servant, who was so sad that the prince had become a frog that he had iron bands bound around his heart to keep it from breaking.

What?

As they drive toward the prince's realm, they hear a cracking sound. The prince thinks his wagon has broken, but it's only Iron Hans's metal bands breaking off of his heart. No need to panic, folks.

What a totally weird part of the story, huh? What is this doing here?

Glad you asked. One aspect of this story is the idea of promises and faithfulness. The important theme is the promise that although the sun (the golden ball) grows cold in winter, spring will return. We see this promise honored by the king, who insists that his daughter must keep her word. Only by keeping her word to the frog will summer return to the golden castle. Now the frog has been reborn into the summer God, and has married the Goddess of fertility. They may travel to her realm, the green earth.

In "John Barleycorn," we hear this verse:

> They plowed they sowed they harrowed him in
> Threw clods upon his head

> And these three men made a solemn vow
> John Barleycorn was dead

Hans is the grain, and the iron bands on his heart are the furrowed bands of earth under which he sleeps through the long, cold winter when his master the sun is a frog in the Underworld. Now that the frog is the handsome God of the sun, the bands may break, and Iron Hans may rise as the green vegetation:

> They let him lie for a very long time
> Till the rains from heaven did fall
> And little sir John sprang up his head
> And he did amaze them all

On another level (myths have many levels), iron breaks enchantment. Faeries hate the stuff, and it will banish them. In folklore across Europe, we are told to carry iron tools at all times to protect ourselves from Faerie enchantment. In fact, the tradition of hanging a horseshoe in the home comes from this belief. And of course we know how the Grimms liked to replace Faeries with witches. That may be the case here.

So Hans wishes to break the enchantment that has been laid upon his master, as he is a faithful servant (as opposed to the princess, who is unfaithful and breaks her promises easily). The iron bands around his heart are there to banish the enchantment. When the prince is free of the curse, the bands around his heart shatter, and the magic is abated.

Iron Hans in both mythic cases represents faith and promise-keeping: the promise from the Gods that we will have grain and food year after year, and the promise of a faithful servant and friend to his master to be loyal while the master is away, imprisoned in dark enchantment.

Both the king and Iron Hans exhibit this faithful behavior. For the king it is more general: he tells his daughter that a promise made must be kept. For Hans it is specific: he will bind his heart to his master, the prince. His faith in his master is rewarded with the prince's return, brought about by the fickle princess. They are two sides of a coin: faithfulness and dishonor, or day and night, light and dark, sun and night. Now the fickle princess will make a new promise, pledging her heart and her body to the prince. This change in her role represents the shifting seasons and the changing year.

Still, it's sad that after despairing over the waning sun, conjuring the sun back by a visit to the ghastly Underworld, transforming the Underworld Frog King back to the Summer God, and squishing a helpless amphibian, the princess is not even remembered in the story's title.

THE FROG KING RITUAL

The story of the Frog King is about faith and fidelity. Sadly, these are virtues lacking in many friendships and romances in our modern world. People seem to make promises casually, never meaning to keep them, and to drift in and out of friendships and romances as the mood suits them.

This ritual is meant to help you find friends and perhaps a lover who will be trustworthy and honest, and who will abide by their promises.

Before doing this ritual, carefully consider that to get respect you must give respect: to have promises kept, you must honor promises you have made. This means taking your word very seriously, and never making promises that cannot or will not be kept. Every day we see people who promised to "love, honor, and obey" for the rest of their lives simply throwing off these promises and divorcing. This is often the role model we had as children: Unhappy with your relationship? Just leave it and find a new one! And while we certainly should flee from an abusive relationship, many people would rather just quit a perfectly workable marriage than put the work into fixing it. Many people see infidelity as the norm today. They make excuses for their behavior, or make empty promises never to do it again.

Friendships are treated the same way. We all see a certain heiress in the news who goes through "best friends forever" like she goes through haute couture gowns. She even had a television show meant to find a "BFF."

And we seem to live in an age where our political leaders promise whatever they think we'd like to hear. We all remember a certain "read my lips" politician.

The point is, in our modern world we have very little in the way of role models for a trustworthy, faithful friendship. If you are not a trustworthy friend—if you lie, break promises, and move from one friendship to the next—think carefully about why that is before performing this ritual. If you use this ritual to find a true friend, and then you dishonor that friendship, you will be breaking a heart, and you will be reneging on a magical vow you have made.

If, however, you are truly ready for a lasting friendship with someone who will not prove disloyal, here is a ritual for finding such a thing. The ritual should be performed at the full moon, and it may take many performances of the ritual to see solid results. As with any spell, do not get discouraged. Perseverance and repetition pay off in magic as they do in life.

You will need:

- A standard altar, with three white candles (one taller than the other two) and a wand
- Your broom
- A golden ball (if you don't happen to have a ball of solid gold, a sports ball painted gold is perfectly acceptable; toy stores also stock gold-colored bouncing balls)
- A spade (to dig)

- You will be asked to bury the ball in a garden, a plot of soil, a forest, or a park; anywhere with a little dirt will do, so have a place in mind

The ritual is best done in a quiet, dark place. Outdoors is preferred, but in a quiet, dark room is great, too. You should be comfortable in dress, whether that is skyclad, robed, in pajamas, or street clothes.

Set your altar with three candles with the tallest in the middle surrounded by a shorter candle to each side, forming a triangle at the center of the altar, and set your wand where it will be easily reached.

Before you begin, light the candle at the center of the triangle. Say, "Winter turns to summer, summer to winter. May the light of this candle see me through each season with trusted friendships."

If you have a broom, sweep three times around the circle, thinking of the magical energy the broom generates and of how you will use this energy to find a true friendship.

Now take up your wand and walk once around the circle, saying:

"Cold winter brings sorrow. I need a friend to console me, hold me, promise true friendship to me. So be it!"

When you return to your starting point, use the small taper candle to light the left-hand smaller candle using the flame from the tallest candle. Say, "This candle is the despair of winter."

Now take up your wand again and walk around the circle, saying:

"Summer brings green and warmth. I need a friend to share laughter and promises. So be it!"

When you return to your starting place, light the second shorter candle with the taper, as you did before. Say, "This candle is the warm breath of summer."

Now walk about the circle a third time, saying:

"So the circle turns, season to season. Only love remains unchanged."

Next, sit and look at the burning candles for a few moments. Take the golden ball in your hands, and hold it to your heart.

"The sun in cold winter is dark, not bright; cold, not warm. My heart is tired of cold promises and careless friendship. Like the sun in long winter, I bury all thoughts of those who have proved untrue to me."

Hold the ball another moment, then place it beside the altar.

Take up your wand and hold it up to the sky.

"You spirits of air, water, fire, and earth! Hear my call! I seek true friendship. Bring into my life a friend who will be as Iron Hans, always faithful, ever caring for me, aware of my feelings and my heart. Let this friend be one who feels my heart like her (his) own! Like Iron Hans, let her (his) heart be bound to mine!"

Now put your wand down and take up the ball again.

"The summer breaks through cold winter, as the Frog Prince broke from the Underworld to the bright sky. This ball is the sun, which will shine over my true friendship. Like the king, I will keep my promises ever to my dear one. Like Iron Hans, my heart will be bound to hers (his).

"I bury this ball certain fathoms within the ground, that like the winter sun it may dream, and seek for me in its dreams the friend (lover) I crave. When it rises from the cold earth, it will see two hearts as one, my friend beside me! So be it!"

End this portion of the ritual by extinguishing the winter candle, saying, "Cold winter, I welcome you. Heal my heart in its long sleep!"

Now extinguish the summer candle, saying, "Summer, warm my emotions, so that I can feel my friend's heart as my own!"

Walk around the circle with your wand, opposite the way you cast, saying, "I carry this circle within me as I bury the winter sun!"

This part of the circle is done. Now you must take the golden ball of the sun to the area where you will bury it. Wrap it in plastic or place it in a small box, and bury it where you may find it again.

FOLLOW-UP

At the next full moon, go to the spot where you buried the ball. Dig it up, and look at it, saying:

"The summer sun shines again. The Sun God returns! The iron bands of my heart are broken! Come sun, and bring true friendship to me! So Mote It Be!"

Place the ball under your bed or on your nightstand, and look at it every evening before you go to bed. You may even want to cast your circle again, and walk three times around the circle holding the ball. When doing so, say:

"I carry the golden sun, which speaks my prayers of true and lasting friendship!" Repeat this each time you walk around the ritual space.

You may have to perform this ritual two or three times, but your honest, faithful friend or lover will come. Appreciate them!

Chapter 9

RAPUNZEL: A RITUAL TO CELEBRATE A YOUNG WOMAN COMING OF AGE

In this familiar tale, a girl is traded for her father's life after a sorceress catches the man stealing rapunzel, a cabbage, from her garden. The girl grows up in seclusion, knowing only the sorceress as her motherly guardian. When she meets a very determined young man, she falls in love, but both lovers must fight fate and the sorceress to have a happy ending to their tale. We will use this story as the basis for a young woman's coming of age ritual, a rite of passage observed in many ancient cultures. Once again, story quotes will be from the Margaret Hunt translation of the Grimms' 1812 collection.

In a marble hall as white as milk,
Lined with skin as soft as silk,
Within a fountain crystal clear,

191

A golden apple doth appear,
No doors are there to this stronghold,
Yet thieves break in to steal its gold.
(Traditional)

Like this traditional riddle, we have a puzzle before us: a tower stands in a deep forest, surrounded by briars. There are no doors, no stairway, no gate. Yet deep within sits a treasure: a beautiful girl with hair of gold, named for a plant and traded for a father's life. She spins all day, singing a lonely, seductive song. How did she get there, and who may enter this prison which has no guard and no lock?

The riddle's answer is an egg, and our puzzle's answer is, of course, Rapunzel.

The opening motif of "Rapunzel" is very similar to two other tales collected by the Grimms. In "Beauty and the Beast," a man exchanges his youngest daughter for his life as payment for picking a rose in a sealed garden; in "Rumpelstiltskin," a woman promises her baby as a prize if a Faerie will spin her straw into gold; and in this tale, a man ransoms his newborn for his own life after entering a walled garden to steal a cabbage called rampion rapunzel.

Rapunzel's story begins with a couple who wish for a baby. The woman becomes pregnant, and begins craving rampion, a cabbage growing in a garden that she can see from her window. The trouble is, the garden is in a walled area guarded by a dread enchantress.

It was generally believed in the Middle Ages that when a pregnant woman craved a certain food, it was very important to provide it to her. It is sound medical philosophy. After all, her craving may be brought on by needing some nutrient in the food. So this woman's husband decides to brave the threat of the sorceress, and he scales the garden wall.

At first all goes as planned. He returns with a handful of the cabbage. Wifey eats some, and all is fine. But like any food of the Underworld (for that's what this particular cabbage is), eating the cabbage only makes her want more, and so Hubby sets out the next evening for more espionage.

Espionage is maybe not Hubby's forte: this time the sorceress catches him. She threatens to kill him, but he begs for mercy and explains his predicament. The sorceress takes pity on him. Well, pity enough to spare his life if he will give her the unborn baby. Not what I would call true mercy. Our hero agrees to the bargain, and skedaddles out of there.

We see this kind of trap set throughout folklore. In *The Mabinogion*, a human hunter named Pwyll sees a white stag and wants to hunt it. Trouble is, it's being hunted by someone else's dogs, who are white with red ears. Not the sharpest tool in ye olde toolshed, Pwyll has his own hounds chase the white dogs away and fell the white stag. At that moment, the horned Underworld God Arawn shows up. He tells Pwyll that having hunted a deer that was by all rights his, Pwyll now owes the enchanted creature his life. But he agrees to spare Pwyll if the human will take his place in the Underworld and fight his enemy. Pwyll agrees, and spends a year in Arawn's land, culminating in a fierce duel.

In both cases, it's a setup. The sorceress wants a child, and we can imagine she has enchanted that rampion in some way to lure the pregnant woman and her husband into the walls of her Underworld garden. The ruse worked, and the man pledges his daughter's life for his own.

Now the wife goes into labor, and the enchantress appears in the bedchamber and takes the newborn. She names her Rapunzel, after the cabbage the girl was traded for, and raises her in solitude, protected from the world.

This is one of the very rare Grimms' tales in which we actually see the passage of time, and learn that the girl who started out as an infant is now old enough to be courted: "Rapunzel grew into the most beautiful child under the sun. When she was twelve years old, the enchantress shut her into a tower, which lay in a forest, and had neither stairs nor door, but quite at the top was a little window." In medieval Europe, twelve was marrying age, and the sorceress, afraid the girl would be courted, places her in the secluded keep. The only entrance is a high window, which is reached by climbing the girl's long braid.

A king's son is passing by, and hears the girl singing high in her tower. He admires her beautiful voice, but he cannot gain entry into the structure: he is thwarted by the riddle of Rapunzel. But not for long. He watches until he sees the sorceress call the familiar greeting: "Rapunzel Rapunzel, let down your hair!"—a passage we all grew up hearing and repeating.

The prince tries the same call to the tower, and is rewarded by a visit to the stronghold, where he beholds the girl. In a sequence reminiscent of the balcony scene in *Romeo and Juliet*, he climbs up and pledges his love for this young woman he's only just met, and they begin a tryst.

Rapunzel schemes to run off with her handsome lover, but before she can, she accidentally spills the beans to the woman she calls "dame gothel," a common German term for a godmother. The enchantress grows furious at Rapunzel's dalliance, and takes her to a desert. She then lays a trap for the prince (something we know she is very good at). She impersonates the girl, and allows the prince to climb into the tower, where she taunts him. When he learns his lover is gone, again much like Romeo, he jumps from the tower. Unlike the Shakespearean hero, the prince does not die, but is blinded by the briar thorns below.

Now he wanders the world eating "nothing but roots and berries," lamenting for his lover. But his wanderings take him in time to the very desert where Rapunzel is hidden. She has given birth to twins by him, and is singing to his children when he hears her song and recognizes her sweet voice. They embrace. She cries when she is reunited with her love, and her tears heal his eyes. He then carries her back to his kingdom, where they will be married and live "for a long time afterward, happy and contented."

Like many of the Grimms' tales, "Rapunzel" is a complex tale with many levels of meaning and magical lore.

CABBAGE PATCH KID

The story of Rapunzel starts with a wish: "There were once a man and a woman who had long in vain wished for a child. At length the woman hoped that God was about to grant her desire." The couple's wish to step outside the natural progression of life, and have a child when they want one rather than when Nature blesses them, leads to trouble. In our modern world, pregnancy is often planned and either avoided or allowed (or even helped along by fertility medicine). But in medieval Europe, it was believed that God or Nature alone decided when a baby was to be created, and the couple's wish is seen as tampering with Nature. This sin is added to by the woman's sin of avarice: "These people had a little window at the back of their house from which a splendid garden could be seen, which was full of the most beautiful flowers and herbs. It was, however, surrounded by a high wall, and no one dared to go into it because it belonged to an enchantress, who had great power and was dreaded by all the world." The woman desired two things she could not have: a baby, and the flowers and plants from the garden of the enchantress.

Now the woman becomes pregnant, and she becomes fixated on the lovely cabbages behind the neighbor's wall. Her husband fears she will get sick, so he climbs the wall to steal the vegetable. He manages once, but the woman is guilty of avarice and now of gluttony; she wants more.

Here is one of our first underlying motifs, and one that will come up again and again in this story: cabbage.

You may or may not have strong feelings about cabbage, but in folklore, cabbage is a pretty potent little vegetable. It holds the same mythic place as the rose, which we saw in connection with Rose-Red and with Briar Rose. Each of these plants has lush folds in its flower, so each is used in folklore to represent the vagina and a woman's sexuality. We see the rose in "The Summer and Winter Garden" ("Beauty and the Beast"); the rose there represents Beauty's sexuality, which, like the fragile rose, the Beast wishes to possess but must wait until the flower is ripe. The cabbage appears there, too, when Beauty has rushed to her father's side with a promise to return to the Beast's castle; as the Beast pines away for Beauty, he lies dying in a cabbage patch. Beauty returns, and revives the Beast with her kiss: she replaces the floral vagina with her actual sexuality, which brings the Beast back to life: women hold the power of rebirth and nurturing, and this is expressed literally through their vagina, the door to life. The rose and the cabbage are vegetative symbols for this power. Certainly this is one reason roses are given as gifts between lovers.

This exchange of a young woman for a sexual flower comes up across English folklore, in songs like "Tam Lin." I've mentioned that song, in which Janet, a lovely young heiress, is forced into a sexual relationship with a Faerie after picking one of his roses.

So here we have these cabbages, vaginal flowers in folklore, behind the wall of the enchantress's garden. The mother-to-be wants one. They represent her sex drive and her incredibly strong desire to birth a child. But we see the nature of the sorceress here, too. She locks these plants into her garden, shielding them from the world. Her own sex is hidden, closely guarded. She will trade for the unborn girl because she feels girls must be protected from their own maturity, and she will lock the girl away just as she has locked away the garden plants.

The mother's gluttony forces her husband to sneak in and steal the cabbage (just as the prince will sneak in and steal Rapunzel's virginity later in the story). The man is caught, and like Beauty's father, is forced to trade his child's life for the vegetable. Because the wife has sinned (wishing for a baby against natural timing, and the sins of avarice and gluttony), she will lose the child she bears. In fact, her sin of avarice will be punished by symbolically changing her daughter into the cabbage she lusts for.

Just as in "Beauty and the Beast," Dad is responsible for the ordeals of the child. In both tales it is Dad who steals the plant from the walled garden, and then promises his daughter to save himself. The enchantress appears at the moment of the girl's birth and claims the child. She names her for the fertile cabbage for which she was traded.

The dame gothel, or godmother, shields the girl from the world, so when the girl reaches the age of twelve, she locks the girl in a tower in the forest.

On one level, we know that the forest is the Underworld. Just like Briar Rose and like Rose-Red, it seems the girl is in a hibernation, a stasis before she enters womanhood. The tower represents her virginity, carefully guarded from the world. The fact that the tower has no doors represents maidenhood. The world can see a young woman growing into maturity, but none may yet possess her. She waits for the prince, the man who will waken desire in her when the time is precisely right.

HAIRWAY TO HEAVEN

We saw a riddle at the start of this chapter. The riddle has many characteristics of Rapunzel's imprisonment inside the tower of her chastity. The riddle describes a treasure, a "golden fountain," set within an impenetrable castle. The gold is the egg's yolk, which is the part of the egg from which new life grows. Rapunzel is also a treasure held in an impenetrable tower. Her imprisonment is an analogy to Rapunzel's newfound fertility, the eggs inside her that must be protected while she is still young and fragile. But like any maturing girl, just as the chick wants to burst out of that egg, Rapunzel wants more than a lonely tower and an aged stepmother. Rapunzel, on one level, is very much the virgin Goddess, the seed of spring, waiting in the Underworld for the right time to blossom and grow, to bring life to the world after dreary winter (like the yolk hidden and guarded in the shell).

Rapunzel is not the only one who inhabits this Underworld keep. The tower is also dame gothel's sanctuary. She seems to have issues with her own sexuality, and has hidden her sex away behind the walled garden, fearful of men entering. When one enters, she wishes to kill him, but realizes that his entry (sex) is the only way she may have a child. She allows it, on the condition that a baby is given to her. But her distrust of men and her discomfort with her own sexuality continues. When her own child is old enough to begin having sexual urges, the woman locks her away, attempting to protect her from the issues the enchantress herself faces.

The enchantress is much like Demeter, mother of Persephone, who attempts to prevent her daughter from pursuing a sexual love with Hades and wants to keep Persephone with her forever, keeping her daughter innocent and childlike.

It doesn't work, of course. Demeter cannot hold Persephone, for the young Goddess must become pregnant so that spring can return. The sorceress and Rapunzel take on the same mythic roles: the enchantress wishes to stop Rapunzel's natural urge to experience love, sex, and procreation. The girl's natural cycle will prevail.

Beside being a symbol of the Spring Goddess, Rapunzel has many characteristics of a changeling, a human who lives a Faerie life (or vice versa). A human child, she is traded for a cabbage from an Underworld garden, and raised by an enchanted being.

Changeling child and Spring Goddess, Rapunzel is bound to the seasons and to the earth. Through her the spring must quicken, and life must be engendered. Rapunzel sings her haunting song from the tower, and a young man is drawn near.

Throughout Faerie lore, we see a young man drawn to the enchanted singing of a Faerie woman. In *The Odyssey*, Odysseus encounters the Sirens, whose songs lure sailors to the rock island where they sit. The sailor sinks and dies, his only thought the love of the beauty he may never possess. The mermaid too sings to lure sailors into the deep, as does the German Lorelei, who lives in the Rhine river and drowns her suitors.

In the tale of Ossian, the hero, who is the son of Finn McCool (who we met in our discussion of "Cinderella"), hears a woman singing on a hillside. Her voice is beautiful beyond words. It is Niamh (Neve) of the Golden Hair, who has come to take Ossian to her land of Tir N'an Og (the Island of the Young).

Like these Faerie women, Rapunzel (who has been raised by an enchantress and uses magic to charm men, in the form of her Faerie-inspired voice) sings to lure a man to the tower. Like each of the men in the myths, the suitor will come to grave harm by this. Just wait and see.

At first the prince watches, waiting to find how the girl can be reached. The enchantress herself shows him the way, by calling out to Rapunzel to lower her hair.

Hair is an amazing thing. For starters, it is one of the very few parts of our body that we can lose and grow back. If you were to trim off your hands, or your ears, you'd be pretty much out of luck. But lop off as much of your hair as you like. Like a lizard's tail, it will grow back. For this reason, hair represents regeneration and rebirth. It holds our strength, our power to renew the world around us and to exert our control upon our world. When biblical Samson lost his hair, he no longer had strength to control his life. When it grew back, he took back his power.

Various religions prohibit the cutting of hair for this reason. In Orthodox Judaism and in certain forms of Islam, men are forbidden from cutting their beards. Jewish men in the Orthodox movement may not cut the hair around their ears. The hair gives these men strength and spiritual power to communicate with the Divine.

Hair is also extremely sexual, and holds a woman's power to seduce and delight. As children we are vividly taught "boys have short hair and girls have long hair." While this message may be a horror to feminist thought, we all acquire this message at an impressionable age, and if we see a little boy with long hair or a little girl with a crew cut, we still, even as adults, have the urge to respond to the child as the opposite of his or her gender. We grow up with this message, which teaches us that hair defines femininity and beauty. Despite our adult experience of long-haired boys and punk rock girls, we have this imprinting of hair being feminine.

Hair is sexy.

In Rapunzel's case, her hair carries both sexuality and power. Locked in her tower, unable to express her sexuality to society in any other way, she is allowed to grow her long, beautiful hair. Like her name, it is an expression of her femininity, her lure. But the enchantress uses the hair to reach the chaste girl, to protect her from the men her hair might attract. The girl's hair has the power to end her seclusion, for it is the one way for a lover to gain entrance to her lonely garret. Looking back at the riddle so similar in character to this tale, her hair is the way for "thieves" to "break in and steal its gold." But paradoxically it is also her captor's entrance into her prison.

The prince learns the hair trick by watching Rapunzel's captor use the girl's hair, and he can now use the luxurious hair for what it is meant to do; he calls to Rapunzel, and climbs the ladder of tresses to embrace the girl. At first Rapunzel is frightened, having never seen a man; but her natural desires take over, and the two plan an escape. Getting the prince out is no problem; Rapunzel must now find a way to get herself down. She asks the prince to bring silk that she can use to make a ladder. The hair that allows her lover to reach her traps Rapunzel herself in the tower. Coming of age, the sexuality that draws others to her traps Rapunzel herself in the cycle of love and procreation, as it does most of us.

HAIR TODAY, GONE TOMORROW

But Rapunzel, raised alone with only her captor for company, has developed no subtlety. In an unguarded moment she blurts out her secret to the old woman, who flies into a rage. The enchantress locks Rapunzel into a new prison in a desert; the desert is devoid of life. Since Rapunzel sneakily let her natural urge to mate and procreate come through, the enchantress will lock her in a place where life cannot grow, where she will not have sex or make babies.

The woman now sets a trap for the prince, using a trick neither Rapunzel nor her lover considered: cutting off Rapunzel's hair and using it as a ladder. Had the young lovers thought of this, they might have escaped unscathed. But like the stepsisters in "Cinderella" cutting their feet, Rapunzel would mar her beauty by cutting her own hair. The woman cuts it, stealing Rapunzel's beauty and sexuality. She now poses as the girl, lowering the hair to the prince.

Like the wolf in "Little Red Cap," the enchantress wears the guise of a friend, pretending to be Rapunzel. But she is an enemy, using Rapunzel's hair to lure the prince, just as the wolf used Grandma's clothes and bed to lure Red. The prince arrives, but now sees only the old woman. She tells him what has happened, and in despair he leaps from the tower, and is blinded by the briars below.

He wanders for years, blind and despairing. We have seen again and again that a journey into the forest in fairy tales is always a journey into the Underworld. Now the prince is living in the deep forest Underworld, blind to our world. In many ways he is now like Orpheus: the wife of Orpheus, the Nymph Eurydice, was killed by a serpent bite. Like the prince, Orpheus traveled into the Underworld in hopes of retrieving Eurydice from death.

Orpheus is a Sun God, the son of Apollo with the Muse Calliope. His presence is very foreign in the dark, dreary Underworld. In the same way, the prince represents love and life, while Rapunzel has always lived in the dark tower in the forest and has been prohibited from creating new life. Now the prince must experience this dark, lifeless Underworld, as Rapunzel has, before he may be reborn, and like any God follow the Goddess back into our world so life may be renewed:

"Then he wandered quite blind about the forest, ate nothing but roots and berries, and did naught but lament and weep over the loss of his dearest wife. Thus he roamed about in misery for some years, and at length came to the desert where Rapunzel, with the twins to which she had given birth, a boy and a girl, lived in wretchedness."

The fact that the prince ate roots and berries, things that grow in the ground, is further evidence of his Underworld journey. But he is drawn to his love, though he does not plan it: his long time in the Underworld, blind and relying only on his inner senses, has given him a psychic ability to connect with dreams and inner urgings. His visions and instincts have guided him to Rapunzel in her desert solitude. There she is with the twins he has given her: with the instinct of young women anywhere, she has broken through the deathly energies of even this dark, lifeless place and has brought new life into the world.

Now we see another Orpheus-like passage: "He heard a voice, and it seemed so familiar to him that he went towards it, and when he approached, Rapunzel knew him and fell on his neck and wept." Orpheus was a singer, and used his song to persuade Hades and Persephone to allow him to take Eurydice from the Underworld. Here it is also a song that allows the two lovers to be reunited.

This element of the story may also have a historic reference that crept into the telling. In 1192 King Richard of England (Richard the Lionheart, who appears in the Robin Hood myth cycle) was captured by Duke Leopold V of Austria and held for ransom. It is generally held that Richard's favorite troubadour, Blondel, rode about Austria from castle to castle singing out Richard's favorite song. Blondel found Richard when, from a high tower, Richard sang the refrain back to the troubadour. This folkloric tale may have found its way into the story of Rapunzel, adding a familiar and romantic motif to the preexisting story.

TOGETHER AGAIN

Rapunzel is now rescued from her Underworld prison. Her lover, the father of her two children, has come to take her back to our world, as Orpheus would have taken Eurydice. But the prince is damaged. He is blind, so present in the Underworld that he has lost sight of our world, where life may grow. Rapunzel is so emotional when the prince holds her that she cries: "Two of her tears wetted his eyes and they grew clear again, and he could see with them as before." This is the final proof that Rapunzel is the maiden Goddess, the Underworld queen who may now leave the Underworld and bring life to our world.

On another level (and isn't there always another level?), Rapunzel the young woman may leave her long prepubescent hibernation. She has made the transition from an obedient girl to a sexually mature woman with a husband and a family. The sorceress has lost her hold, and we never see the old woman again in the tale. Unlike the cruel parents of Cinderella or Snow White, the sorceress is not punished. She was protecting the girl from what she thought was harm: she may have been overprotective, perhaps a little psychotic, but she was not malicious.

We are told that Rapunzel had two children by the prince, a boy and a girl. These twins represent the cosmic life force, the universal male and female or yin and yang, expressed Divinely as the God and the Goddess. We see that not only has Rapunzel the Underworld Goddess created life in the face of death, but she has unleashed the procreation force into the world; the boy and girl child will grow to be next year's Goddess of spring and God of the forest, as the Goddess eternally rebirths herself by her stay in the Underworld, and she eternally gives birth to the dying-reborn God. Rapunzel has triumphed over death and stagnation by creating new life and allowing the life cycle to continue in its own harmonious rhythm, a feat neither her birth mother nor the sorceress could accomplish.

THE RAPUNZEL RITUAL

When a young woman comes of age, it is vastly important that her maturity and abilities be recognized by her family and community. Ancient cultures have always ritualized this: from the Jewish tradition of the bat mitzvah to the Hispanic quinceañera, to its roots in tribal rituals such as the Brazilian Tupinambá Girl's Rite or the Apache Na'ii'ees. In each ritual a girl has to be sequestered in some way, endure an ordeal of some sort, and then be reintroduced to her family and friends as an adult. This is vitally important for the girl to gain confidence in her new role as a woman. A young woman who has endured these types of rituals can say she has suffered for her community, and can name the day she became a grownup.

As important as these rites are, by and large our society does not have them. Years ago, a sweet-sixteen party or "coming out" ball might have sufficed as a vague shadow of these traditions, but even those seem to be trivialized, commercialized, or completely forgotten in our modern world. This is one of a myriad of reasons that our young women have so much difficulty maturing and finding their niche in a confusing culture.

When does a girl mature and become a woman? In many ancient cultures, it is when puberty begins, which in a girl might be defined as her first menses. But young women may menstruate very young, long before they are ready to see themselves as mature. The mid-teens are often a time of yearning for an independent identity, and the years between fifteen and seventeen are a very good time for a girl to go through this type of ritual. But it is never too late. I recently saw a friend whom I've known since her childhood decide at the age of twenty that she was ready for her rite of womanhood, and she asked several respected women of the Pagan community to perform it for her. For her sequester, she slept overnight in the deep woods. She was then able to ritually rise to womanhood, even though she'd been living as a grown woman for some time.

Rapunzel suffered during her long period of sequestering, guided by her immediate family (her adoptive mother) and honing the skills she would need as a mature woman. She endured a test in living through her days in the desert, and in healing her lover the prince. We will use the model of Rapunzel to create a ritual for young women of our culture to ritualize their own maturity.

PREPARATION

This ritual is meant to be done by a group of women closest to the young woman being celebrated. Her mother, older sisters, grand-mothers, and aunts might be included. Her adult friends should be there, especially women she admires or learns from, as well as any friends who have already gone through such a rite.

The young woman herself should carefully consider the ritual for some time before going through it, perhaps weeks or months. It is important for her to consider that although she may act childish, after this day she will be treated as a young adult, and be expected to respond as one. The women performing the ritual should carefully question just what that means to the young woman. The young woman should also grow her hair out for as long before the ritual as possible, as a lock of her hair will be cut off in the ritual.

If the women performing the ritual feel the young woman is capable, she should be sequestered for a time. Like my friend, she might sleep in the forest in a small tent for a night before her ritual. Or she may stay in seclusion in a room or lodge prepared especially for her. The important element is that the young woman be alone with her thoughts in her "tower." She should fast, and prepare for the ritual. She should have no phone, television, video games, or Internet, and no contact with friends. She might journal, or do some type of art or music celebrating the change she is about to go through.

THE RITUAL

Once the young woman has prepared, the community of women is ready to perform her ritual.

You will need:

- An altar with a wand, a bell, a small amount of rose oil, some rose petals, a small ornate pair of scissors, and a pretty tray or small plate
- A light ritual robe or shift, and a garland of flowers for her hair
- A beautiful dress for the young woman, as nice as can be obtained, which should be hidden from her until it is brought out in the ritual

In preparing for ritual, the young woman should be bathed by her mother or older sisters in a bath full of roses. During this time, in the area where the ritual will be performed, the women may cast the circle with the wand, walking three times around. They may call upon specific Goddesses or iconic female figures, or simply ask for the presence of the Goddess, or the Great Mother.

When the circle is cast and the young woman is ready, she should be helped out of the bath. The garland or flower crown should be placed on her head.

Woman: "This crown represents the flower of your childhood. These beautiful blooms are like the blooms of spring that lead to the fruits of summer. Flowers herald the seed of that which will grow tall and strong. Wear this crown one last time, and enjoy its beauty, before you take on the role of the woman who you will become."

The young woman should be dressed in the white robe, shift, or gown. A path of rose petals should be strewn between the bath and the ritual site, and she should be brought on this path by a family member or close friend.

The young woman is to be brought just outside the ritual area, and must stand before all of the women who are assembled. In this ritual we will use the term *woman* to cue the women in the ritual to speak. Any of the women assembled for the ritual may speak any of the lines. There may be several cues in a row, and it should be decided before the ritual which woman will speak which line. "Girl" will mean the young woman going through the rite of passage. She will be cued to answer as she wishes, but she should be gently encouraged to speak, rather than simply nod or remain silent. It is very important that the young woman understand that her voice is valuable and important, and that her words are respected by the community.

She now stands at the edge of the cast circle, facing the women who have gathered.

Woman: "Who stands before the circle of women?"

Girl: "_____." (She says her name.)

Woman: "Why do you come here?"

Girl answers.

Woman: "All here know you well, as a girl. We remember you from the time of your birth. We have many dear memories of your childhood. We recall them now." (The women may take turns telling stories or sharing memories of the young woman as she grew up. This can take as long as is necessary.)

Woman: "Is it your will now to grow beyond the girl we have all known, and become the woman we all dream you might be?"

Girl answers.

Woman: "To be a woman is to remain strong when life would make us weak, to remain confident when life would have us surrender, to nurture though you may go hungry, tired, or cold. Would you take on these difficult responsibilities?"

Girl answers.

Woman: "How do we know you are ready to be made a woman?"

Girl answers.

Woman: "You have been sheltered in the high tower these ___ (young woman's age) years, protected from the harshness of the world. Are you prepared to face the world as it is, rather than the child's world you have always known?"

Girl answers.

"Know this, child: life may be difficult, hard choices must be made, the deep forest is full of thorns and briars, and is not as pretty as the lofty tower of your childhood. By this rite would you leave the tower and walk on the earth? Do you choose to enter the circle of adult women?"

Girl answers.

Woman: "We each sacrifice something of ourselves in living our lives, in giving ourselves to our work, in giving our love, and in tending to those precious to us. Reflect for a moment now upon the sacrifices each woman here has made in her life so that you might grow strong, healthy, confident, and sure." (Silence for a moment as the young woman reflects. A bell might be rung to end the silence.)

Woman: "Here you may take a moment to thank any woman here who has sacrificed for you, inspired you, or guided you."

Girl addresses the women in the ritual, thanking them for anything they might have done for her.

Woman: "To become a woman you must prove that you too are willing to sacrifice. You have grown lovely child's hair upon your head these ___ (young woman's age) years. As a sign that you are truly ready to sacrifice, to give of yourself, will you allow us to take your tresses as a tithe to the Goddess, the Mother of All?"

Girl answers.

A woman closest to the young woman (mother, sister, aunt) cuts a lock of the young woman's hair and places it in a tray upon the altar.

Now the young woman is led into the center of the circle.

Woman: "By this sacrifice you show that there is Goddess inside you, willing to give so that life may be honored, preserved, and nourished. This hair will be woven into a charm; when you face hard choices, when you find you have little strength for life's challenges, when help seems far away, wear this charm and reflect that in your heart and your spirit you are always with the women present here, for they love you and accept you wholly as part of the circle of Goddess!"

Woman: "Like the Goddess who enters the Underworld, you must enter with nothing but the love in your heart. Are you ready to stand before us, and show that you enter with nothing but the love, confidence, kindness, mystery, and subtlety that these women have taught you?"

Girl answers.

The flower crown is taken from her head.

Woman: "These flowers are the beauty of your youth. You have chosen to remove them, for you have grown to be a woman. But you will ever recall their beauty and joy. The girl you have been will live inside you, and inside of us, always."

Woman: "I anoint you with rose oil. Bless your heart that you may always carry within it the child you once were, and always look ahead at the woman you will become, for we are always becoming!"

Woman anoints the young woman with rose oil over her heart.

Woman: "Now that you are woman, you may be arrayed as a woman!"

A beautiful dress is presented, and the young woman is helped into it. All women present admire her in her beauty. New flowers may be placed in her hair, and personal gifts of jewelry or charms may be given at this time.

Woman: "_____ (young woman's name), you have stood before us, ready to be seen as a woman; you have given us your hair in tithe to the Goddess who lives inside you; you have shown us that you have grown to be our equal and peer, our confidante and companion in life. From this day forward you take your place among us! Blessed Be!"

All hug the young woman. Each may offer their blessings and wishes for her. Gifts may be given at this time.

When this is done, a woman walks widdershins around the circle to end the ritual.

Woman: "We end the circle, but carry it always within our hearts. We are the circle, and the circle is us. We are bound by it, and carry it like a flame. Welcome, _____ (young woman's name), to the circle!"

A fuss should be made for hours, with a feast, stories, and joy being had by all. In the aftermath of the ritual, a charm or necklace should be made containing the young woman's hair, and this should be presented to her to wear or to keep safely hidden away.

Chapter 10

STRONG HANS: A RITUAL TO CELEBRATE A YOUNG MAN COMING OF AGE

A boy who has been kidnapped by criminals finds he has the strength to free himself and his mother. In time he sets off upon what becomes a supernatural adventure, in which he finds a dwarf, a treasure, and a captive princess. This typical Hero's Quest will set the stage for a young man's coming of age ritual. The story quotes are once again from the Margaret Hunt translation.

What happens when Snow White takes Hansel and Gretel on a walk to Jack's beanstalk? Well, we may never know, but this lesser-known Grimms' tale has so many familiar elements that you'll probably recognize little pieces of each of these stories. What is interesting about "Strong Hans" is the strange, twisting plot that takes Hans below ground, back above ground, and into the air and the water. In each place he faces challenges that must be met with both brute strength and subtle cunning. He exhibits patience, deduction, resourcefulness, and mastery, and hones each of his skills as he goes. Through his epic quest, Strong Hans defeats evil, corrects injustice, provides for his family, and finds love. And has a big stick. Make of that what you will.

At the outset, the tale is pretty unremarkable. The narrative starts off with echoes of "Hansel and Gretel." A husband and wife live in the deep forest with their toddler son, Hans.

The story tells us: "It came to pass that the mother once went into the wood to gather branches of fir, and took with her little Hans, who was just two years old. As it was springtime, and the child took pleasure in the many-colored flowers, she went still further onwards with him into the forest."

The whole further-into-the-forest thing should set off a bunch of alarms. In any fairy tale, going further into the forest always leads to trouble. Sure enough, trouble finds them: "Suddenly two robbers sprang out of the thicket, seized the mother and child, and carried them far away into the black forest, where no one ever came from one year's end to another."

Again reminiscent of Hansel and Gretel, who were held captive by a sorceress in the deep forest, mother and son are now taken by robbers in the darkest part of the woods. Like Hansel and Gretel there is no one there to save them, and they must rely upon their own resources. Unfortunately, Hans is only two years old, and has little in the way of resources. Yet.

The woman is made to work for a cave full of robbers (just like some versions of "Snow White" or "The Robber Bridegroom," in which the house in the woods was not full of dwarfs but full of robbers or dragons). She is treated well, and Hans grows up with these unlikely stepfathers, a twist on the evil-stepmother motif. The captain of the robbers becomes Hans's principal stepfather and the focus of his need to establish his own identity by escaping to find his true father (the way Cinderella retained her identity by visiting her true mother's grave each day). But Hans begins to grow extremely strong. He makes himself a club from the branch of a fir tree, awaiting the moment he will be strong enough to use it against his "evil stepfather." At the age of nine, he decides to try the weapon.

"In the night, when the robbers came home from their robbing expedition, Hans brought out his club, stood before the captain, and said, 'I now wish to know who my father is, and if you do not tell me at once I will strike you down.' Then the captain laughed, and gave Hans such a box on the ear that he rolled under the table."

This is the first point at which the story stops being a fairly predictable Grimms' tale, and becomes something a little more sophisticated: "Hans got up again, held his tongue, and thought, I will wait another year and then try again, perhaps I shall do better then."

Hans is showing us a bit of his remarkable nature. Although he's only nine, he is able to perceive that patience is an ally to him.

When a year has passed, Hans confronts the captain again, who laughs at him and strikes him as before. But this time Hans is strong enough to return the blow, and he "beat the captain and the robbers with his club, that they could no longer move either their arms or their legs."

At this point, Hans has gained a degree of maturity: he has impressed his mother with his skill, proving to her that he no longer needs her nurturing: "His mother stood in a corner full of admiration for his bravery and strength. When Hans had done his work, he went to his mother, and said, 'Now I have shown myself to be in earnest, but now I must also know who my father is.'"

Still, at this point the story is not noteworthy. We haven't seen any real magic, no shapeshifting, no enchanted vegetables, no prophetic birds, no late-night trysts with bears, or any of the things that make the Grimms' tales magical and mysterious. Thus far we simply have a hostage scenario turned around by a ten-year-old. But wait, things are about to change.

Hans takes an extraordinarily large bag of the robbers' booty, his mother takes the key, and the two head back to his father's house in the forest. There is Dad, sitting on the porch.

This is another rare tale that shows us the passage of time in a child's life. When Hans finds his dad, we are told: "But Hans, although he was not twelve years old, was a head taller than his father." This is meant to show us that Hans is growing very large and strong, but it also serves to show us that Hans is maturing. He has returned to his father at an age when most boys at this time would leave home to become apprenticed, and learn to make their way in the world. But Hans is prepared for this. He shows his father the treasure he has brought home, and the bag of loot is so heavy it breaks the floor of the little cottage in the forest. Again, we are shown that ten-year-old Hans is strong enough to carry a bag that the floor of his childhood home cannot support.

Hans and his parents buy a farm, and Hans is so strong he is able to plow without the help of his bulls. But having proved to both his parents that he is capable, Hans knows that he must leave home and seek his fortune in the world: "The next spring, Hans said, 'Keep all the money and get a walking-stick that weighs a hundred-weight made for me that I may go a-travelling.'" With his huge stick, Hans leaves the safety of the farm, leaves his wealth with his family, and goes into the world on his walkabout.

This is where our story begins to take some strange, unexpected turns, and magic begins to slowly creep in. Hans begins his journey into the forest: "There he heard something crunching and cracking, looked round, and saw a fir tree which was wound round like a rope from the bottom to the top, and when he looked upwards he saw a great fellow who had laid hold of the tree and was twisting it like a willow-wand. 'Hullo,' cried Hans, 'what are you doing up there.'" The "great fellow" is twisting the fir trees like a rope to hold firewood. Hans names him "Fir-Twister," and takes the man along on his travels. Remember that it was a fir tree that his mother was looking for at the story's start, when she and Hans were taken captive, and a fir tree that provided Hans with his weapon against the robbers.

Next, Hans "heard something knocking and hammering with such force that the ground shook at every stroke. Shortly afterwards they came to a mighty rock, before which a giant was standing and striking great pieces of it away with his fist." He found a man harvesting stones to build a home so that wolves and bears do not disturb him while he sleeps. Odd, right? Hans calls this man "Rock-Splitter," and takes him along.

They roam further into the forest, where "the wild beasts were terrified, and ran away from them." It is not long before the three find a home. "In the evening they came to an old deserted castle, went up into it, and laid themselves down in the hall to sleep. The next morning Hans went into the garden. It had run quite wild, and was full of thorns and brambles. And as he was thus walking round about, a wild boar rushed at him, he, however, gave it such a blow with his club that it fell directly. He took it on his shoulders and carried it in, and they put it on a spit, roasted it, and enjoyed themselves." In this strange aside, Hans proves that he is stronger than wild animals of the forest.

"Then they arranged that each day, in turn, two should go out hunting, and one should stay at home, and cook nine pounds of meat for each of them. Fir-Twister stayed at home the first, and Hans and Rock-Splitter went out hunting."

Now the story takes another strange twist, with the inclusion of a strange, Rumpelstiltskin-like dwarf. "When Fir-Twister was busy cooking, a little shriveled-up old mannikin came to him in the castle, and asked for some meat. 'Be off, you sneaking imp,' he answered, 'you need no meat.' But how astonished Fir-Twister was when the little insignificant dwarf sprang up at him, and belabored him so with his fists that he could not defend himself, but fell on the ground and gasped for breath. The dwarf did not go away until he had thoroughly vented his anger on him."

Fir-Twister does not tell the others he's been bested by a dwarf. He lets Rock-Splitter find out for himself the next day. The same dwarf confronts Rock-Splitter, who denies the creature a meal, and again the dwarf beats the man.

Now it is Hans's turn to stay home. But unlike the other two, when the dwarf asks for meat, Hans shows his generosity by giving the creature a meal. The dwarf is not satisfied, and makes to attack Hans. Hans beats the little creature, and watches the dwarf flee.

Now another odd thing happens. So strong and agile throughout the tale, "Hans was about to run after him, but fell right over, flat on his face. When he rose up again, the dwarf had got the start of him. Hans hurried after him as far as the forest, and saw him slip into a hole in the rock." It's a little odd that we see Hans fall while he is chasing the dwarf. We now see that Hans has human failings, and is vulnerable despite his strength.

Hans shares his tale with his companions, and they admit they'd been thrashed by the dwarf: "Hans laughed and said, 'It served you quite right. Why were you so mean with your meat. It is a disgrace that you who are so big should have let yourselves be beaten by the dwarf.'" Hans does not understand his companions' lack of empathy, and thinks they deserved their beatings for not offering meat. In a sense, he believes doing the right thing would have made his fellows stronger, as it did himself.

Now the three go in search of the dwarf: "Thereupon they took a basket and a rope, and all three went to the hole in the rock into which the dwarf had slipped, and let Hans and his club down in the basket." Hans is the only one to climb down, and he finds the dwarf with a beautiful young woman as his captive. She is tied up, and the dwarf grins at Hans "like a sea-cat." Hans kills the dwarf with his club, and frees the maid.

He sends the maid up in the basket, but having gained wisdom, Hans realizes that his fellows have lied to him before, and that they may deceive him again. Sure enough, they abandon Hans in the dwarf hole, and claim the maiden as their own prize.

Now we have a last plot twist, and a final touch of magic. In a sequence much like Sinbad and his lamp, Hans finds a magic ring with which he can command the air spirits. He orders the spirits of air to free him from his prison in the dwarf's holes, and "they obeyed instantly, and it was just as if he had flown up himself." Now with their help, he finds his false companions in a boat on the sea with their captive maiden.

Hans makes another mistake: he jumps into the sea with his heavy club, which almost drowns him. But he is saved by the air spirits, and slays his former friends. He takes the maiden to her parents, and of course marries her.

What an odd little tale!

THE HERO'S QUEST

We've already noticed how many elements of the tale are familiar: in fact, the entire tale is very familiar. It is a fairy tale version of the Hero's Quest. In any Hero's Quest, a hero, usually a young man, must travel a great distance to prove himself and find some treasure or right a great wrong.

"Strong Hans" resembles several great Hero's Quest myths. One very similar story is that of Jason and the Golden Fleece. In it, Jason's father, Aeson, is killed by his own half-brother, Pelias. Jason is spared by the cunning of his mother. We have a similarity right away, in that Hans's father is absent from his life because of the kidnapping robber captain, and his mother's usefulness to the robbers saves Hans's life. When he returns as an adult to take Pelias's throne, Jason is sent by his evil stepfather to retrieve the Golden Fleece. He takes a group of strong men, including Hercules. In "Strong Hans," Hans himself assembles a group of strong companions (though we never truly learn the reason).

We've already mentioned a similarity to the story of Sinbad the Sailor (a small portion of the *Thousand and One Arabian Nights*). Sinbad journeys on a Hero's Quest, broken into seven voyages. The Arabic sailor finds a magical lamp, like Hans's ring; is aided by an enchanted flying creature, a roc, as Hans is aided by the air spirits; and, like Hans, Sinbad is abandoned by his shipmates. Sinbad also finds great treasure in his journeys.

Other bits of Hero's Quest tales are all over the story of Strong Hans. In the Irish story of Cú Chulainn, that hero learns that his fiancée, Emer, has been imprisoned in a castle by her father, Forgall. Cú Chulainn leaps over the castle wall, kills all the soldiers within, and leaps back over the wall with Emer in his arms to escape. This is very close to Hans's rescue of the maid trapped by a dwarf, especially as Hans must fly or leap out of the dwarf's cave.

Hans is much like Cú Chulainn in many other ways: the Irish hero uses magical weapons, just as Hans uses his big stick; the Irishman's name derives from a great feat of strength when he was a boy; he killed a vicious watch dog belonging to a smith named Culann, and agrees to take the dog's place in guarding the castle, taking the name "the hound of Culann." Hans exhibits the same type of strength, fighting ability, and loyalty as a lad when he defeats the robbers and frees his mother.

Like any hero myth, Strong Hans begins with a great peril arising in the course of the hero's birth or childhood. For Perseus it is his grandfather's fear that Perseus will kill him; Moses is cast in a basket on the Nile; Oedipus is left to die because his father fears the infant will kill him. In all of these tales, the hero is too young and vulnerable to save himself, and a God or Goddess must rescue him (more about that in a moment).

Hans and his mother being taken by the robbers in the forest is the great peril the infant boy finds himself in. Like these other heroes, Hans is a toddler, and cannot defend himself and his mother. But the captain in "Strong Hans" treats the mother well, acting as a father (more so than the stepmothers of "Cinderella" or "Snow White").

Hans is smart. We see his mother teaching him to read and to relate to historical heroes: "His mother told him stories, and taught him to read an old book of tales about knights which she found in the cave." Hans understands that patience is important, and waits years to have the strength to free himself and his mother.

He makes his weapon out of a fir tree: "When Hans was nine years old, he made himself a strong club out of a branch of fir." This is interesting, since it was fir that got him and his mother into this mess; remember that the tale opened with "It came to pass that the mother once went into the wood to gather branches of fir, and took with her little Hans, who was just two years old."

THE FIR AND THE FOREST, OR, FIR SURE!

Fir is an evergreen, often used as a Christmas tree. In the Celtic Ogham alphabet, Fir is *Ailm*, the equivalent of our letter A, and means "will" or "desire." In Greece the tree is sacred to the Goddess Artemis who presides over childbirth, and in Bulgaria, the fir tree is called *elha*, and is associated with young women reaching puberty (coming to an age of bearing children). Its association with the winter solstice makes it a symbol of the Saxon God Jul and the Roman Saturn, who die in the hunt or harvest and are reborn with the sun at the solstice. In Scandinavia the fir is associated with the God of the forest, who is usually seen holding a fir tree in his hand. It is also connected with land ownership, and represents the lord of the manor.

It's no wonder then that the fir comes up again and again in the story of "Strong Hans." In the very beginning, when his mother takes Hans with her to gather fir branches, we see Hans associated with the Forest God, who will bless the boy and make him very strong. I mentioned earlier that many heroes in these types of tales are watched over by a God or Goddess in their infant perils. The fir tree under which Hans is kidnapped contains the spirit of the Forest God, who will watch over Hans during the toddler's ordeal with the robbers.

Hans joins forces with the Forest God again, directed by that deity to build his club of the fir in order to defeat the robbers. This is a magical weapon, imbued with the spirit of the forest that has been watching over Hans for nine years now.

But when Hans first wields the club, it is useless. Remember the Bulgarian meaning of the fir: Hans is not yet mature, so the magic will not work for him. He is patient, and, in another year, stronger and more mature, the magical weapon works just as it is meant to. He frees his mother and returns to the home of his father, after thrashing the false father, the robber captain.

The passage describing their exit of the robbers' cave is an interesting one: "They left the cave, but how Hans did open his eyes when he came out of the darkness into daylight, and saw the green forest, and the flowers, and the birds, and the morning sun in the sky. He stood there and wondered at everything just as if he were not quite right in the head." Hans is the true lord of the forest, protected by the God that holds the fir tree. After his long imprisonment, Hans is looking at his forest kingdom for the first time. Hans is awed by the beauty of his kingdom. Perhaps his long banishment in the robbers' cave makes him truly appreciate the riches his kingdom holds.

Fir is associated with rightful ownership of the land: the robber captain was a trespasser in the forest, illegally hoarding stolen loot there. Hans's father is the rightful landlord of the forest, so the fir leads Hans and his mother home with no difficulty.

Once mother and true father are reunited, Hans provides for his family, taking on the role of fir-tree wielder, true master of the land. He uses his robber loot to build a new home for his family and to create a prosperous farm. By defeating the robbers, he proved himself to his mother; by providing for his family, he proves himself to his father. He is now matured enough to be master of his immediate family. But guided by the Forest God, he knows he must leave, to complete his Hero's Quest in the wide world. We can assume without being told that his walking stick is made of, yeah, you guessed it, fir. Hans is taking a part of the forest with him wherever he goes, to show his place in the world, and to bring with him the blessings of the Forest God.

Hans sets out from home, and immediately runs into an odd sight: a man gnarling a fir tree. Fir-Twister is marring the fir tree, destroying its true nature. While Hans and Fir-Twister are united by the tree, Hans has a natural connection to the forest, using the tree as a symbol of lordship; Fir-Twister is not happy with the tree in its natural state, and is reshaping it for his own purposes. In a sense he is industrialism to Hans's agriculture. We see right away that Fir-Twister is not rooted to the land, and is not to be trusted. Rock-Splitter is just as distrustful of the land. He explains that when he tries to sleep "bears, wolves, and other vermin of that kind come, which sniff and snuffle about me and won't let me rest." The forest sees Rock-Splitter as an intruder, and wild animals harass him in his sleep (or perhaps he just dreams this, his rest disturbed by his own discomfort in the forest).

A RIDDLE EMERGES,
AND A DWARF DESCENDS

Why does Hans invite Fir-Twister and Rock-Splitter to travel with him? The story has become diluted enough that we are not given a reason for the epic journey of Hans, a holy grail that Hans must search for in this quest: let's see if we can figure out what the grail at the end of the quest might once have been. We see Hans assemble a crew of giants just as Jason did with the Argonauts, as Sinbad did with his sailors, and just as Moses did by bringing Aaron to speak for him and by uniting the Hebrews to present a unified front. Hans takes his small army of giants to an abandoned castle, where the three take turns hunting and cooking.

An abandoned castle in the forest is just the sort of place you'd expect to meet Faeries. In the song "Tam Lin," Janet is repeatedly warned not to go by Carter Hall because it is haunted by the changeling Tam Lin. She goes despite the warnings, picks a "double rose," and next thing she knows she's in Tam Lin's bed. In *Dracula*, the Count's power is strongest when he is in his castle in Transylvania, and he must sleep in soil from that estate when he is in England. So it is no surprise that Fir-Twister encounters a dwarf, come to beg his share of the food.

You may think you own a house, apartment, or castle. You may think the place is yours, and any other creature living there, be it animal or Faerie, is a guest in your space. But in the mind of a Faerie they own the place, and have for longer than you can reckon. And when a Faerie owns a place, they're usually happy to share it with humans in exchange for a tithing of some food or a little alcohol. Well, the little dwarf is no exception. He expects his tithing if these rogues are going to share his abandoned castle. But Fir-Twister is not at home in the natural forest, and does not know the way of the enchanted ones. He refuses the dwarf his tithe, and the dwarf pummels him for it.

Next it's Rock-Splitter's turn, and he is just as outside his element when dealing with the natural world. The dwarf makes short work of him as well.

But Hans knows the ways of the forest, and so knows how to tithe to the Faeries. He gives the dwarf food. When the dwarf is not satisfied, the Faerie finds he has no power over Hans because Hans has satisfied the tithe. Hans, who has given justly, is able to beat the dwarf (literally) at his own game.

Hans attempts to follow the dwarf out of the castle, but trips and falls (perhaps due to some dwarf magic?). He manages to mark the spot where the dwarf disappears and brings his companions to help him locate the dwarf's hovel.

We asked what could be the purpose of Hans's quest. This is a clue. In similar Hero's Quest tales, the hero assembles a crew or army to aid him in his task; this is the only time in the tale when Hans mobilizes the small army of giants he has assembled. He does this to find the home of the dwarf: almost as if Hans knew he would encounter the dwarf, and would need to assemble an army to handle the situation when he did. We can assume that in the original tale the Forest God was guiding Hans, and knew what Hans would need as he went. The fir walking stick would have been the God's contact point with Hans.

Dwarfs, like dragons, are hoarders of treasure. This probably comes from the fact that dwarfs are creatures of the deep earth, and mine gold and silver. Tolkien knew this, of course, when he placed his dwarfs in the Mines of Moria. We see a treasure-hoarding dwarf in "Snow-White and Rose-Red," and of course the dwarfs in "Snow White" go off to mine precious metals each day (even in the Disney version, though there they whistle as they do so). In our modern mythology, Santa Claus, who is a dwarf or a gnome, hoards treasure to give out at Yuletide. In older tales Santa was always accompanied by a dwarf or elf, often one who would beat bad children as Santa handed gifts to the good ones.

Hans follows the dwarf, knowing that he will find some treasure in the creature's abode.

Now you may be saying, "Well, it's obvious what his quest was for; he was there to find the girl." It's a good theory, and maybe quite valid. But in most Hero Quests, the girl, while lovely, is never the primary focus of the quest. Perseus, for instance, must get Medusa's head. He meets Andromeda on his way, and can only save her because he has successfully completed his quest; he uses Medusa's head to kill the gorgon who is about to swallow his lady love.

Odysseus, you say, was trying through his whole quest to get home to his wife. But really the quest was to outfox Poseidon by getting home, and then to kill off the suitors (the would-be evil stepfathers of Odysseus's son). The wife was simply the midpoint of the home, and she was actually Odysseus's ally as she held the suitors off for twenty years until he could get back and kill them. The true quest of Odysseus was for the magic that would allow him to escape Poseidon's wrath.

So Hans, while he does get a bit distracted by the girl, is there for something else. He has assembled an army to get it, and has met a pretty girl along the way. Though, like Perseus, he cannot rescue the girl without the object of his quest: the power ring that allows Hans to control the element of air.

AIR HEAD

All right, so why the element of air? That seems a bit random.

Fair enough. Let's backtrack a bit. Hans is rooted to the forest and his alliance with the Forest God. We see that right from the start, when Hans's mother is gathering fir branches to have Hans blessed by the God. The forest, and its God, represent earth. The fir is used in the celebration of Yule and Christmas, the winter solstice that Pagans place in the north, the direction of earth. Hans proves that he is lord of the land, the earth.

Next we see the fiery passion of Hans and his strong will, in his careful preparation for his escape from the robbers. We also see his physical strength. These are all the domain of fire. We also see that Hans is capable of deep love. He frees his mother, and provides generously for his father. Later he falls in love with the girl on first sight. He is kind and spiritual. All the province of water.

Having attained initiations in three of the four elements, Hans is ready for air, the highest element. In the Tarot, air represents thought and intelligence, and it also bodes trouble and care. Hans is ready for true wisdom. Air is also youth and birth; Hans is ready, by his initiation into the four elements, to be reborn as a new man, a true hero, proven and tempered by fate and experience. Finally, in Tarot air is the suit of swords (although some people put wands in air, but bear with me). One reason for swords being in air is that like a sword, intelligence and reason cuts away the unwanted, useless, or harmful. The sword is also aligned with the flaming swords held by the angels (creatures of air) at the gates of Eden, preventing any but the initiated from entering the garden.

The sword is a powerful magical weapon, wielded with intelligence and care, cleaving away the unnecessary or harmful, guarding the secrets of the garden from the uninitiated. While Hans has wielded the weapon of earth, the fir staff of his God throughout the tale, he is ready to gain the use of the air spirits and their swords. This would make him, as you gamers say, invincible.

Through the guidance of the Forest God, Hans knows he will find a powerful magical weapon in the treasure hoard guarded by the dwarf. He creates a magical weapon, his staff, and assembles an army: Rock-Splitter and Fir-Twister. He then follows the dwarf to its lair.

His army betrays Hans (like Sinbad's sailors, and like the Hebrews who betray Moses while he is on Sinai). In doing so, they put the maiden in danger: like the wolf or the dwarf in "Snow-White and Rose-Red," they mean the girl no good, and may rape or kill her. Hans's command of the air spirits enables him to fly out of the dwarf's subterranean abode. But not fully initiated, Hans attempts to use his old magical weapon, the staff, "without thinking what he was doing, club in hand into the water, and began to swim, but the club, which weighed a hundredweight, dragged him deep down until he was all but drowned."

He must pass one final test, wise use of his magical weapons: "Then in the very nick of time he turned his ring, and immediately the spirits of the air came and bore him as swift as lightning into the boat." He may now rescue the girl and punish his unfaithful comrades: "And then he sailed with the beautiful maiden, who had been in the greatest alarm, and whom he delivered for the second time, home to her father and mother, and married her, and all rejoiced exceedingly." Hans is now made complete, initiated into the mysteries of the warrior hero, and united with the female component of his reign: the Goddess to his God, you might say, fresh from the Underworld where she sat beside Hades in the form of the dwarf. She may now reign in our world with Hans the Lord of the Forest. And indeed, "all rejoiced exceedingly!"

THE STRONG HANS RITUAL

Throughout the tale of Strong Hans, we see Hans's growth and strength echoed in the fir tree. At first Hans is brought into the forest and meets the fir tree itself, a symbol of the Forest God. He then makes a club out of the tree to defeat the robbers. When it is time for Hans to make his way in the world, to journey on his epic quest, he makes a walking stick out of the fir.

Each time Hans is called upon to rise to a different challenge, we see the fir tree take on a new character: denizen of the wild forest, magical weapon, tool of support, symbol of wisdom and guidance.

The symbols of tree, wand, and club have always been associated with male strength, power, and wisdom. Looking over the mythic record, we see Odin hanging from the World Tree to gain wisdom and power; we see the Sumerian God Utu gain his strength and vision from Huluppu, the World Tree that grows along the Euphrates River. This is probably the myth underlying the Genesis tale of Adam, who is given the charge of protecting and honoring the Tree of Knowledge that grows in Eden, also along the Euphrates River (Genesis 2:17). In eating from another tree in the garden, the Tree of Life, Adam is forced to mature into a farmer, rather than leading a childlike, idyllic life in Eden.

We've already seen that the branch of the fir tree represents ownership of land, and with it the growth of crops on that land. Images of a staff-wielding God of the harvest are abundant in Britain. The 180-foot chalk carving of the Cerne Abbas Giant etched into the earth near Dorchester is just such a God, carrying a huge club and revealing his own club-like phallus. Women to this day will bring their partners to the chalk figure late at night to have sex over the phallus, believing that this will ensure fertility and bring a baby to their marriage. A chalk figure in East Sussex known as the Long Man of Wilmington is 220 feet tall, and though not as graphic as the Cerne Abbas Giant, carries twin clubs as a symbol of fertility.

English Morris dancing acts out the use of these clubs in a ritualized fertility dance, done to this day in the English Cotswolds and carried with the English throughout the world. In this dance six dancers, facing each other in rows of three, prance and leap with short sticks, and at the apex of each twirl bang the sticks against their partner's, then bang the energy into the ground. The dance is performed each year at Whitsun, the British festival of May, and at the harvest festival. The sticks are a symbol of the virility of the traditionally male dancers (after World War I, when an entire generation of British men were sacrificed, women began dancing as well to keep the dance alive; in the past century the dance has been done as a "mixed" Morris, by both men and women). The banging of the sticks into the ground represents the transfer of virility into the field where crops will grow and be harvested. The staff is a smaller version of the Maypole, a great wand placed into the fields of each British village, and danced around by young men bearing ribbons: the ribbons are traditionally made of the garments of young ladies of the village who have reached courting age.

For centuries the staff was commonly carried as both a tool and a weapon by men throughout Europe. Known in England as the quarterstaff, because it was the bearer's full height plus a quarter of his height, the staff was used in all phases of activity, including defense. In the tale of Robin Hood, Robin and Little John meet while fighting with quarterstaffs over who will cross a log bridge, itself a staff and a symbol of virility and strength. In the tale of Ivanhoe, the hero is both a great archer and a master at the quarterstaff.

In our ritual we will use the staff as a symbol of male strength and maturity, echoing these myths and tales, and Hans's tie with his fir-tree staff. If you are able to obtain a fir-tree staff for the ritual, that is superb; otherwise a staff of any good, strong wood—such as ash, oak, or birch—will be fine.

This ritual is done to honor a young man whose time has come to be regarded as able to take on adult responsibilities, and to be seen as a peer by the adult men in his family and his community. There is no specific age for this. Different spiritual paths set the age differently: for Jews it is thirteen, for the Amish it is sixteen, but in your spiritual community and in your family you should feel that this young man is ready to act as an adult, and to be seen as a peer by the adult men around him. He should feel ready to make a commitment to the Gods and to his family that binds him to this decision.

Beside a staff, you will need an altar with a central candle, a mirror on the altar that will be hidden by a green cloth as the ritual begins, and beside it one special candle in the favorite color of the boy being honored. You will also need an athame or small knife, and food to share.

Begin by having the young man being honored spend the day meditating, and reflecting on what it means to be an adult man. If he is a physical lad, he might want to walk or hike alone for some hours and focus on his thoughts. If he is not as physical, perhaps simply meditating in a forest or garden would suit him. He should not have distractions such as television, games, or playful peers around him during this time.

When he is ready, the men performing the ritual should assemble and send for him. As he approaches the circle, one man should take the ritual knife (athame) and challenge the boy, by holding the knife to his chest.

"In days of old, young men ready to take on adulthood pledged that they were willing to die for their families. Strong Hans bravely fought to free his mother. Are you now willing to pledge your life to the love of those in this circle?"

The boy answers.

"Then join us!"

The boy is allowed into the center of the circle, while the men stand around him. Now a man takes the hand of the man next to him, and says:

"From hand to hand the circle is cast."

That man takes the next hand, saying, "From hand to hand the circle is cast," each man repeating this until a circle is formed around the boy. The man who began the casting, when the circle returns to him, says, "The circle is cast!"

Now a man calls the east:

> "Spirits of east, hear my voice
> Spirits of east, your children call
> We who would learn from you
> Of the beginning of things

Of wisdom and the seed that rides the winds
Spirits of east
Join us in this circle
Join us in this rite"

Next a man calls the south:

"Spirits of south, hear my voice
Spirits of south, your children call
We who would learn from you
Of sweet passion
Of swift action as the Ancients knew it
Spirits of south
Join us in this circle
Join us in this rite"

A man in the west speaks:

"Spirits of west, hear my voice
Spirits of west, your children call
We who would learn from you
Of strong emotion
Of love as the Mother first dreamed it
Spirits of west
Join us in this circle
Join us in this rite"

A man in the north speaks:

"Spirits of north, hear my voice
Spirits of north, your children call
We who would learn from you
Of the hidden green places
Of trees, and the silent beauty of winter
Spirits of north

Join us in this circle
Join us in this rite"

Now a man takes the boy to the altar and says:

"Great Horned God, Forest Spirit, you whose force is in the fir tree! Come to us. Know _____ (say young man's name), who stands before you ready to be made an adult: a man of knowledge, strength, skill, and dedication.

"To show that he wishes to pledge himself to you, he will light your candle."

The boy lights the candle at the center of the altar. The man who was speaking continues:

"To show that he wishes to pledge himself to you, Forest Spirit, he will bear the great staff!"

The boy is handed the staff. Once he is holding it, a man who is special to him (his father, brother, uncle, cousin) says:

"_____ (name of young man), repeat after me:"

(The boy repeats each of these pledges.)

"Brothers, I am come before you to pledge myself to you.

"I pledge my hand in service and aid to my family, friends, and community!

"I pledge my heart in love: love of family, love of friends, love of a partner, love for a child or any who come within my nurture.

"I pledge my wisdom to help determine our future, and to solve problems that arise and are within my ability to solve.

"I pledge to the Forest Spirit that I will live by a code of morality and justice as I understand these, never knowingly bringing harm to my brothers and sisters!

"So may it be, now and all of my days!"

A man says:

"If this is so, kiss the staff you hold, and vow to honor it as a sign of your pledge."

The boy kisses the staff.

A man says:

"_____ (name of young man), you have grown and learned with us as your teachers, mentors, and providers. Now we send you on a Hero's Quest. You will need to answer several riddles, though each one, you will find, has the same answer. Are you ready?"

The boy answers.

The man says:

"Then let us begin. You will hear us pose many questions. Consider each one, but wait to answer until all have been asked of you. In the end, you will arrive at the Hero's answer:

"Who can you rely on when peril is great?"

The boy is pushed to another part of the circle and is addressed by a different man:

"Who can you count on when things seem hopeless?"

The boy is pushed to another part of the circle and is addressed by a different man:

"Who can cheer you up when you feel listless?"

The boy is pushed to another part of the circle and is addressed by a different man:

"Who is your greatest ally?"

The boy is pushed to another part of the circle and is addressed by a different man:

"Who can be your worst enemy?"

The boy is pushed to another part of the circle and is addressed by a different man:

"Who can drag you down and stop you cold if you let him?"

The boy is pushed to another part of the circle and is addressed by a different man:

"Who can give you the cheer you need when things don't look so good?"

The boy is pushed to another part of the circle and is addressed by a different man:

"Who is your best friend?"

The boy is pushed to another part of the circle and is addressed by a different man:

"Who knows right from wrong?"

The boy is pushed to another part of the circle and is addressed by a different man:

"Who can show you what is missing?"

The boy is pushed to another part of the circle and is addressed by a different man:

"Who can always find a way to put food on the table?"

The boy is pushed to another part of the circle and is addressed by a different man:

"Who is able to fulfill all of your dreams?"

The boy is pushed to another part of the circle and is addressed by a different man:

"Who can you trust?"

Now, the man closest to him (his father, brother, uncle) takes him arm and takes him to the altar:

"The answer to every one of these riddles is hidden here. Can you find it?"

The boy is given a moment. If he cannot figure out what to do, the man who is holding his arm lifts the green cloth, revealing the mirror, and says:

"Here is the answer you seek!"

The boy is given a moment to peer into the mirror.

A man asks, "What is the answer to each of these questions?" The boy is allowed to answer.

Now he is handed a match, and told:

"Now you know the answer to these riddles. But we are all here to guide you, help you, and give you counsel and aid along your journey. So that we may find you whenever you have need of us, no matter where you are, light this candle as a beacon."

The boy lights the special-colored candle.

Each man in the circle takes a turn vowing:

"When you need me, I'll be there for you."

The vow moves around the circle. When each man has said this, all may sit. Food is passed around the circle, and each man may take a turn telling a story of something he remembers the young man doing or saying, especially something that showed the man a special trait or talent the young man possesses.

When this is done, all should stand.

A man goes to the altar, saying:

"Forest Spirit, we thank you for joining us in the circle and witnessing _____ (name's) pledge of honor and adulthood. Though we extinguish your candle, we know it is but a symbol, and you will be here always for each of us."

The center candle is extinguished.

The man in the east says:

"Spirits of east. We thank you for joining us in our circle. As you return to your lovely realms, we bid you farewell!"

All say, "Farewell!"

This is repeated in the south, west, and north.

Now all join hands with the young man included. First man says:

"We end the circle, but carry its joy in our hearts." He lets go of the hand to his right.

The next man says this and lets go the hand to his right. Each man does the same until all hands are dropped. Than the man who began says:

"The circle is ended. Blessed Be."

All should feast together and spend a while socializing and being joyful. The young man should have a huge fuss made over him during the festivities.

Chapter 11

THE ROSE:
HONORING THE SPIRIT OF DEATH

In this short Grimms' narrative, a sickly girl struggling to do her chores meets a strange, delightful boy who helps her work. He gives her a rose, and tells her that when the rose blooms she will see him again. Soon after, the girl's mother finds the girl has died peacefully, and at that moment the rose has bloomed. In a ritual, we will honor the spirit of death, ever present in our lives. Story quotes are from the Margaret Hunt translation of the 1857 printing of Children's and Household Tales.

Medieval Europe suffered long periods of plague, little ice ages, ghastly wars, and famine. The Grimms' tales are rife with horrors such as mothers unable to feed their children, sickness claiming children's lives, and death leaving helpless orphans. While feared and dreaded, death could be a release from disease and poverty.

Folklore shows us that death could arrive at any time, and in many guises. Not always a robed skeleton, death could be encountered as a fetching maiden, a stranger in a feast hall, or as a well-dressed gentleman met on a lonely road. Death might even come as a sweet child in the towering growth of the Black Forest.

The great Neil Gaiman, commenting on his portrayal of death in the *Sandman* series, once mentioned a belief among students of the Qabalah that Death must be very attractive, otherwise no one would follow Death into its dread world. Gaiman portrays his Death character as a quirky, optimistic goth girl, full of wit and charm. To Gaiman and his readership, this is a very attractive figure of death.

To the little girl in the Grimms' "The Rose," laboring for her family deep in the woods, Death is a child who is friendly, strong, and helpful. The tale begins: "There was once a poor woman who had two children. The youngest had to go every day into the forest to fetch wood. Once when she had gone a long way to seek it, a little child, who was quite strong, came and helped her industriously to pick up the wood and carry it home, and then before a moment had passed the strange child disappeared."

We can vividly imagine this tiny girl, pale and with dark circles under her eyes, struggling day after day to drag home enough wood to light the stove and warm the house. The pile probably seemed never enough, and the sickly child must have endured many cold nights in the wintry Black Forest. Until one day a potential friend and playmate simply appeared, picked up the huge pile of wood, and handily, cheerfully followed the girl home with it.

This opening passage sounds like a story of a Kobold or a Brownie, some helpful Faerie coming to the child's aid. It is often said in folklore that Kobolds take the form of children, and are hard workers. Women in Germany would use various spells to coax a Kobold home with them, for this type of Faerie will work all night as the household sleeps. What housewife would not want a happy Brownie tidying up and scrubbing away?

"The child told her mother this, but at first she would not believe it." A poor and desperate mother working slavishly with nothing on her mind but feeding her children thinks her youngest daughter is playing a game, perhaps out of loneliness. Mom chalks it up to an imaginary friend, an invisible companion used to ease the girl's lonely days in the deep woods.

But the child, to whom the experience is quite real, insists upon being believed: "At length she brought a rose home, and told her mother that the beautiful child had given her this rose, and had told her that when it was in full bloom, he would return. The mother put the rose in water."

Now the story takes a morbid twist: "One morning her child could not get out of bed. The mother went to the bed and found her dead, but she lay looking very happy. On the same morning, the rose was in full bloom."

This eerie tale is one of the ten "Children's Legends" that were added to *Children's and Household Tales* for the second printing in 1819. In that printing the main character was a boy, but in the subsequent printings from 1857 on, the child became a girl. The Grimms might have felt that girl children are seen as more vulnerable, sweeter, and prettier, and would elicit more empathy from the reader.

Although this legend is quite brief, only a paragraph long, it contains a myriad of lore and a strange riddle: who is the mercurial boy the child meets in the forest, and what does the rose signify?

DEATH: THE FALSE KNIGHT

Folklore is quite full of meetings with strangers that seem random, but that have profound impact. In the Middle Ages there were folk songs about a boy meeting a "false knight" on the road. The false

knight would ask the boy a series of questions that seemed unanswer-
able, but the clever boy would answer each riddle. By successfully an-
swering his questions, the boy escapes death. Here are some typical
verses from a version of this traditional song:

> Oh where are you going? said the false knight on the road
> I'm going to my school, said the wee boy and still he stood
> What is on your back? said the false knight on the road
> My clothing and my books, said the wee boy and still he stood
>
> I wish you were in yonder sea, said the false knight on the road
> A good boat under me, said the wee boy and still he stood
> The boat will surely sink, said the false knight on the road
> And you will surely drown, said the wee boy and still he stood
>
> I wish you were in yonder tree, said the false knight on the road
> A ladder under me, said the wee boy and still he stood
> The ladder it will break, said the false knight on the road
> And you will surely fall, said the wee boy and still he stood
>
> Has your mother more like you? said the false knight on the road
> Aye and none of them for you, said the wee boy and still he stood
> I think I hear a bell, said the false knight on the road
> It's a-ringing you to hell, said the wee boy and still he stood
> (Traditional)

These sorts of riddle songs are often about meetings with ghosts
and murderous Faeries. In the traditional "Whittingham Fair," or
"Scarborough Fair," an ancient song from British folklore that came
to be well known after a version of it was recorded in the sixties by
Simon and Garfunkel, it is the ghost of a woman's dead lover who
asks the woman to accomplish several impossible tasks in order to
bring him back to life:

Tell her to make me a cambric shirt,
Parsley, sage, rosemary, and thyme
Without any seam or needlework,
Then she shall be a true lover of mine

Tell her to wash it in yonder well
Parsley, sage, rosemary, and thyme
Where never spring water or rain ever fell
And she shall be a true lover of mine

Tell her to dry it on yonder thorn
Parsley, sage, rosemary, and thyme
Which never bore blossom since Adam was born,
Then she shall be a true lover of mine
(Traditional)

Of course the woman cannot do these things, so the man remains dead. The herbs mentioned in each refrain are a protection from evil, be it Faeries or death, that the woman must wear about her person to rid herself of this demanding ghost.

African culture in America called the stranger on the road *Papa Legba*. Myths of this figure from African religion transformed in the southern United States into tales of meeting the devil at a deserted crossroads. The devil would appear as a well-dressed stranger in these tales, and offer the human what he most wanted. But if you agreed to the bargain, you lost your soul to the diabolical stranger. Blues legend has it that the iconic singer-guitarist Robert Johnson gained eternal fame by selling his soul to a stranger at the crossroads. In the song "Crossroads," Johnson promises his soul to Papa Legba for fame as a bluesman. He indeed became legendary after recording the song in 1937, which is considered one of the most famous blues performances of all time. But Johnson never lived to see his fame. He died a year later, poisoned by a jealous lover.

THE BOY WITH THE ROSE

Often the handsome or lovely stranger one meets is Death himself (or herself). This is not always a tragic thing. Folklore makes a strong case for death as a release from sorrow, not a punishment, as it seems to be for the sickly child in our tale. Our poor child has met a stranger in the deep forest while doing labor that is literally killing her. Our first clue that this stranger has come to give the child release is in the task the mysterious child does, carrying the sickly girl's heavy firewood. We also realize immediately that this is no ordinary child, as we hear "before a moment had passed the strange child disappeared." This mercurial being has appeared like a Faerie, willing to help the struggling girl.

Now the girl is given a rose, which she shows to her mother to prove she is not lying.

We have spoken in our chapter on "Briar Rose" about this flower's sexual symbolism. But throughout European lore the rose has long been a symbol of death and rebirth. The rose blooms beautifully for a few short days, then withers and dies so that its seed may fall, leaving only the thorny vine. This is an analogy for the sweetness of life, which is short, and for the thorny bitterness of death.

The blooming rose signifies not only death, but also rebirth. Although the lovely flower dies in a few days, each spring the reborn flower comes back to life, tokening rebirth from death, the energy of the Goddess and her promise that life will always continue, though death may take those we love from us.

So it is with the poor girl in "The Rose." The helpful stranger gives the sickly, pale girl a rose as a token of their meeting. He tells her she will see him again when the flower blooms. The mother puts the flower in water, a sign of her love for the child even in the face of poverty and drudgery.

One morning like any other, the child dies. There is no dramatic death scene or lingering disease: the mother tries to wake the child, and she will not wake. In the forest around them birds sing, foxes prowl, life goes on in abundance. But a mother finds her child has died, and weeps at the girl's bedside. The stranger Death has visited her one last time, and as a symbol of her release, the rose he gave her has bloomed. The lovely flower represents the mother's love, which will continue beyond death; it also shows that the girl will be reborn into a better life, in which she may thrive and prosper as Nature intended for her. Death has proved himself her true friend.

THE ROSE RITUAL

Death: the final frontier. Rich or poor, young or old, hardworking or lazy, cute or less blessed, smart or less smart, death is the end of the road for all of us. It is part of our daily lives, a fact of life we learn to accept. When we were children, most of us had a pet who died; some of us had loved ones who died. The acceptance of death goes even deeper: to eat, we must kill. We eat animals who have given their lives for us. Even vegetarians must harvest to live. Each year we kill John Barleycorn to make our food and drink. Death provides us with leather, glue, wood for our floors and walls, pet food, musical instruments, and fuel for our cars, buses, and airplanes. Every aspect of our life can be traced back to the death of a plant or animal.

For centuries we have honored the creatures whose deaths sustain us. In earliest times hunters would do elaborate ritual dances thanking the animals who died for their meat and skin. One such dance is still done in England, Canada, and the United States today—the Abbots Bromley Horn Dance. Done with racks of antlers that carbon-date to the eleventh century (which replaced even older antlers at that time), the dance is a survival of a Pagan hunting ritual that honored the deer that provided the village of Abbots Bromley with food each year. In English lore, we still sing the song "John Barleycorn," honoring the grain from which we make ale and brandy. These traditions exist to help us remember that only through death can life be sustained.

Honoring death does not mean hoping for death. Healthy people have an instinct for survival, which means that no matter how bad things might seem, we remain afraid of dying. Ancient rituals exist to keep death from our door—to deflect death, you might say. An ancient, biblical example of this is in Exodus 12, in which the God of Israel instructs the Jews to slaughter a lamb and paint its blood on their doors and gates so the angel of death will spare their houses. A memory of this rite is enacted each year at Passover.

The Jews were only one of many peoples whose rituals were meant to fend off death. Throughout Europe in the Middle Ages, each town and village enacted the *Danse Macabre*, or Dance of Death, especially around Halloween (Samhain in Gaelic), when because of the harvest and the hunt the veil between our world and the Underworld is thinnest. In this dance, people dressed as Death, and as skeletal kings, queens, knights, and maidens dance through the village to eerie music. It was hoped that Death would see the grim procession and believe he had already visited this town, and therefore pass it by and be on his way. This tradition ultimately gave us "trick or treating" on Halloween; people would dress as Death or as ghosts and accept symbolic gifts of food in exchange for keeping their lives for another year.

Death can be allegorical. In the Tarot, card thirteen, Death, is traditionally seen as the Grim Reaper, a skeletal figure with a sickle, taking lives of men, women, and children. In the Rider-Waite Tarot deck, the card was changed. There Death is a figure on horseback carrying a white rose. In his wake, a bishop, a king, and a beautiful maiden succumb to death. The bishop wears a hat that looks like a fish's head, a reminder that the Death card is equated to the sign Pisces in this system; throughout history, fish were buried with planted grains to fertilize the ground so the grain might grow. The grain is then harvested, sustaining our lives.

The Death card is a reminder of this cycle of life-from-death. It is also a symbol of the death of some facet of our life: childhood dies so that adulthood may blossom; a project dies so another may emerge; a love or friendship dies, and one day a new one develops, better for the lessons we've learned from our experience. In a reading, Death might mean a huge change or profound growth.

In our ritual we will honor the spirit of Death as an agent of change, a constant motivator, and a teacher of life's lessons. We will honor the spirit of loved ones or heroes who have succumbed to death, and whose memories and ghosts drive us to reach our own goals and dreams.

You will need:

- A standard altar with a wand and a single candle, plus a small candle for each magician
- A white rose
- A special token of a loved one or admired person who has died

This ritual may be performed with one person or a group: if you are in a group, assign lines to each person present. The ritual may be done at Samhain (pronounced SOW-*an*), the Celtic name for Halloween, a time when the veil between our world and the world of death is hazy, and ghosts may feel our presence. You may also do the ritual anytime you feel the need to honor a loved one or hero who has died. The circle may be done in a dark, quiet room, or outdoors.

Begin by assembling in silence. Each magician should carry a lit candle into the circle as he or she files in, and sit quietly with the candle burning for a short time. Begin when each feels ready.

"We gather here tonight to honor Death, without whom Life could not exist. We honor the spirit of Death who sustains our lives, and who will claim each of us when the time comes. Death, we honor you!"

Each magician takes a turn touching their candle to the single candle on the altar; the first touch will light that candle, but each flame should touch the altar candle. When each is done:

"The light on our altar is Life itself, always bright, always present. We honor the light of life before us. Blessed Be!"

All: "Blessed Be."

"In our hands we hold the light of life: our own life, and the life of those who came before us. Each of us has a loved one who has died. Each of us holds dear the spirit of someone who has gone before. Their light has gone out, their spirit moved on from this world. Please say the name of the person you honor as you lightly blow out your candle."

Each magician says a name as she or he blows out the candle. Various names will be heard around the room: of departed relatives, friends, or figures from history. Let each take a moment to say the name and snuff their candle, then proceed.

Pick up the wand and move to each direction in turn:

"Spirit of east, creature of air. I call you to join us in this circle. Bring to us laughter in the face of sadness and grief. Teach us that life continues through youth and birth! Blessed Be!"

"Spirit of south, creature of fire. I call you to join us in this circle. Bring us the will to continue though death claims those we love. Teach us that life is fragile and precious! Blessed Be!"

"Spirit of west, creature of water. I call you to join us in this circle. Bring us the depth of love, sorrow, grief, and hope to deal with the death that affects our lives. Teach us to hold ever in our hearts the love of those who have gone before us! Blessed Be!"

"Spirit of north, creature of earth. I call you to join us in this circle. Bring us the solidity of earth and calm, the peace of the ground beneath us. Teach us that like the rose that blooms on the grave, life goes on. Everything changes, nothing is lost! Blessed Be!"

Sit back in the center and replace the wand on the altar. The leader picks up the rose that is on the altar, and says:

"Oh Death! Thou spirit of change and transformation. We honor you! We have come to know you from the beginning, you who claim all, you who change all. Everything changes, nothing is lost!"

All repeat: "Everything changes, nothing is lost!"

The leader says, "Death, you give us life! You give us the cow, the hen, the sow in the meadow, that we may feast and live."

All reply, "Everything changes, nothing is lost!

The leader says, "Death, you give us the grain in the field, John Barleycorn, that we may bake bread, brew ale, and make pasta and cereal. We live and thrive from your gifts!"

All reply, "Everything changes, nothing is lost!"

The leader says, "Death, you are a teacher. You give us knowledge of those who have passed, who inspire us, who drive us. In your humbling presence we realize we must bring our light into the world before it is snuffed out. Guide us, Death, to achieve, to work, to create, to birth life, to nurture life!"

All reply, "Everything changes, nothing is lost!"

The leader continues, "This white flower is a symbol of our lives. It blossoms in beauty, casting its love and peace on all those who view it. But in time it will whither and fade. Yet painters will paint it; writers will write its ode; lovers will ever remember it as a token of their passion; the grieving will lay it as a sign of remembrance on the earth.

"Take this flower now, each of us, and bless it with your joy, your grief, your love, and your sorrow."

Each magician takes the rose and holds it as they think of someone they have lost, of someone gone who has inspired them, or of the plants and animals they have consumed today. When the rose returns to the leader, he or she says:

"Death crushes us all. This rose bears a lovely bloom, but in time it will fade and die, as we all die in time. Everything changes, nothing is lost!"

All: "Everything changes, nothing is lost!"

"We are given a short time on this earth. In that time we must strive to make our mark. We must create, be it art, music, joy, life, our work or our teachings. We are inspired by those who have passed. The dead teach us that life is precious. They teach us that we have no time to lose. We must always strive, for Death may claim us as She pleases.

"We honor those whom Death has taken. Dear ones, close to our hearts, just beyond the Veil. We call to you!"

The rose may be replaced upon the altar. Each person in the circle should now pick up the token they've brought that reminds them of a departed person or a hero in their lives. All in the circle may now speak, taking turns honoring a person who has died. This could be someone who was dearly loved, someone they knew well, someone they did not know well, or a hero or historical figure who has inspired them.

This is an example, but each magician must use his or her own words and thoughts:

"I honor George, my dear friend who died these four years ago. I hold his photograph in my hands. Ever loyal to me, he showed me what could be accomplished through will, perseverance, and a refusal to give in. George was a man of few words, but when he spoke it was always with love and careful thought. George has inspired me to achieve many things, and he is missed in this world. George, we honor you!"

Now the next magician speaks, and so on in turn.

When each magician has spoken, each will replace his or her token on the altar. Then all take up the candles that were first carried into the circle.

"Everything changes, nothing is lost! The memories, the ghosts, the spirits that have left this world continue with us, guiding us, warning us, nurturing us. We light a candle now that will carry us into our future, that we may ever remember those we honor tonight!"

Each walks deosil around the circle, lighting their candle from the center candle. When each has finished, the leader walks the line out of the circle. All may dance and sing together, celebrating their lives and the lives that have gone before.

When they are done, however long that takes, one magician shall re-enter the circle, and approach the candle on the altar.

"Death, you are ever present. May you be an influence on us, an agent of change. May you drive us to create, to make life, to enjoy the time we are given, to remember always those who have made the journey in your embrace! We extinguish your light. Blessed Be!"

Snuff candle.

"Spirits of east, we thank you for joining us in this rite! Hail and farewell!"

Repeat in the south, west, and north.

Walk deosil around the circle, saying:

"We cast this circle back into the earth, until we need to call upon its energies again. We who are alive, who share this magical time and space, give thanks for our lives and for each other! Blessed Be!"

All should hug, kiss, embrace, and share joy and a meal. When all is done, the rose should be placed in a special location until the bloom is gone. Then it may be pressed, or its pedals used in a ritual bath or for a spell.

AND THEY LIVED
HAPPILY EVER AFTER

The children have emerged from the forest, wiser and stronger for their trials there. The wolf is dead, the beast is transformed, the bear sleeps again through the long winter. The princess is awake, and begins her life anew. Hans and his bride ride the air to their new home. The storyteller smiles and says, " . . . and they lived happily ever after."

But the tale doesn't end there for us. We hold these tales in our hearts, living by their lessons, recalling their profound effect on our childhood selves, bearing the memories of their little heroines and heroes into our adult lives.

I hope this book has brought you into a deeper understanding of fairy tales, and has given you a whole new point of view on the tales collected by the Grimms. Not the cute, sweet stories you remember, are they?

Where do we go from here? Further. Like the study of pretty much anything, the study of fairy tales and folklore is something you pursue over time. The more you come to know these quaint, beautiful, magical tales, the more you understand them intellectually and the more you feel their magic viscerally. As I wrote in the chapter on "Beauty and the Beast," fairy tales may be understood on many levels, and each level raises our awareness of magic, of Nature, and of ourselves.

I strongly suggest you find these tales in their original form on the Internet, or in any collection of the original Grimms' tales. Reading these tales in their original form, rather than trusting your memory or calling to mind film adaptations, is important to your understanding of fairy tales and folklore, and to the kernel of magic held inside them. Read over each tale a few times, and see if you can follow my thoughts about its origins and magic. Come up with some interpretations of your own. I would also recommend reading Bruno Bettelheim, Maria Tatar, and Catherine Orenstein, all of whom you'll find mentioned in the bibliography. These are great commentators on the meanings of these tales in our modern lives.

Try the rituals and spells, remembering that anyone can learn to do ritual magic. It just takes practice and a little dedication. Study the Tarot, think about the elements of ritual, and read some the material I've suggested.

After all, it's your ever after!

BIBLIOGRAPHY

Amrani, Estelle Nora Harwit. "The Kinaalda Ceremony—A Dance into Womanhood." 1988. Online at http://www.mlms.logan.k12 .ut.us/~ckircalli/sing down the moon/womanhood ceremony.htm.

American Agriculturist, eds. *Broom-Corn and Brooms*. Ottawa, ON: Algrove, 2000. Originally published in 1887.

Ashliman, D. L., trans. "Cinderella." (Translation of "Aschenputtel," in Grimm, Jacob, and Wilhelm Grimm. *Kinder- und Hausmärchen*, final edition [Berlin, 1857, no. 21].) Translation ©D. L. Ashliman, 2001–2006. Online at http://www.pitt.edu/~dash/grimm021.html.

———. "Death of the Seven Dwarfs. A Legend from Switzerland." (Translation of "Tod der sieben Zwerge," in Rochholz, Ernst Ludwig. *Schweizersagen aus dem Aargau*, vol. 1 [Aarau, Switzerland: Druck und Verlag von H. R. Sauerländer, 1856, no. 222, p. 312.]) Translation ©D. L. Ashliman, 2009. Online at http://www.pitt.edu/~dash/ dwarfs.html.

———. "Little Broomstick." (Translation of "Besenstielchen," in Bechstein, Ludwig. *Deutsches Märchenbuch* [1845]. See also Scherf, Walter, ed. *Sämtliche Märchen* [Darmstadt, Germany: Wissenschaftliche Buchgesellschaft, 1983], 416–20.) Translation ©D. L. Ashliman, 1998. Online at http://www.pitt.edu/~dash/type0425c .html#broomstick.

———. "Little Red Hat." (Translation of "Das Rothhütchen," in Schneller, Christian. *Märchen und Sagen aus Wälschtirol: Ein Beitrag zur deutschen Sagenkunde.* [Innsbruck, Austria: Verlag der Wagner'schen Universitäts-Buchhandlung, 1867.]) Translation ©D. L. Ashliman, 2007. Online at http://www.pitt.edu/~dash/type0333.html#italy.

———. "Little Snow-White." (Translation of "Sneewittchen," in Grimm, Jacob, and Wilhelm Grimm. *Kinder- und Hausmärchen*, 1st ed. [Berlin: Realschulbuchhandlung, 1812], v. 1, no. 53, pp. 238–50.) Translation ©D. L. Ashliman, 1998–2002. Online at http://www.pitt .edu/~dash/type0709.html#snowwhite.

Aubrey, John. *Miscellanies Upon Various Subjects.* 1696. Downloaded from the Gutenberg Project website, http://www.gutenberg.org/ ebooks/4254.

Basile, Giambattista. "Sun, Moon and Talia," from *Il Pentamerone.* Translated by John Edward Taylor. London: David Bogue and J. Cundall, 1848. See also http://www.public.iastate.edu/~lhagge/sun,moon .htm.

———. *Stories from the Pentamerone.* Translated by E. F. Strange. London: Macmillan & Co., 1911.

Bechstein, Ludwig. *Deutsches Märchenbuch.* 1845. Trans. D.L. Ashliman. Online at http://www.pitt.edu/~dash/type0425c.html.

———. "Besenstielchen," in *Sämtliche Märchen* (Walter Scherf, ed.). Darmstadt, Germany: Wissenschaftliche Buchgesellschaft, 1983. The original source is Ludwig Bechstein, *Deutsches Märchenbuch* (1845). Translated as "Little Broomstick," by D. L. Ashliman (© 1998). Online at http://www.pitt.edu/~dash/type0425c .html#broomstick. Used with permission.

Bettelheim, Bruno. *The Uses of Enchantment: The Meaning and Importance of Fairy Tales.* New York: Random House, 1976.

Bray, A. E. *Traditions, Legends, Superstitions, and Sketches of Devonshire*. London: John Murray, 1838.

Brownmiller, Susan. *Against Our Will: Men, Women, and Rape*. New York: Simon and Schuster, 1975.

Carter, Angela. "The Company of Wolves," in *The Bloody Chamber*. London: Gollancz, 1979.

Child, F. J. *English and Scottish Popular Ballads*. New York: Dover, 1965.

Croker, Thomas Crofton. *Fairy Legends and Traditions of the South of Ireland*. Philadelphia: Lea and Blanchard, 1844.

Dickens, Charles. *A Christmas Tree*. London: T. N. Foulis, 1907.

Dickens, Charles (Yolen, Jane, ed.). *A Christmas Carol by Charles Dickens*. New York: Tor Books 1990.

Eyre-Todd, George. *Byways of the Scottish Border: A Pedestrian Pilgrimage*. Selkirk, Scotland: James Lewis, 1890.

Farrar, Janet, and Stewart Farrar. *Eight Sabbats for Witches*. London: Robert Hale Ltd., 1981.

Fortune, Dion. *The Training and Work of an Initiate*. York Beach, ME: S. Weiser, 2000.

Freud, Sigmund. *Three Essays on the Theory of Sexuality*. London: Hogarth, 1915.

Graves, Robert. *The White Goddess*: New York: Farrar, Straus and Giroux, 1966.

Grimm, Jacob. *Deutsche Mythologie*, 4th ed. 1877.

Grimm, Jacob, and Wilhelm Grimm. *The Annotated Brothers Grimm*. Ed. Maria Tatar. New York: W. W. Norton and Company, 2004.

———. *Grimm's Household Tales*. Translated by Margaret Hunt. London: George Bell, 1884.

———. *Kinder- und Hausmärchen* (Children's and Household Tales), vol. 1, 1812; vol. 2, 1814. Berlin: Realschulbuchhandlung. Trans. D. L. Ashliman, 1999–2008. See http://www.pitt.edu/~dash/grimm.html#jointpublications.

Guest, Lady Charlotte. *The Mabinogion*. London: Bernard Quaritch, 1877.

Hunt, Margaret, trans. and ed. *Grimm's Household Tales*. Translation of Jacob Grimm and Wilhelm Grimm's *Kinder- und Hausmärchen* [Children's and Household Tales] (1812). London: George Bell, 1884.

Keats, John. *The Poetical Works of John Keats*. London: Macmillan, 1884.

Klein, Kenny. *The Flowering Rod*. Stafford, UK: Immanion Press 2009.

———. *Through the Faerie Glass: A Look at the Realm of Unseen and Enchanted Beings*. Woodbury, MN: Llewellyn, 2010.

Lang, Andrew, ed. *The Blue Fairy Book*. London: Longmans, Green, and Company, 1889.

———. *The Red Fairy Book*. London: Longmans, Green, and Company, 1891.

Levi, Eliphas. *Transcendental Magic: Its Doctrine and Ritual*. New York: S. Weiser, 1970.

Lintrop, Aado, trans. "The Great Oak and Brother-Sister." (Traditional.) *Folklore*, vol. 16. Tartu, Estonia: Folklore/Electronic Journal of Folklore, 2001. © Folk Belief and Media Group of ELM, Andres Kuperjanov. PDF available online at www.folklore.ee/folklore/vol16/oak2.pdf.

Markstrom, C. A., and A. Iborra. *The Kinaalda Pubertal Rite of Passage and Identity Formation among Navajo Girls*. (April 2002). Paper presented in the symposium "Alternative Conceptions of Identity Among First Nations and American Indian Adolescents" at the 2002 Biennial Meetings of the Society for Research on Adolescence, in New Orleans, LA.

Megli, "An Introduction to the Four Branches." Mabinogistudy.co.uk. Online at http://www.mabinogistudy.co.uk/introduction.html.

Olson, R. L. *The Quinault Indians*. Seattle: The University of Washington, 1936.

Orenstein, Catherine. "Dances with Wolves: Little Red Riding Hood's Long Walk in the Woods." *Ms. Magazine*, Summer 2004.

———. *Little Red Riding Hood Uncloaked: Sex, Morality, and the Evolution of a Fairy Tale.* New York: Basic Books, 2003.

Pike, Lynn Blinn. *Sexuality and Your Child.* Columbia, MO: Department of Human Development and Human Studies, University of Missouri-Columbia. (Pamphlet GH6002, p. 1.)

Perrault, Charles. *Les contes de ma mère l'Oye* (The Tales of Mother Goose). First published in 1697. Content and analysis at http://www .surlalunefairytales.com/ are ©1998–2010 by Heidi Anne Heiner.

Regardie, Israel. *Ceremonial Magic: A Guide to the Mechanisms of Ritual.* London: Aeon Books, 2007.

———. *The Tree of Life: An Illustrated Study in Magic.* (Edited and annotated by Chic Cicero and Sandra Tabatha Cicero.) St. Paul, MN: Llewellyn, 2000.

Schofield, Roger. "Monday's Child Is Fair of Face," in *Family History Revisited: Comparative Perspectives,* edited by Richard Wall, Tamara K. Hareven, and Josef Ehmer, 57–73. Cranbury, NJ: Associated University Presses, 2001.

Shakespeare, William. *The Complete Works of William Shakespeare: Moby Project.* Cambridge: Massachusetts Institute of Technology, 1993. Online at http://shakespeare.mit.edu/.

Sheba, Lady. *The Book of Shadows.* St. Paul, MN: Llewellyn, 2004.

Smith, Jessie Willcox. *The Little Mother Goose.* New York: Dodd, Meade and Company, 1912.

Tatar, Maria. "Introduction. Snow White," in Jacob Grimm and Wilhelm Grimm, *Children's Stories and Household Tales.* New York: Norton, 2004.

Yolen, Jane. *Touch Magic.* New York: Philomel Books, 1981.

INDEX

TO WRITE TO THE AUTHOR

If you wish to contact the author or would like more information about this book, please write to the author in care of Llewellyn Worldwide Ltd. and we will forward your request. Both the author and publisher appreciate hearing from you and learning of your enjoyment of this book and how it has helped you. Llewellyn Worldwide Ltd. cannot guarantee that every letter written to the author can be answered, but all will be forwarded. Please write to:

Kenny Klein
℅ Llewellyn Worldwide
2143 Wooddale Drive
Woodbury, MN 55125-2989

Please enclose a self-addressed stamped envelope for reply,
or $1.00 to cover costs. If outside the USA, enclose
an international postal reply coupon.

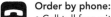

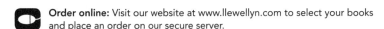

Through the Faerie Glass

A Look at the Realm of Unseen and Enchanted Beings

KENNY KLEIN

What are Faeries really like?

Seducing virgins, abducting babies, luring mortals toward madness and death . . . contrary to today's sanitized depictions, the pixies, elves, wood nymphs, selkies, and other magical creatures embodied in folklore can be quite nasty. Kenny Klein draws on folkloric record—legend, myth, song, and sagas—to reveal the true nature of Faeries: where they live, what they do, and their sexuality, fears, and talents for disguise, enchantment, and prophecy. He also offers practical tips for those who dare to visit their world.

Entertaining and enlightening, this unique guide examines human interactions with Mab the Faerie Queen, Puck the prankster, Jenny Green Teeth, and other legendary fey. Discover how these historic tales intersect with Pagan customs and Judeo-Christian mythology—and survive in today's fairy tales, music, and holiday traditions.

978-0-7387-1883-5, 312 pp., 6 x 9 $16.95

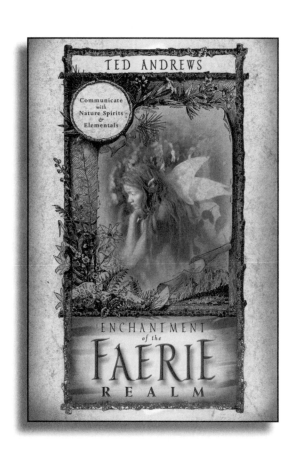

Enchantment of the Faerie Realm

Communicate with Nature Spirits & Elementals

TED ANDREWS

Forests, lakes, mountains, caves—even your garden—are alive with Nature's spirits. *Enchantment of the Faerie Realm,* by popular author Ted Andrews, can help you commune with elves, devas, nymphs, gnomes, and other Faerie folk. With just a little patience and persistence you can learn to recognize the presence of these mysterious, magical creatures.

978-0-87542-002-8, 240 pp., 6 x 9   **$14.95**

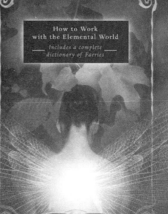

A Witch's Guide to Faery Folk

How to Work with the Elemental World

EDAIN MCCOY

Have you ever seen a Faery? As you will discover in A *Witch's Guide to Faery Folk*, by Edain McCoy, people all over the world have reported encounters with a race of tiny people, neither human nor divine, who live both inside and outside the physical human world. Our Pagan ancestors actually lived, worked, and worshipped with these elusive creatures on a regular basis.

In many instances today, Pagans let the Faery people fill the role of elemental archetypes. Perhaps, they are called on, but only to witness rituals, not participate in them. A *Witch's Guide to Faery Folk* changes this forever.

This book shares two ways to contact the Faery people. First, it shows you where and how to find them in our world. Second, it teaches you to use guided meditation to visit them in their world. Third, it describes how to work with them when casting spells and doing rituals.

A unique dictionary listing the names, lore, and characteristics of 230 Faeries makes learning which ones to work with easy. Whether it is the Erdluitle (for weather work), Tomtra (to help raise a Cone of Power), or any of the others, this book will open new vistas for spiritual development and growth.

978-0-87542-733-1, 384 pp., 6 x 9 $17.95

To order, call 1-877-NEW-WRLD
Prices subject to change without notice
Order at Llewellyn.com 24 hours a day, 7 days a week!

NANCY ARROWSMITH

field guide to the
Little
people

a curious journey into the hidden realm
of elves, faeries, hobgoblins & other
not-so-mythical creatures

Field Guide to the Little People

A Curious Journey into the Hidden Realm of Elves, Faeries, Hobgoblins & Other Not-So-Mythical Creatures

NANCY ARROWSMITH

The beloved cult classic *Field Guide to the Little People* has been out of print in English for thirty years. Copies have been as hard to find as a Will-o'-the-Wisp! Llewellyn is proud to bring this book back so everyone can have this "scientific" manual revealing the histories, characters, lineages, appearances, and examples of the fairies and seventy-eight other kinds of their kin, from Hobgoblins to Leprechauns, Sirens to Red Caps. The text is based entirely on the author's extensive research into historical folklore—nothing is invented. Plus, we've made this book better than ever, with eighty amazing new illustrations by Sabrina the Ink Witch.

So, whether you want to know about the Alven, White Ladies, Church Grims, Hey-Hey-Men, or any of their mystical mates—spirits who are so often just beyond our sight yet bring so much magick to our world—you'll want to make this timeless resource a part of your bookshelf!

978-0-7387-1549-0, 336 pp., 6 x 9 $24.95

Amber K

&

Azrael Arynn K

Ritualcraft

Creating Rites

for

Transformation

& Celebration

RitualCraft

Creating Rites for Transformation and Celebration

AMBER K & AZRAEL ARYNN K

From Sabbat events to magick ceremonies to handfastings, ritual is at the heart of Pagan worship and celebration. Whether you're planning a simple coven initiation or an elaborate outdoor event for hundreds, *RitualCraft* can help you create and conduct meaningful rituals.

Far from a recipe book of rote readings, this modern text explores rituals from many cultures and offers a step-by-step Neopagan framework for creating your own. The authors share their own ritual experiences—the best and the worst—illustrating the elements that contribute to successful ritual. *RitualCraft* covers all kinds of occasions: celebrations for families, a few people, or large groups; rites of passage; Esbats and Sabbats; and personal transformation. Costumes, ethics, music, physical environment, ritual tools, safety, speech, and timing are all discussed in this all-inclusive guidebook to ritual.

978-156718-009-1, 624 pp., 7 x 10 $29.95

To order, call 1-877-NEW-WRLD
Prices subject to change without notice
Order at Llewellyn.com 24 hours a day, 7 days a week!

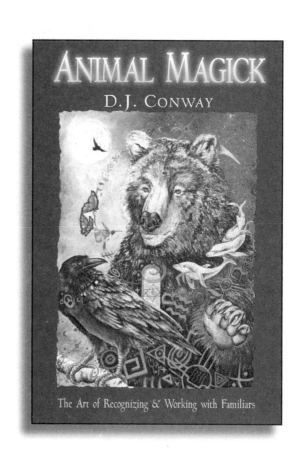

ANIMAL MAGICK

D.J. CONWAY

The Art of Recognizing & Working with Familiars

Animal Magick

The Art of Recognizing & Working with Familiars

D. J. CONWAY

The use of animal familiars began long before the Middle Ages in Europe. It can be traced to ancient Egypt and beyond. To most people, a familiar is a witch's companion, a small animal that helps the witch perform magick—but you don't have to be a witch to have a familiar. In fact, you don't even have to believe in familiars to have one. You may already have a physical familiar living in your home in the guise of a pet. Or you may have an astral-bodied familiar if you are intensely drawn to a particular creature that is impossible to have in the physical. There are definite advantages to befriending a familiar. They make excellent companions, even if they are astral creatures. If you work magick, the familiar can aid by augmenting your power. Familiars can warn you of danger, and they are good healers.

Most books on animal magick are written from the viewpoint of the Native American. This book takes you into the exciting field of animal familiars from the European Pagan viewpoint. It gives practical meditations, rituals, and power chants for enticing, befriending, understanding, and using the magick of familiars.

978-1-56718-168-5, 288 pp., 6 x 9 $15.95